Rose's Vintage

ROSE'S VINTAGE

KAYTE NUNN

NERO

Published by Nero,
an imprint of Schwartz Publishing Pty Ltd
Level 1, 221 Drummond Street
Carlton VIC 3052 Australia
enquiries@blackincbooks.com
www.nerobooks.com

The National Library of Australia Cataloguing-in-Publication entry:
Rose's vintage / Kayte Nunn.
9781863957991 (paperback)
9781925203707 (ebook)
Love stories.
Wineries—Australia—Fiction.
A823.4

Author photo: Jane Earle
Cover image: Wells, Stocksy
Graphic: Ohn Mar, Shutterstock

For Andy, for keeping the home fires burning.

prune

verb

to trim (a tree, shrub or bush) by cutting away dead
or overgrown branches or stems, especially to encourage
growth

CHAPTER 1

I f ever there was a place for the zombie apocalypse, this
could be it, thought Rose, shivering in the wind, which
felt like it had blown direct from Antarctica to the Shingle Valley. Parallel rows of bare, withered vines stretched
across the landscape as far as the eye could see, stark against
the washed-out grey sky, while in the distance the dark
shadows of what she presumed must be the Shingle Hills
loomed, looking very much like a giant's crumpled, discarded handkerchief.

It was eerily quiet. The wind whipped her hair around
her face and she stamped her feet and flung her arms about
her body in a vain attempt to bring some circulation back to
her numb fingers. They had frozen into claws from being
curled around the steering wheel of her little yellow car for
hours. When she'd bought it in Sydney last week, she'd forgotten to check whether the heater worked.

That had been her first mistake. Her second had been failing to pack anything approaching winter wear. She'd never imagined Australia would be this cold. This wasn't the sunshine-and-board-shorts culture she'd been led to believe existed year-round in the land downunder. *Home and Away* had a lot to answer for. Jeans, Birkenstocks and t-shirt – even one with long sleeves – offered little protection against the freezing wind that cut clean to her bones.

A few minutes earlier, the car's tyres had slipped in thick mud as she trundled up the tree-lined dirt road, her head bumping uncomfortably on the roof of the tiny vehicle. It had been a long drive, but a straightforward one once she'd escaped the tentacles of the city and sailed north over the Harbour Bridge. She'd found Kalkari Wines easily enough, spotting the timber sign with the curlicued name embossed on it in black as she hurtled along the road heading out of Eumeralla, the small town that sat smack in the centre of the valley.

One day when Rose was a child, she and her brother Henry had played a game in the backyard, trying to dig a hole all the way to Australia. She had kept at it long after he lost interest, digging a crater so large it could have swallowed her whole. When their mum saw it, she blew her top and insisted they fill it in, chuntering that Rose had damaged the roots of her precious hydrangea bush, and that Rose could have buried herself alive. Rose remembered being indignant at the injustice of it; she'd worked hard at digging that hole. Now, she felt like she had kept on digging and had finally popped out the other side.

It was nothing like she'd expected.

She mentally snapped the elastic on her big-girl pant-
ies, took a deep breath of the icy air and walked up to the
cellar door, a low timber-and-stone building beside the public carpark. Behind it loomed a very large, industrial-looking
shed with a corrugated roof. The sign next to the cellar door
stated opening hours of 10 a.m. to 4 p.m. She looked at her
watch. Just after eleven. She tried the handle. The door
didn't budge. Peering through the dusty glass, she could see
a few wine barrels and a bar running the length of the room,
but no signs of life.

To her right a lone magpie cawed mournfully. *One for
sorrow*, thought Rose. She saw signs in everything, from bad
news coming in threes to black-and-white birds foreshad-
owing doom. *This isn't looking good.*

Doing her best to ignore the magpie, which had
cocked its head at her inquisitively, she headed to her left,
leaving the carpark behind, and followed the other drive,
marked 'private'. As she rounded the bend, she came upon
a house – and let out an involuntary gasp. Even on such a
gloomy day, it was an impressive sight: sandstone walls with
huge rectangular windows were topped by a gabled dark
shingle roof with chimneys at either end. A pair of grand
sandstone columns flanked a vast iron-studded timber door,
and the square front porch was bookended by a couple of
straggly lavender bushes in tarnished copper urns. As she
looked at the house framed by the hills behind, Rose
thought she'd never seen anything quite so intimidating or
so beautiful in her life. She had a distinct feeling of deja vu:
that she'd seen it before, known it before …

Get a grip, girl!

Nerves were making Rose's pulse race – she wasn't used to subterfuge. That was all Henry's doing. Feeling a little anxious and a lot like an intruder, she knocked timidly on the door.

And then knocked again, louder this time.

Getting no response, she walked around to the back of the house and found a wide verandah scattered with assorted kids' paraphernalia: rusty bikes, a half-built Lego tower and an array of different-sized muddy boots, lined up from tiny to gargantuan. A few ruddy chickens scratched around in the dirt. Signs of life there at least.

'Hallooo!' Rose called out. 'Hi there! Anyone home?'

'Ain't nobody here but us chickens.' The old jazz tune sprang to Rose's mind.

Just then she heard the rumble of an engine and the scrunch of tyres on gravel. She hurried round to the front of the house again to see that a battered four-wheel drive had screeched to a halt at the front door, scattering gravel as it braked. Rose watched as a willowy, platinum-haired girl, who – with her puffy ski jacket and knitted beanie – wouldn't have looked out of place on the slopes of St Moritz, climbed down from the front seat. Close up, she could see that the girl had the kind of peachy clear skin that looked as if it was lit from within and a small diamond piercing that twinkled in her nose. She looked all of about seventeen.

'Hi,' said Rose, 'I– I wasn't sure if anyone was home.' The arse-freezing cold made her teeth chatter.

'It's okay,' said the girl, pushing her fair hair behind her ears and looking down her pert little nose at Rose. 'You must be the new au pair.'

'That's me,' said Rose, not sounding particularly convincing even to her own ears. Until two weeks ago, she'd never imagined in her wildest nightmares that she'd be fronting up on the underside of the world, pretending to be an au pair in such a godforsaken place. She'd been, if not exactly happy, then at least in a comfortable groove, with a steady job, a flat and a boyfriend. Now she was completely adrift, cut off from all that she'd once thought was solid.

I can do this.

The girl looked at Rose with Teutonic directness in her clear blue eyes, and Rose nearly lost her nerve. 'Good. The agency said they were sending someone. Mrs B's back is very bad, and it's bullshit crazy at the moment. You'd better come in,' she said. 'It's a bit mad around here, and he is – how do you say? A moody bugger. But the kids are good. Well, most of the time.' She opened the passenger door and began unbuckling a little girl, who looked about two years old. Rose glimpsed a cloud of dark hair escaping from beneath an apple-green fleecy hat.

Rose knew who 'he' was. Henry had briefed her in London. Mark Cameron. Founder and proprietor of Kalkari Wines. Thirty-eight years old. After a stellar career working for one of Australia's biggest wine conglomerates, he'd turned his back on corporate life and chosen instead to risk his reputation and financial stability setting up Kalkari. He'd bought fifteen acres of run-down vineyards in the Shingle Valley about ten years ago, together with the imposing

Kalkari House. He'd added considerably to the original vineyards since then, and, according to what she'd read, now had some 160 acres under vine in the Shingle Valley. By all accounts he was just starting to turn the wines around, with his latest vintage getting some rave reviews from the press in Britain and America, as well as Australia. Mark had a glamorous Spanish wife, Isabella, and they had a son, Leo. Henry had shown her a photo of Mark and Isabella pulled from the internet. They made a striking couple. Clearly Henry's information was a tad out of date though, judging by the little girl in the car.

'I am Astrid,' the blonde bombshell said, unloading her charge, 'and this is Luisa. Say hello to—? Sorry, what is your name?'

'Rose. Hi, sweetie! Lovely to meet you,' Rose said, directing a wide grin at the little girl. It wasn't the children's fault that her reasons for being here were less than honest, and she was a sucker for cute little girls with dimples in their cheeks in any case. She wondered where Leo was; there was no sign of him in the car.

'Oh, you're English,' Astrid said. 'They didn't tell me that.'

And you're German, thought Rose, equally surprised.

'Anyway, let's get inside. It's freezing out here.' Holding Luisa by the hand, Astrid led the way through the imposing front door and into a flagstoned hallway that was bare save for a couple of side tables and an ancient-looking frayed rug. She made a swift left and Rose followed, a few footsteps behind, doing her best to absorb her surroundings as she went.

The kitchen was a large, square room with a huge lemon-yellow enamelled range, pale granite surfaces and white glazed butcher's tiles. The earlier clouds had begun to clear and sun streamed in through two large timber-framed windows, and in the centre of the room was a scarred table surrounded by several wheel-backed chairs. The table was barely visible beneath the remains of what had obviously been breakfast, and the floor was sticky and strewn with what looked like Cheerios. The cavernous butler's sink and the draining board beside it were piled high with an assortment of dirty dishes. *If a bomb went off in the room it would make no discernable difference*, thought Rose.

'As I said, Mrs B has not been in for a couple of weeks, and I've got my hands full looking after Luisa and Leo,' said Astrid waving her hands at the mess unapologetically. She unbuttoned Luisa's coat, shrugged off her own and then grabbed two mugs from the table, giving them a quick rinse before putting the kettle on. 'Leo's at school at the moment; you'll meet him later.'

Luisa looked shyly at Rose from beneath dark, impossibly long lashes as she peered at her from behind Astrid's legs.

Holy maracas! She sure takes after her mother.

'Like bunnies?' Luisa asked with an uncertain tone.

'Why yes, I most certainly do,' replied Rose seriously.

Thump, thump, thump. Luisa trundled out of the room with the unsteady gait of a toddler in a hurry.

'She's gone to find her favourite teddy,' said Astrid, clearing a space at the table and setting a mug of tea down in front of Rose. 'Milk? Sugar? Here you go. The agency said they were having trouble finding anyone who could start so soon, but it seems they did, which is good, I think. I couldn't stand it for much more, stuck out here all on my own.' Astrid barely paused for breath. 'While you're here and Mrs B is off, you will do the cooking, cleaning and shopping. And you will look after Luisa and Leo on my nights and day off and help me out. You can cook, can't you? We especially wanted someone who can cook,' she said insistently.

'I think I can manage that. And yes, I know my way around a kitchen. But where is Mrs Cameron, or Mr Cameron? I thought one of them would be here to show me around.'

'Mark's off to a conference today. He's left me in charge.' Astrid stuck out her chin defiantly.

'Oh.' Rose wasn't sure how she felt about being bossed around by someone who was by all appearances still in her teens, but she reined in her ego. She only needed to suck it up for a few weeks, get what she came for, and then split – take off for the beach perhaps. It had to be warm *somewhere* in this humongous country.

She still couldn't quite believe that she'd agreed so easily to Henry's harebrained scheme. There were more holes in his plan than in the moth-eaten pullovers her father favoured. If she'd been thinking more clearly, she'd have dismissed it outright, but she'd been preoccupied with her boyfriend Giles's – make that ex-boyfriend, she corrected herself – abrupt ending of their relationship and his sudden departure for a new job in Brussels. As it was, she had jumped at the chance to flee the country herself, and put as much space between the 'gutless wonder' (as Henry had called him when she told him what had happened) and herself as she could.

When they were growing up, her brother always looked out for her. Eight years older and infinitely wiser, Henry had fought Rose's childhood battles for her, seeing off some of the older girls at school who picked on her for her height (by the age of eleven she'd towered over everyone in the class), pipecleaner legs and woefully unfashionable clothes. She also had the kind of wide mouth that made her the butt of frog jokes. Her cheeks still flamed at the memory of those days.

In his own odd way, she guessed Henry was probably still trying to look after her now – but it had resulted in him persuading her to leave all that was familiar behind. Okay, so she had been jobless, heartbroken and homeless (Giles had sublet their flat – well, technically it was *his* flat – after informing her he was leaving town), which were all pretty compelling reasons to go along with Henry's plans.

She hadn't wanted to stay in the flat anyway. Without Giles there it was as hollow as her heart, sadness lingering like the smell of burnt garlic. Henry had sent a mate with a panel van to collect her stuff and arranged to store it in his garage. Offering her his spare room, he had allowed her a couple of weeks of wallowing. Then one morning before he left for work, he had knocked on the bedroom door.

'C'mon, sis, you can't stay in there forever. It's not doing you any good at all.'

Taking in her dishevelled appearance, stringy hair and red-rimmed eyes, he ushered her towards the shower, gathering up dirty coffee cups and stale peanut-butter-covered toast crusts as he did so.

'You go and clean yourself up; I'll take care of everything else.'

'But I was about to buy the Instyler Tulip Auto Curler!' she protested. 'It's on special offer to callers for the next ten minutes! Ten pounds off.' Rose had been gorging on the 24-hour infomercial channel. Anything to take her mind off things.

Henry was immovable.

Grumbling under her breath about bossy older brothers, she nevertheless did as she was told, picking up a box of tissues like it was a hospital drip she was attached to and shuffling towards the bathroom, barely registering the worried look on his face.

Later, over a mug of tea to which Henry had added nearly half the sugar bowl, she listened as he outlined his plan.

'You're depressed,' he announced.

'No shit, Sherlock. Don't you think I've got every right to be?'

He ignored her question. 'I know just what you need.'

'Oh yeah? You and Dr Phil both, huh?'

Henry held up his hand to stop her. 'The way I see it, you've got nothing to keep you here.'

'Well, thanks for that,' she said sarcastically. 'Are you telling me that my life is completely pointless now? 'Cause that's what it feels like from where I'm sitting.'

'Don't be daft, Rosie, you know I didn't mean it like

that. You're footloose and fancy-free – nothing tying you down. People would kill for that. The world is your oyster. It's time to get out there instead of burying yourself half-alive here.'

'Given that I'm skint and virtually homeless – oh, and broken-hearted, in case you'd forgotten – I'd say that kind of limits my options.'

He waved her concerns away, 'Details, darling, details.'

Rose marvelled at her brother's ability to see the bright side of every situation.

'As your caring but incredibly interfering older brother,' he said, then paused. 'I've got a proposition for you. Call it a favour if you like. I want you to do some digging for me and report back. It's a bit of a way away, but as it happens, there's a job on offer at a vineyard I'm interested in. A mate of mine over there mentioned it, when I was telling him how miserable you were. They're after someone who can cook a bit, so I thought you might be able to manage that.'

She threw the box of tissues at him.

Having grown up with Henry, and remembering him as a gangly, pimpled teenager, Rose often forgot that her brother was now considered a bit of a big shot in certain circles. He'd started his career as a wine merchant with Berry Bros. & Rudd, and now, thanks in part to an old schoolmate, had interests in a number of vineyards in Argentina and Spain. He'd always been ambitious, even when they were kids. He was the one who'd convinced their dad to drive him to Iceland one scorching summer (the frozen foods store, not the country: he wasn't that crazy) and bulk-buy ice-creams to sell on to their school friends for a tidy profit.

Henry had always known exactly where he was going and had wasted no time getting there. Recently, after a discreet tip-off, he'd bought a couple of struggling Spanish wineries on the cheap and put in new management to turn them around, using his connections to shift the inventory into the UK. If what Rose heard was true, he was doing rather well out of it. So when Henry said 'digging', she knew he wasn't talking about the kind that involved spades and soil.

As Henry outlined his plan, Rose's first thought was that he was off his head. Australia was the other side of the world, a gazillion miles away, and she'd never even heard of the Shingle Valley.

'Here's the number of the au pair agency that's dealing with the job,' he said, thrusting a slip of paper at her. 'Call them. They'll love you, I know it. If nothing else, it'll take your mind off that little twerp.'

'Hey, that's my ex-boyfriend you're referring to, if you don't mind! I thought you liked him.'

'I revised my opinion when he was such a shit to you.'

Henry had been insistent. He could sell sand in the Sahara, even to someone who knew his wiles as well as Rose did, and so Rose had found herself agreeing to his plan. 'Against my better judgment, let it be noted,' she had protested.

She'd been on a plane before she'd had time to properly think it through.

Thump!

Rose was startled out of her reverie by the return of Luisa, who had thrust a sodden, grimy lump of what had possibly once been a pink velour rabbit at her.

'Ugh,' she said, recoiling before she could help herself.

'Bunny!' exclaimed Luisa, undaunted.

Rose looked up to see Astrid laughing at her.

Oh Christ. What had she let herself in for?

CHAPTER 2

The welcome from Astrid had been as cool as the air temperature, but Rose decided not to dwell on it. She wrapped her hands around the mug, wincing as the feeling returned to her extremities. At least the tea was hot.

'So when do I start?'

'Now, of course,' said Astrid sternly. 'How did you get here? Do you have a car?'

'Um, yes, I'm parked around by the cellar door. I wasn't sure where to leave it.'

'No problem. I'll show you where to drop your stuff. There's a room for you in the barn.' Astrid drained the last of her tea, stood up and grabbed her coat from the back of one of the chairs. 'Come on then.'

Rose perked up at the sound of a barn. She followed Astrid, who had swept Luisa and her manky bunny up into her arms, to the back door and across the garden. A barn. How romantic! She had visions of a New England-style conversion, all soaring spaces and white walls, overstuffed loose-covered cream sofas and thoughtfully placed glass bowls of blousy peonies in shades of blush pink ...

Hmm, perhaps not.

Rose surveyed the dilapidated structure in front of her. This barn stretched the definition of habitable and clearly hadn't been occupied for quite some time. Its roof was a cobbled-together patchwork of rusted corrugated iron, and the plaster on the walls crumbled at her touch.

Walking inside, she discovered that a thick layer of dust coated the windowsills, the floor – any horizontal surface, actually – and the windows were cobwebbed and grimy. There was a cavernous white-walled sitting area with a couple of faded sofas; the far end of the space had been sectioned off to form a couple of bedrooms; and there was also a small bathroom with a deep, claw-footed rust-stained tub and a shower over it. Rose peered into one of the bedrooms and found an unmade bed with a lumpy mattress, several curling paperbacks on the bedside table, and an ancient, very dusty dresser. It lacked the *Home Beautiful* touch, that was for sure.

'I'll leave you to get settled,' said Astrid, hurrying out of the door with Luisa still in her arms, back to the relative warmth of the main house.

Rose sat for a moment on the bed, shivering in the chilly air, torn between a desire to drive back to Sydney as fast as four wheels could take her, and the lure of huddling up under a blanket and sleeping off the last vestiges of her jet lag.

She did neither.

Silently cursing her brother, and kicking herself for agreeing to his plans, Rose walked back to the cellar door. Retrieving her car, she followed a track that wound around the back of the winery to the barn. Arriving at her destination, she popped the boot, grabbed her backpack and threw it into the barn's living room.

She needed clean sheets, a broom and plenty of bleach, so she set out purposefully towards the house again. If she was going to stay, even for only a few weeks, she might as well have somewhere halfway decent to sleep.

As Rose made her way back she caught sight of a tall, rangy figure striding towards her. He had his head down, his hands jammed into the pockets of his jeans, and as he got closer she could see a definite scowl on his face. Rose knew immediately who it was: Mark Cameron. But he didn't appear to notice her until they were almost shoulder to shoulder. She was just wondering if she should say something to him when he glanced up and blinked at her. He looked as if he had been a million miles away.

'Hello, can I help you? I'm afraid the cellar door's not open today.'

His voice was low and husky and Rose gave an involuntary shiver. She found herself staring into eyes as green and as dark as bottle glass. She realised they were on a level with hers, not something that she encountered all that often – she was used to being taller than most men. It was a little unnerving to gaze directly into such a forbidding scowl.

'Er ... um, actually, I'm not here for the cellar door.'

'Well, we're not running any winery tours at the moment either,' he said abruptly. As he finished speaking recognition dawned on his face, softening its harshness. 'Oh, you must be Rose. Of course. Sorry, I completely forgot that you were coming today. Have you met Astrid? Been shown around?' He held out his hand and she took it in hers. She felt a prickle of electricity at his touch. His grip was firm, his skin dry and smooth, though his nails were ragged and stained purple. 'Always judge a man by his hands,' her nanna had insisted. 'His hands and his shoes.' By shoes, Nanna had meant brogues, from Loake or Lobb, no doubt. Rose briefly wondered what she'd have made of Mark's rough-and-ready hands and his mud-encrusted boots.

'Yes. Thanks, Mr Cameron. I was just getting settled in the barn.'

He grimaced. 'It's not in the best state, but at least it's dry.'

'It'll be fine.' Rose didn't know what else to say. She didn't want to be a stuck-up princess and complain about her digs when she'd barely been there five minutes.

'Good. Now, if you'll excuse me, I've got to get on. I'm off to a conference for a few days – bloody inconvenient – but Astrid will fill you in on everything.'

Rose nodded. She wasn't sure if the conference was inconvenient for him or her.

'Oh, and it's Mark by the way. Mr Cameron is my father,' he said with a brief wink as he turned to leave.

'Well he wasn't so bad,' thought Rose to herself later as she returned from the house with rubber gloves, mop, bucket and an industrial-sized bottle of disinfectant, and set about sanitising, dusting and de-cobwebbing her new home, rehousing several daddy longlegs in the process. Thankfully there were no enormous arachnids of the kind Australia was famous for.

Finally satisfied, she wiped her hair away from her cheek and glanced at her watch. Two o'clock. No wonder her stomach had been growling for the past hour. She looked around at the now spick-and-span room – all her clothes were neatly put away, her backpack stowed under the bed. Stepping into the living area, she confirmed with satisfaction that she could now at least see out of the windows, the cushions were plumped and the floor swept. *You could almost eat off that now*, she thought. *Speaking of which ...*

Heading back to the kitchen, Rose bumped into Astrid and Luisa. They had their coats and boots on again.

'We're going to feed the chooks,' said Astrid.

'Shooks!' repeated Luisa, eyes wide with excitement. 'Shooks! Shoooooks!' she shouted at the top of her voice.

'Can I come too?' Rose asked, thoughts of food momentarily forgotten. The faster she got to know her way around Kalkari the better. The first step was to get her bearings on the sprawling vineyard estate.

'If you like. Lead the way, Luisa.'

Rose followed them meekly out into the yard.

Luisa toddled across the scrubby lawn towards a wooden chicken house. Astrid shook a carton of feed, and several of the rusty-coloured birds Rose had seen when she first arrived began to strut jerkily towards her. 'That is Maggie,' Astrid said, pointing to the largest chicken. 'Then there's Stephanie and Nigella. And over there is Nugget.' Bringing up the rear, marshalling his hens, was a fine-looking rooster with colourful tail-feathers. Rose laughed to herself. Only Australians would call a chicken Nugget.

Luisa was excitedly chasing the hens around the yard, trying in vain to catch one. Astrid got closer, scooped up Nigella and placed her in the little girl's arms. Luisa beamed with joy, dimples denting each chubby cheek.

'Shooks!' she cried excitedly.

'Don't squeeze her. Be gentle,' warned Astrid, as she leaned into the hen house.

'Do you get many eggs?' asked Rose, addressing Astrid's petite bottom, which was now sticking out of the hen house.

'Yes, they lay well. We are never short of eggs,' Astrid replied. After a moment she asked, 'Have you eaten?'

'Actually, I was on my way to the kitchen when I bumped into you. I'm so hungry my stomach thinks my throat's been cut – I didn't really have time for breakfast this morning.' Rose placed her hand over her belly.

Astrid gave her an odd look.

Perhaps she doesn't understand the English idiom, thought Rose.

'Well, there's not much in the fridge, but there's a loaf of bread, some cheese and a jar of Mrs B's chutney in the pantry, if you like.'

Rose left the two of them playing chase around the

yard and made her way back to the kitchen. Astrid had moved the breakfast dishes, but there were now the remains of lunch on the table. Rose piled everything up to one side of the still overflowing sink, resolving to deal with all the dishes after some sustenance. Making herself a doorstop cheese-and-pickle sandwich, she sat down and grabbed an old magazine that had been hidden under the debris on the table. As she slowly flipped the pages, absorbing the mouth-watering photos of lavish food, she began to wonder exactly when Mrs Cameron – Isabella – would make an appearance.

She finished her sandwich and decided to put the kitchen to rights. Hidden behind a cupboard, she discovered a cleverly concealed dishwasher – praise the Lord! – and began to scrape dishes and stack them into it. Peering into the cupboard under the sink, she found detergent, sponges and everything else she needed, and set to work scrubbing and polishing, wiping sticky surfaces and sweeping the stone floor.

When she'd set off from Sydney early that morning, she'd not imagined that her day was going to pan out quite like this, and she shook her head, as much at herself and what she was getting herself into as at the state of the place. It had sounded like an easy task when she'd been sitting in Henry's London flat as he explained what he needed her to do. Now she was actually here though, it was all too real. And involved far too much washing up for her liking.

Astrid and Luisa had gone out after feeding the chooks, and Rose was just sitting down with a cup of instant coffee, having finally cleared up the kitchen, when she heard a car pull up in front of the house. She heard Astrid's strident tones, a giggle from Luisa, and then another voice too.

They came tramping into the kitchen and Rose saw that the third voice belonged to a scruffy-looking dark-haired boy of about six or seven, wearing grey school trousers that stopped several inches above his ankles and a red V-neck sweater that looked equally shrunken. His big toe poked through a hole in his sock. This must be Leo.

'Hullo,' he said.

'Hey, Leo, I'm Rose,' she said, giving him her best fake-cheery smile.

'Rose has come to help us out because Mrs B's sick, Leo,' said Astrid. 'She's from England.'

Rose wasn't altogether sure she liked Astrid's emphasis on the word 'England'. She made it sound like a communicable disease. But perhaps Rose was just being over-sensitive. Best to give Astrid the benefit of the doubt – she wasn't here to make an enemy of the nanny.

Leo's eyes, however, lit up. 'Cool. Have you seen Tottenham play? Harry Kane's *awesome*! I really, really want to see him play. Would you take me there?' His words tumbled out in a rush.

Rose liked his enthusiasm. He seemed like a nice kid. 'Actually, Leo, I have been to White Hart Lane. More than once in fact. They're my dad's favourite team. And mine too.'

Leo's eyes grew wide. 'That is so cool! Wait til I tell Joe.'

'Joe?' asked Rose.

'Best friend,' explained Astrid.

Luisa, not wanting to be left out, came over to Rose and held her arms up for a cuddle. Rose hoisted her onto her knee as Astrid opened a sweet-smelling white paper bag.

'Bakery treats,' she said, piling glossy jam tarts, coconut-flecked sponge and caramel squares topped with a thick layer of dark chocolate onto a plate. 'You have been working hard,' she said grudgingly, casting her eyes around the now spotless kitchen and lifting the heavy kettle onto the range. 'I didn't think you'd do so much today.'

Rose helped herself to a slice of fudgy caramel and chocolate shortbread and self-consciously adjusted the waistband of her jeans, which was biting into the flesh around her stomach. Astrid hadn't exactly rolled out the welcome mat, but it was nice to have her efforts acknowledged at least. The cakes weren't bad either.

After Leo had done his homework and the kids had eaten some fish fingers that Rose had discovered, rimed with frost, in the depths of the freezer, she walked back to the barn to sluice off the dust from the day's efforts. She was filthy and couldn't wait a moment longer to get clean; she just hoped there would be some hot water.

Making her way across the yard, she stopped abruptly as she spied an upright silhouette frozen against the skyline. It was a kangaroo. As Rose's eyes adjusted to the dusk

light, she saw another – and another. Rose chuckled gleefully to herself. She couldn't believe her eyes. She'd seen the
yellow road sign with the image of Skippy on it on her
drive into the valley, but she hadn't thought she'd actually
see any. *Real kangaroos! Bloody Nora!* Wait till she told
Henry. She stayed and watched as they became used to her
presence and returned to nibbling the sweet grass, but she
didn't linger long. It was freaking freezing outside, kangaroos or no kangaroos.

Inside the barn it was barely a degree warmer than outside, though at least there was hot water. Showering and
towelling off quickly, she then piled on every one of the four
t-shirts she'd brought with her, plus a musty pullover that
she'd found in one of the drawers in the chest. The wool was
scratchy, and the colour – Coleman's mustard yellow – made
her skin look sallow, but she wasn't exactly in a position to
be fussy. At least it covered her bum. She was grateful that
the thick sheepskin of her new ugg boots was keeping her
toes toasty.

Back at the house, all was quiet. Rose followed the
sound of voices and came upon Luisa and Leo in a small living room off the kitchen, sitting on a faded burgundy sofa,
its velvet completely bald on the rolled arms. Astrid was
reading to Luisa. Rose nearly cracked up, hearing her asking,
'But vere is de green sheep?', but kept silent, not wanting
Astrid to think she was making fun of her.

Rose got her chance to find out more about Mark and the absent Isabella over a late dinner with Astrid after the kids were in bed. There wasn't much in the way of supplies, but thanks to Maggie, Stephanie and Nigella, and an overgrown herb garden she'd discovered at the side of the house, she was able to throw together a potato and parsley frittata. As it finished cooking, Astrid appeared in the kitchen, holding up an unlabelled bottle.

'The house wine,' Astrid said, reaching for a couple of glasses.

'Yes, please,' said Rose. The exhaustion of the day's cleaning, her early morning drive from Sydney and lingering jet lag was hitting her badly now. 'That'll go down nicely.'

'You really can cook. This is good,' mumbled Astrid through a mouthful of frittata.

'So I said,' said Rose, bristling slightly, though inwardly pleased at the compliment. 'I trained at Le Cordon Bleu in London. But my last job was in a cafe,' she admitted. 'And I've flipped more burgers than I've plated up *haute cuisine* meals so far.' She told Astrid the story that she and Henry had agreed on: that she was here to take a bit of a break and experience the country, perhaps do some more travelling eventually.

'Me too.' Astrid nodded. 'I've been in Oz for about eight months. I spent a couple of months up in Queensland working at a kids' club in a resort, then found this job in March. Leo and Luisa are a bit of a handful though. But then, who wouldn't be if their mother walked out on them?'

Rose looked up from her plate. Isabella had walked

out? She hadn't been expecting to hear that. Though it did perhaps explain why the house was in such a state and Leo's clothes were too small for him.

'She left at the end of summer,' Astrid continued. 'She went back to Spain, with a Spanish winemaker who was here to help with vintage. Mark had no idea. She was the complete nightmare, so Mrs B tells me. Señora Demanda, she calls her. The cleaning, the cooking: nothing was good enough. I think that's half the reason Mrs B got sick: Isabella made her work so hard. Luisa still asks where her mama is, but Leo won't talk about it, won't talk much at all in fact. When he met you today, that is the best I've seen him; he was so excited to talk to you about the football.'

'Oh, that's so sad.' From what she'd seen that day, they were perfectly nice children. 'The poor things. And how long is Mark away for?'

'He'll be back at the end of the week. Mark has the black moods sometimes. It's not always easy.' She didn't elaborate further and Rose didn't press the subject. She needed to tread carefully and not arouse any suspicions. She was sure she'd find out more soon enough.

The conversation moved on to Astrid and where she'd grown up – Rose had been close in her assumption of Germany: Austria, in fact – and before they knew it, the bottle was empty and the remains of the frittata had grown cold on the plate. Rising to clear the dishes, Rose was surprised at the stiffness that had invaded her body. She'd spent a few days seeing the sights of Sydney before she'd arrived in the Shingle Valley, without so much as a twinge, but clearly a day of vigorous cleaning was another matter entirely. Her spirits sank a little as she realised there was probably plenty more cleaning in store tomorrow, if the state of the kitchen was anything to go by. She said goodnight to Astrid and prepared to head back to the barn.

As she opened the back door, an icy draft of air hit her in the face like a slap, instantly sobering her up. 'Christ, it's cold.'

'Yep. In the Tyrol, it is very cold; that's why I came to Australia. I thought those two extra letters would make a difference. Pah! They do not!' Astrid shivered theatrically. 'Oh, I forgot to tell you, we get up at about seven. I have to get Leo to school by half of the eight.'

'Right. I'll be in the kitchen before seven-thirty and get breakfast on,' said Rose. 'It's good to be here,' she added. She wasn't sure why she'd said that; the words came out before she had a chance to think about them. They were hardly true.

'Yes, I am happy too,' replied Astrid. It seemed that their shared dinner had thawed her initial frostiness.

'Night then,' Rose called.

It was so cold in the barn that Rose could see her breath and the wind whistled through huge gaps under the door and window frames. Not having thought to pack warm pyjamas and knowing that the flimsy sleeping tee and old pair of Giles's boxers she had with her wouldn't cut it, she wriggled out of her jeans and pulled on a pair of leggings she'd thrown into her pack at the last minute. She kept her t-shirts and socks on and shivered under the covers, glad that she'd found a couple of heavy blankets in the wardrobe earlier. She resolved to ask about heaters, or at the very least a hot water bottle, tomorrow.

For a fleeting moment her mind turned to Giles. She had vowed to keep her thoughts on a tight rein where he was concerned, but he snuck into them whenever her guard was down. Before she knew it, she was reliving their last few days together. It was like prodding an open wound: although she knew no good would come of it, she couldn't help herself. She shivered again, and not just with cold, as she remembered the day her life had begun to go completely tits up.

Friday the thirteenth. Of course. And Mercury had been retrograde. She really should have known better.

It had turned out to be a day of endings: it was also the last day of her job at The Pine Box, the cafe where she'd worked for the previous five years. Although most of the time there she'd felt like she was ready for a pine box herself by the end of a shift, being dismissed without notice stung more than she cared to admit. And all over something as stupid as a steak.

The red-faced, puffed-up tosser with the bad haircut had complained so loudly that Arthur, the other cook, and the one who was responsible for the steak, had come out of the kitchen to investigate. 'It's as tasteless as an Axminster carpet,' the customer had bawled. Hearing the man going off at Arthur, Rose came out from behind the swing doors.

If there was anything that made her blood boil, it was people who thought they were powerful picking on those they considered beneath them. She'd been the target of her fair share of bullies at school and after she'd left, had vowed never to stand by and let it happen to anyone else. Seeing red, she'd tipped the jug of gravy she'd been carrying over the ignorant bugger's plate, sloshing it onto his lap, soaking his trousers and scalding his nether regions. 'That'll add some flavour to it, you rude sod,' she'd said.

Needless to say it hadn't ended well. She was out on her ear before her shift had even finished.

With her twenties very nearly over, Rose's life hadn't exactly panned out the way she'd thought it would when she was nineteen, the ink barely dry on her culinary diploma, ready to take on the world. Two of her classmates from Le Cordon Bleu had recently opened a restaurant that was London's darling, another had her own line of gourmet produce − available at Fortnum's no less − and her best friend was sous chef at Le Du, Bangkok's hottest restaurant *du jour*. If Facebook was to be believed, most of her old school friends were happily married; heavens, two had just had babies and Nancy, who she'd known since primary school and always the one most likely to breed − had three under five. All Rose had was a set of expensive chef's knives, and ten years' experience, mostly working a deep-fryer.

Then, just to reinforce the fact that the entire planetary system had decided to conspire against her, Giles, the man she'd thought she would end up married to, the one she was going to share the dream house in the country and a khaki-green Landrover with and make two or maybe even three apple-cheeked children with, announced that he was moving to Brussels. Without her.

Never mind that they shared custody of a poo-brown ('toffee', the Habitat sales assistant had convinced them) leather sofa and five years of memories: apparently she was supposed to have known that it wasn't a 'forever thing'. After dropping his bombshell that evening, he'd buggered off out before she'd even had the chance to tell him about being fired from The Pine Box. The prospect of a double episode of *The Great British Bake Off* – which she'd really been looking forward to – and the fact that there was a bowl of salted-caramel cookie dough in the fridge failed to make her feel even the slightest bit better. Even she couldn't think about food at a time like that.

Rose wriggled further into the blankets, trying to keep out the frigid air and wondered again why on earth she'd gone along with Henry's suggestion. Giles had no idea where she was – in a stronger moment, she'd deleted him from Facebook and his number from her phone. What if things in Brussels didn't work out? What if he changed his mind and realised he'd made a big mistake and came back and found her gone? What if she'd made a big mistake in coming here? She suddenly felt very far away and very alone.

CHAPTER 3

Waking up, Rose reluctantly poked her nose over the blankets and lowered them to her chin. For a minute she couldn't work out where she was. Then the events of the previous day came flooding back. Ah yes. The Shingle Valley. Arse-end of nowhere.

Checking her watch and seeing that it was nearly seven, it took all her determination to throw back the covers. It was far too cold to even think about a shower, so she made do with a quick splash of water on her face and pulled her hair back into a messy ponytail. She noticed ice on the inside of the barn's windows as she prepared to head over to the house. Looking outside, she could see a white-tipped winter wonderland – an overnight frost had carpeted everything with a fine layer of crystals.

This is insane. I'm going to freeze to death.

In the kitchen, she set about scrambling eggs for the kids' breakfast, made a pot of tea and set the table. The kitchen's oil-burning range warmed the room, and the tips of Rose's fingers and toes slowly defrosted.

Leo came into the kitchen first, flashing her a brief look of acknowledgment before sitting down and opening up the book he was carrying. His animation of the previous day was nowhere to be seen. Luisa and Astrid came next, Astrid chasing Luisa with a hairbrush as she tried to catch her and tame her wild curls.

'Come here, miss minxy,' Astrid said, as Luisa hid behind Rose's legs.

'Wosie?' asked Luisa.

'Yes, poppet?' Rose had fallen hard for Luisa's delectable dimples.

'I don't like my hairbrush.' The toddler stuck her thumb in her mouth and looked dolefully up at her.

'Aw, sweetie, if you brush your hair, it'll grow long and silky like a mermaid's,' Rose offered, trying to console her.

'What's a mermaid?'

'A beautiful lady who swims like a fish and sings to sailors as their ships go by.'

Luisa brightened. 'Hokay. I be a mermaid,' she said, and submitted to Astrid's brushstrokes.

'Thanks,' said Astrid, grinning at her.

With breakfast over, and with Luisa's hair restrained in two pink butterfly clips, Astrid set out to take Leo to school. 'Luisa has a swimming lesson this morning, so we won't be back till lunchtime. Mark left money for food and anything else we need in the jar over there.' She indicated a cream-coloured earthenware pot sitting on a high shelf over the range. 'The nearest supermarket is in Eumeralla, and there's a farmers' market there on Saturday. We can all go to that if you want.'

'Sounds good,' said Rose, who was already in the process of writing a long shopping list. She had woken up with new resolve. She might as well take this job seriously while she was here. Clearly Astrid hadn't had time to stock the pantry in recent weeks, and there was precious little in the way of staples, let alone fresh food and veg. Eggs, herbs from the garden and homemade preserves seemed to be the only things they weren't short of. And wine, of course.

Rose finally got the car's temperamental heater to sputter to life, and motored along the road to Eumeralla. The 'valley of plenty', Henry had called the Shingle Valley when he'd described it back in London; it had sounded so lovely and lush. The reality was not so Elysian: endless rows of emaciated vines lined her way, interspersed with small triangular ponds that gleamed an icy silver in the pale light. A shallow river, frozen at its edges, snaked its way along the valley floor. She passed shaggy, conker-brown cows and grubby white sheep. Horses in fields of bleached grass huddled together for warmth, steam blowing in clouds from their nostrils. The bleakness of the landscape did have a kind of raw beauty though, she had to admit.

As she approached Eumeralla – 'Settled in 1833', the sign proclaimed – she drove past neatly kept weatherboard cottages with bullnose verandahs, some with rose bushes out the front, their few stray blooms bright spots of colour fluttering in the breeze. The town itself offered a clutch of old stone buildings gathered either side of its wide main street, interspersed with smaller timber houses and shops. As she slowed down to look for the supermarket, Rose spotted a Chinese restaurant, two pubs with upstairs verandahs, a hardware store, a large general store, a town hall, a war memorial and a small park. Pulling into a space on the side of the main street, she unfolded her legs from the tiny car and spied a cafe. 'Sacred Grounds', read the A-frame sign on the pavement outside. 'Dark, bitter and hot for you.'

Ha. Someone round here has a sense of humour.

Ordering a cappuccino, Rose took a stool by the window and watched the town residents going about their business. Across the street near the park, a straggling line of schoolkids followed their teacher. Rose strained her eyes to see if Leo was among them, but these children looked a little older than him, and their wide-brimmed hats obscured their faces. A couple of gnarled old men wearing thick jackets and leaning on walking sticks had stopped on a bench just along from the cafe to watch the world go by. A young mum pushing a pram laden with shopping was headed in the opposite direction towards a crossroads.

It was a far cry from London, or even Bondi, where she'd spent the previous week.

Finishing her coffee and gathering her things, Rose

headed in the direction of the supermarket. It was not exactly her local Waitrose. There were quite a few things on her list that the store didn't seem to stock. Getting used to completely different brands and even names of things – what exactly was bocconcini anyway? – was time-consuming, and it was late morning by the time she eventually returned to Kalkari.

That afternoon, Rose decided to cook. Anything to take her mind off Giles. She found an old apron on the back of the pantry door and got started. It was soothing to be back in the kitchen, and the familiar motions of chopping and kneading made her feel a tiny bit more at home in this alien place. It also didn't hurt that the kitchen was the only place in the house that was warm. First up, she made a huge pot of bolognaise, some of which she froze and the rest of which went into a lasagne for dinner that night. She'd been able to find dried yeast in Eumeralla and now weighed flour for a loaf. She chopped onions, carrots, celery and herbs, smashing her knife down on the board as she thought of all the things she should have said to Giles when he'd been surprised she was so upset at his casually announced departure. 'But babe, you knew it wasn't going to last,' he'd said. 'We're fundamentally such different people.' *Yeah, only one of us is an arsehole*, she thought savagely, dismissing her doubts of the previous night and wishing she'd had the presence of mind to say that to him at the time. Putting the knife down and taking a deep breath, she added the now pulverised vegetables to a deep pan containing a whole chicken and a generous amount of barley, and set it to simmer on the range.

Then she began to measure out flour, butter, eggs and cocoa.

'What you doin'?' a little voice behind her piped up. Luisa had crept unnoticed into the kitchen, her cheeks rosy from sleep and her dark hair wild about her face.

'Hey, sweetheart. You're just in time. I could really do with some help here. Would you like to make these biscuits with me?' Rose asked.

Luisa nodded vigorously, her dark curls jiggling with the effort, and Rose hoisted her up to stand on a chair next to the bench and handed her a wooden spoon. 'Can you stir that?' The little girl was thrilled to be helping out, and Rose's heart melted completely. She really was a poppet.

Astrid followed Luisa in and sat down at the table.

'Hey,' said Rose brightly. 'Everything's under control here, especially now I've got my helper.' Rose indicated Luisa, who was eating chocolate chips from a packet on the counter.

'I called in to see Mrs B on our way back from swimming,' said Astrid.

'Oh yes?' said Rose, suddenly concerned that her time at Kalkari might be over before it had begun. Aside from discovering that Mark's wife had walked out, she still had serious sleuthing to do for Henry.

'She's feeling better but not hurrying to come back to work. She's quite old, and I think it has all become too much hard work for her.'

'Oh, that's good,' said Rose, feeling relieved that she wasn't going to be kicked out before she'd barely got her foot in the door. She might be stuck out in the middle of nowhere, but she had made a promise to Henry, despite her misgivings, and she didn't want to let him down.

'She said she misses the kids though. She will come to babysit on Friday night so we can go out. There's not much going on around here, but the pub in town is okay and they sometimes have a band. I've been stuck here by myself for so long, it'd be great to get away, just for a few hours. I've got cottage fever.'

'I think you mean cabin fever!' laughed Rose, though Kalkari House was more mansion than cabin. Letting Luisa gouge the cookie dough off the spoon with her fingers, Rose slid the baking sheets into the top oven of the range. 'Sounds great.' She was keen to see what the area had to offer and perhaps get some intel on Kalkari from some of the locals before Mark returned from his conference.

Having heard from Astrid how moody he could be, Rose was apprehensive about her new boss, not least because she was there under false pretences.

On Friday night, sure enough, Mrs B arrived to babysit. Rose warmed to her immediately. A tough old bird, broad of beam and firm of handshake, she quickly took in the scrubbed-up surroundings and appetising smell of a casserole on the range. 'Looks like you've settled in well, love,' she said to Rose. 'Truth be told, I've been ready to retire for a while now but I didn't like to leave Mark in the lurch – not with that fancy piece of Spanish Harlem upping and leaving him and those two poor kiddies like she did.'

'That your doing?' she asked, pointing an arthritic finger at a sponge Rose had made that afternoon. Luisa had 'helped' her with the lemon icing and it had dripped haphazardly down the sides.

'Um, yes. Why?' It wasn't one of her best, but Rose couldn't imagine what was wrong with a cake.

'You should keep a look out for the next CWA competition – it's on next month. Everyone enters something, but I'll warn you, we take our baking pretty seriously around here.'

Rose hadn't a clue what the CWA was but didn't get the chance to ask. Mrs B settled herself and her knitting on the sofa and as Leo and Luisa raced down, pyjamaed and sweet-smelling after their baths, gathered them cosily to her. 'Now, chickies, how have you been? Leo, I swear you've grown a foot since I was last here.' The children were obviously thrilled to see her, and Luisa climbed onto her lap, burying her head into Mrs B's soft, cardigan-clad bosom.

Rose escaped to the barn and put on a clean shirt, ran a brush through her long hair, leaving it loose, and applied a slick of gloss to her lips and mascara to her lashes. She seriously considered leaving on her uggs, but changed them for a pair of work boots she'd liberated from the back verandah that were just her size. She wasn't sure what the ugg-wearing etiquette might be at the pub, and she didn't want to stand out as a tourist. But being only a smidge under six foot, she generally stood out wherever she went without even trying. Throwing on a jacket that Astrid had lent her, and winding a scarf several times around her neck, she was ready. Travelling light severely restricted her wardrobe choices, but she somehow doubted that the Southern Cross Hotel was going to be style central.

Driving through the pitch darkness to Eumeralla was eerie, even with Astrid in the passenger seat, and as they cruised down the main street, Rose was relieved to see fairy lights strung up along the eaves of the pub. Astrid had mentioned that quite a few of the local winemakers and winery workers made the place a regular Friday pitstop and, sure enough, despite the cold night, the place was jumping. They had to thread their way through the crowd towards the bar, which was two deep with people waiting to order a beer.

'Hey, Astrid!' called a loud voice.

Rose turned and saw a guy with a freckled face and a mop of curly blond hair, wearing a flannel shirt, waving madly at them.

'Thommo!' Astrid yelled back.

'Hey, how ya goin'?' he said as he reached them. 'Is this the new girl I've heard about?' he asked, looking Rose up and down as if she were a prize heifer.

Before she could stop herself, Rose sucked in her stomach. She might be heartsick, but she wasn't immune to cute boys, especially ones as friendly as this one seemed to be.

'Ha! Nothing happens in this valley without someone noticing,' Astrid laughed. 'Thommo, this is Rose. Rose, this is Thommo. Thommo is from Windsong Estate. Born and bred in the valley. A "man of the land", so he tells me.' Astrid fluttered her eyelashes at him.

'Pleased to meet you, Thommo,' Rose said formally.

'Likewise. Now, let's give you a proper Shingle Valley welcome. What are you both drinking? My shout.'

Rose stuck to a light beer, as she'd offered to drive, but Astrid hoed into a double vodka and tonic enthusiastically, before disappearing amid the crowd in the pub.

Thommo took Rose over to where a knot of people were standing, propping up a narrow shelf that ran around the back of the room. She did a double-take: one of them was pretty much a carbon copy of Thommo.

He thrust his hand out. 'G'day. Charlie. Thommo's older brother.'

'Yeah, by five minutes,' said Thommo.

Charlie then introduced her to Deano, Mick and Angie, a trio who also all looked to be in their mid-twenties, and who worked at Lilybells, one of the valley's largest wineries. With them was Bob, a white-haired old man with a face like a dry riverbed, lines hewn into it from years of blistering sun and wind. Bob was the proprietor of Bob's Run, which, Charlie informed her, was a small winery just further along Shingle Road from Kalkari. Standing over by the far side of the bar was the dreadlocked barista from Sacred Grounds. Recognising him, Rose went to say hello.

As they talked, she surveyed the crowded pub, spotting two steel-haired old crones sitting at a small table by a crackling fire, one skinny as a rake, with long bony arms, and the other solid and sturdy, with thighs the size of hams straining at her flowered skirt. She asked Bevan, the barista, who they were.

'The Trevelyn sisters,' he said. 'Violet and Vera. Rumour has it they grow their grapes with a fair whack of witchcraft.' Rose blinked at him, not sure if she believed him. 'Well, whether they do or not, they produce some of the best grapes in the valley. Everyone clamours to get hold of their fruit. They farm biodynamically, bury cowshit in horns by the light of the moon, brew up compost tea, all that sort of thing.'

'You're kidding, right?'

Bevan was serious. 'No, really, plenty of people swear by the practice.'

'But they don't make their own wine?' she asked.

'No, they're growers. Lotta vineyards around here like that. Sell their grapes to other producers, who blend them in with their own. Guess they don't want the hassle of making the actual stuff, or the headache of selling it.'

Rose was fascinated, and soaked up the conversations she heard swirling around her, even if she didn't understand half of what was being said. As they joined the others, talk turned to something called the Burning of the Canes, which was apparently taking place in a few weeks' time.

'It's a bonfire of the prunings from the vineyard – a kind of death and rebirth thing, a little bit pagan really,' explained Thommo. 'We get to celebrate the end of winter pruning, there's a big feast and, needless to say, plenty of good grog, and we have a bit of a dance. Everyone comes, all the locals, even some bigwigs from Melbourne and Sydney. This year it's at our place.'

'Actually, Astrid's just been telling us that you're a pretty decent cook,' chimed in Charlie, sidling up to her. 'Don't suppose we could borrow you? We could really do with the extra help. Two of the old girls who usually help out have let us down.'

His smile was so charming and everyone had been so friendly that Rose found it impossible to refuse. 'Sure, I guess,' she said, not really knowing what she was letting herself in for but, in her warm, beer-induced haze, happy to agree. 'I'll have to check with my boss first though.'

'Oh, don't worry about Mark. He'll be okay with it,' Charlie assured her.

'Are you sure?' Rose was surprised. She'd gotten the impression from Astrid that he was tricky at the best of times.

'Absolutely – he's all bark and no bite. You'll see,' he said confidently. 'He's a decent bloke.'

Some time later, Rose glanced at her watch. She hadn't realised it had gotten so late. She'd been having a surprisingly good time chatting to Bevan and Deano. She looked around for Astrid, only to find the blonde girl cuddled up against Thommo. Or was it Charlie? Either way, she looked pretty cosy with him, but Rose was tired and ready to call it a night. She caught Astrid's eye.

'Think I'm ready to head home now,' Rose said. She

paused. 'I mean back to Kalkari.'

What had made her call Kalkari home? What was she thinking? She'd been there less than a week.

But apparently Astrid had drunk far too many vodka tonics to notice the slip. 'Hokay,' she slurred. 'I think I might stay here for a bit. One of the boys will give me a lift back.'

'Alright, I'll see you later then.'

Rose promised to get in touch with Charlie and Thommo and let them know about helping out at the Burning of the Canes and then went to get her jacket.

Mrs B was snoring gently on the sofa when Rose let herself into the house. She woke with a start as Rose gently touched her arm. 'Oh hello, dear! There you are. Did you have a nice time?'

'Yeah, thanks. I certainly met a lot of people – Charlie and Thommo from Windsong, and Deano, Mick and Angie from Lilybells, and someone called Bob, from Bob's Run.'

'Ah yes, Charlie and Thommo. I remember when they were running around with scabby knees and snotty noses. Doing pretty well for themselves now, I hear. They've taken over the running of Windsong from their parents. Bob's a good bloke, too. Went to primary school with him. That's going back a few years,' Mrs B cackled. She got slowly to her feet and looked around for her handbag. 'The little 'uns are fine, went straight to bed. I did hear Leo calling out for his mum in his sleep though. Poor little tacker.' Rustling in her bag for her car keys, she let herself out.

Rose decided to wait for Astrid to return. After all, she could hardly leave Leo and Luisa in the big house on their own. She stoked the log fire that was burning in the small living room and lay down on the sofa, pulling a blanket over herself.

CHAPTER 4

Rose was roused from her sleep by the staccato chatter of birds, so loud she could swear they must be perched on the windowsill. No gentle chirrup of birdsong here – more a raucous wake-up call no-one could ignore. She looked at her watch and saw with alarm that it was just after eight in the morning. She was still on the sofa. There was no sign of Astrid, and she felt sure she would have heard her come in. The little sitting room was next to the front door, which was impossible to shut quietly. Not a peep from the kids either, despite the time. She listened. The house was quiet.

She reached for her mobile phone, but there was no message. She'd thought Astrid might be more responsible than this, but then again she'd known her less than a week – hardly long enough to confidently predict her behaviour.

As Rose tried to stretch the kinks out of her back

caused by a night spent with her knees tucked up almost to her chin, she heard the *thump-thump* of Luisa coming down the stairs. 'Assie, Assie …' she called out. Rose was glad she hadn't gone back to the barn last night. What if no-one had been there when Luisa or Leo woke up?

'Hi, sweetie! Did you have a sleep-in? Astrid's out just now, but I'm here.' Rose lifted her up from the stairs into a hug. 'How are you this morning, little one?' she asked, settling her on one hip.

'Good,' said Luisa, nodding her head emphatically.

'Shall we go and change you and get you some milk?'

'Miiilk,' said Luisa, reminded of her favourite drink. 'Warm up,' she demanded.

'Yes, missy, I can do that,' replied Rose, giving her a kiss on her chubby cheek.

In the kitchen, Rose drank coffee and warmed her feet on the range while Luisa splattered milk-soaked Weet-Bix over the table. She had wiped away the crusted mascara from under her eyes, rolled up the sleeves of her thin blouse and pulled back her hair into a messy knot, but she was definitely in need of a shower and a teeth clean. Rose hadn't had a chance to check on Leo, and could only assume he too was having a sleep-in.

She heard the squeak of unoiled hinges and then a bang. The front door.

Oh good, Astrid's back.

There was a heavy tread on the flagstones. Something fell with a whomp on the ground and a set of keys clunked noisily onto the side table. None of this sounded much like Astrid. Rose was about to go and investigate when Luisa scrambled down from her booster chair and ran full pelt to the hallway, calling out exultantly, 'Daddy, Daaaaddy!'

Oh bollocks. Mr Cameron – Mark. And here I am with crumpled clothes, bird's nest hair and last night's make-up half-way down my cheeks.

Sure enough, Mark appeared in the kitchen doorway. He also looked dog-tired, with dark stubble covering his jaw. The jacket he was wearing was frayed around the collar, missing several buttons and hung off him as if it were made for a much larger man. He could have quite easily passed for a vagrant.

'Ah, hello, Rose,' he said, looking around the kitchen. 'Where's Astrid?'

'Hello,' Rose said brightly, ignoring the fact that she was as dishevelled as he was. 'Um, it was Astrid's night off. She stayed in town, I think,' she said, thinking on her feet. 'How was your trip? We weren't expecting you until later today.'

'Got an earlier flight. I've really missed this little one' – he tweaked Luisa's nose – 'and her brother. Where's Leo? I've got a surprise for him.' He turned abruptly and walked out of the kitchen.

He returned, moments later, carrying a wriggling ball of black and white fur in his arms. As he placed it gently on the kitchen floor, the puppy began to sniff out its new surroundings. Rose's heart contracted. She loved dogs, though she'd never been able to have one in London.

'Ohh, hey boy,' she said, rubbing its soft belly. 'And what's your name, hmm?'

'Well, he howled along to Jimmy Barnes all the way home, so I reckon it's Barnsie.' Mark smiled fleetingly and

Rose saw the clouds lift from his expression. *Wow*, she thought, *he's completely different when he smiles.* There was something that drew you to him, like the feeling of wanting to warm yourself at a blazing fire. She could see why even someone as glamorous and sophisticated as Isabella was reputed to be would have fallen for him.

Mark whistled to the puppy, but it ignored him, lapping up the attention from Rose instead. 'Humph. Got my work cut out there, I can see. I thought border collies were supposed to be intelligent.' With that, he marched out of the room, Luisa in his arms, and clomped up the stairs, calling for Leo.

Rose ran her fingers through her hair and grimaced. Not exactly how she had intended to greet her new boss on his return.

As she was going back to the barn for a shower, leaving the kids with Mark, she heard a car heading up the drive. Changing direction and walking around the side of the house, she went to see who it might be. She caught sight of a battered ute with the numberplate, 'CORK 1', and then a flash of Astrid's blonde hair in the passenger seat.

She tumbled out of the ute, looking quite pale. 'Oh, Rose, I'm sooo sorry about last night. My phone ran out of charge. I would have called you but it was so late by the time I noticed, and I thought I'd be back early enough anyway. Thommo offered to drive me back first thing this morning, so I stayed over at his place.'

Rose waved at Thommo before replying. 'Well, I was a bit worried about you,' she said, 'But I stayed in the main house. The children were fine.'

49

'I knew I could count on you. Thanks a lot,' Astrid smiled sweetly at Rose. Rose wasn't fooled. *Girls as pretty and young as Astrid*, Rose thought, *are used to getting away with things.*

'Oh, and by the way, Mark's back.'

'Oh God,' Astrid wailed, suddenly anxious. 'Did he ask where I was? Oh bloody hell, I'm in trouble now.'

Rose thought for a second about letting her sweat on it, but instead reassured her. 'Don't worry, I covered for you. I said it was your night off and that you were in town with friends.' It could only help to get Astrid on her side.

'Nice one,' said Astrid, looking at Rose with a new respect. 'Thanks. I'd better get inside right now.' And with that she leaned back through the window, kissed Thommo lightly on the lips and fled into the house.

'See ya, Rose,' said Thommo, 'gotta fly.' He whirled the car around and disappeared down the long drive.

Later that morning, Rose and Astrid pried Leo away from Barnsie – the puppy had been a huge hit with both kids – and Luisa away from Mark, who had a backlog of work to catch up on in the winery, and drove into Eumeralla for the monthly farmers' market. Astrid had promised it would be fun and she was right. It was completely up Rose's alley. Trestle tables laden with vibrant fresh greens, earth-covered potatoes and khaki-coloured cabbages bigger than her head jostled for space with fresh cheeses, jewel-bright jars of jams and jellies, and handmade soaps. There was a butcher's stand with local meat, and a baker's stall piled high with sourdough loaves, croissants and flaky pastries studded with berries. All around her, people filled capacious baskets with fresh vegetables, meat and cheese, while fortifying themselves at a takeaway coffee stall that was doing a roaring trade.

Astrid pushed Luisa in a stroller, and Leo quickly found a couple of school friends with a football and ran off to the oval for a kick around. Rose stocked up on carrots that Bugs Bunny would have been proud of, their fluffy green tops still attached, a big bunch of spinach tied together with twine and a Halloween-worthy pumpkin. She spotted the Trevelyn sisters from the pub, each with a large basket of greens under their arm, and waved to them.

Her mouth watered at the sight of the shiny fruit- and custard-filled pastries, but Astrid steered her in the direction of a stall selling egg-and-bacon rolls, buying two, smearing them with spicy tomato relish and handing her one. 'Breakfast of champions,' she chortled, through a mouthful of bacon. 'Delicious.'

'Mmmmm,' Rose agreed, tearing off a bit of fried egg and bread and handing it to a hungry Luisa, 'Or breakfast of dirty stop-outs!'

Astrid looked momentarily confused, then laughed, understanding that Rose was teasing her.

They cruised the rest of the market, adding beans, onions, plump heads of purple garlic and a big bag of apples to the supplies, until Rose could carry no more and even the basket under the stroller was groaning with their purchases.

Leo caught up with them, having finished his football game. 'Last one to the car's a squashed tomato,' yelled Astrid, careering off towards the carpark, pushing Luisa. Leo scrambled after her, and Rose, weighed down with bags, brought up the rear.

As they all climbed into the car, Rose made a mental note to ask Mark about the groceries budget, and her pay as well. She felt a bit guilty at the prospect of taking money from him, when really she was there for a spot of industrial espionage, but dammit, she'd worked hard all week. Getting to know Leo and Luisa, and seeing Mark again, even though he hadn't exactly welcome her warmly, had made Rose feel even more uneasy about her undertaking. She needed to email her brother, but she'd have to wait until Wednesday, her day off, before being able to get back into Eumeralla and the free wifi at Sacred Grounds.

As Rose fed the children their supper, Mark walked into the kitchen and cut a thick slice from the loaf on the bench, slathering it with butter. Rose hadn't been expecting him and his sudden appearance was unnerving. There was something about him that made her self-conscious, quite apart from the fact that she couldn't forget that she was there to spy on his winery.

'So, Rose, you're English?' he said before biting into the bread.

'Um, er, yep, that's me.' *Oh God, that sounded completely*

inane. Still, it was a pretty dumb question. 'I grew up in a small village in north Oxfordshire, but I've spent the past eight or nine years living in London.'

'Right. Well, you'll find the Shingle Valley a bit quieter than London I expect.' Mark turned his attention to Luisa, chucking her under the chin while she giggled gleefully and waved her fork in the air. He bent and retrieved a piece of pasta that had fallen under her chair. He dropped it in the bin before exiting the room as suddenly as he'd arrived.

Great conversationalist, then. She was going to have her work cut out to find out what Henry needed to know – it didn't look like the boss himself was going to give much away.

CHAPTER 5

Rose didn't see much of Mark the following week either. He bolted down a quick breakfast with the kids each morning and then disappeared to the winery. He came back to the house when Leo got home from school, helped him with his homework and then played with Leo and Barnsie outside in the fading afternoon light, patiently throwing sticks for the puppy. Much to Leo's delight, the dog returned them every time. He sat with the kids while they ate an early dinner and then returned to the winery for a few more hours. Most nights, Rose left food warming for him on the range.

One night Mark came back to the house while she and Astrid were eating.

'What's this doing open?' he asked, his voice ominously quiet as he held up a wine bottle that was on the sideboard.

'Oh shit,' Rose muttered under her breath. She'd

grabbed the bottle from the back of the pantry. It was so old and dusty she hadn't been able to make out the label. Figuring that it was part of the store of 'house wine' that Astrid had opened the first night, she'd added a generous slosh to the meal that they were eating. 'Um, I needed some wine for the beef casserole. I thought it was okay to use. It was right at the back of the pantry. Did I do something wrong?'

Mark glowered at her. 'It's a twenty-year-old cabernet from my family's original vineyard.'

Rose shrugged, not knowing what to say.

'How the hell did it get into the pantry?' he said, almost to himself. 'Was there any more in there?' This question was directed at Rose.

'Not that I could see. Sorry, Mark, I had no idea …'

'Well, the casserole had better be bloody good then,' he said, a resigned expression on his face. 'Pass me a plate.'

Needless to say, after that, conversation at the scrubbed kitchen table was stilted. He was preoccupied, answering Astrid and Rose's polite questions with monosyllabic responses and scoffing down the food at a furious rate.

Astrid interrupted. 'Mark, the school rang. They want to know if Leo will be playing soccer for the school team. You haven't signed the permission slip. They said they really want him – but they need the slip. It's already late. You should see him play, Mark, he's a very good striker,' she said.

Mark's fork slowed its progress from his plate. 'Find it for me, Astrid, and I'll sign it. Really, I expect the two of you to keep on top of everything to do with Leo and Luisa. I've got enough to worry about with the winery.'

'Yes, of course, sorry. I did give it to you last week, but I'll get them to send another one.'

Mark resumed eating, saying nothing in response. Astrid rolled her eyes at Rose, being careful not to let Mark see her, and the two girls lapsed into silence, unnerved by his stony presence. He didn't even make any comment on the meal, which was a pretty decent boeuf bourguignon, if Rose did say so herself.

Honestly, thought Rose, *Mark Cameron has all the personality and charm of a garden rake.*

The only small satisfaction was in watching him thoroughly clean his plate with a hunk of bread. At least he seemed to appreciate her cooking.

When she wasn't feeding everyone or clearing up after them, Rose spent her time setting the house to rights, beating the dust out of ancient rugs, cleaning windows and polishing the house's motley collection of furniture till it shone. She was keen to see what she could discover for Henry, and cleaning the place gave her the perfect excuse to nose around without attracting suspicion.

She began to feel less intimidated by the grand old home as she ventured into each of the rooms. On the ground floor, she discovered a sunny formal living room which, in complete contrast to the shabby furnishings in the rest of the house, was decorated in flamboyant style, with deep red and fuchsia high-backed sofas and gold and pink curtains.

Isabella's touch was obvious.

One afternoon she hauled the emphysemic vacuum cleaner and a bucket of cleaning supplies up the wide wooden staircase to the first floor, stepping over a pile of abandoned toys and opened the door on Astrid's room. She left the mess of discarded clothes, shoes and make-up alone, guessing that the Austrian girl would prefer her privacy. Down a hallway, she discovered three more guest rooms and a bathroom. These looked to be barely used, but a fine layer of dust had built up, so she wiped and vacuumed and straightened curtains and bedding.

Then, as she walked back along the hallway, she came to a door on the other side that she'd not noticed before. It could only be Mark and Isabella's room. Glancing down the stairwell to make sure she was still alone, she slowly opened the door. The curtains were drawn, the bed rumpled and unmade and there were drawers half open, their contents spilling out onto the floor. The cloying fragrance of stale perfume hung in the air.

As she pulled back the curtains and closed the drawers, Rose noticed a silver frame face-down on the bedside table. She propped it up again and saw it was a photo of Mark and Isabella on what must have been their wedding day. A very glamorous Isabella was laughing up at Mark, her hair framed by a sheer white veil, dark eyes sparkling, as Mark gazed back at her amid a flurry of confetti. They looked young and carefree and as if they were absolutely besotted with each other. 'Nightmare,' Astrid had warned her about Isabella. 'Looks so nice on the outside, but I would not trust her if I could throw her.'

There were no papers or documents on the dresser or side tables, and Rose felt too uncomfortable to start opening drawers and searching. The room was too personal, too intimate. She sighed. She was going to make a rubbish spy for Henry.

Rose also braved the chilly weather and began to explore Kalkari. Early one morning she disturbed a mob of breakfasting kangaroos in a paddock; after that, she kept mainly to the paths alongside the vineyards. Eventually bored of walking, she decided to up the pace with a gentle jog. She'd been a runner back in secondary school, even qualifying for the county championships – her long legs had been good for something – but double shifts and fuelling up on pies and pancakes at The Pine Box had meant that it had been ages since she'd laced up a pair of trainers and done anything more than shuffle to the shops for milk. She couldn't believe how heavy she felt now, and it was hard to ignore her bulk as she hauled herself up the steep slopes of the Shingle Hills. There was no avoiding it: she'd morphed into a heffalump.

Rose had been a lanky, skinny teenager – you wouldn't think it to look at her now, but as a kid her nickname had been Ribs. Unfortunately, those days were long gone. Her tummy almost had a life of its own – it wobbled like a perfectly set panna cotta. The weight gain had been so gradual she'd not really been aware of it, and being tall, she'd been able to hide it easily. But now, looking down at the rolls of creamy skin billowing over the straining waistband of her leggings, she realised it had got out of control. Gasping for breath, she was forced to slow down as the slopes got steeper, but she doggedly kept going, distracted by the brilliant views from the top of the hill above Kalkari.

The valley spread out before her like a scene from a picture book; the rows of vines, laid out in different directions, made a patchwork as far as the eye could see, and small houses and winery buildings were dotted among them like a toytown. Most mornings she was able to make out a few frozen-looking figures among the vines, wrapped up in thick coats and beanies. With baskets by their sides and secateurs in their hands, they were trimming the bare grapevines splayed out along rows of wire trellises. It must be a bit like pruning rose trees, she supposed. It looked bloody miserable to be stuck out in the cold for hours on end.

She always arrived back at the barn red-faced and huffing like a steam train, but the exercise and the hard work in the house meant that her pants were feeling a little less tight. It pleased her more than she thought it would.

Mobile coverage at Kalkari was woeful, so one morning Rose took her laptop and drove to Sacred Grounds. She sent her brother an email update – not that there was much to report at this stage. She hadn't been able to check out the cellar door or winery yet – Mark was always there – and that was where she was likely to find the info that Henry was after. Both were locked up whenever Mark wasn't around. She'd seen a car coming and going – presumably the manager or someone – but Mark always stayed long after the car left. And she had no idea where the keys were kept.

She also sent a quick email to Philippe and Frostie, the friends she'd stayed with in Bondi before coming to Kalkari, moaning about the cold and the lack of decent coffee anywhere other than at Sacred Grounds, before catching up with the news on Facebook. London seemed such a long way away now. She checked, and checked again, but there was no email from Giles. She hadn't really expected anything, but a small hope that she'd been trying her best to ignore had still glimmered deep inside her that maybe, just maybe, he'd had second thoughts, that he'd realised he couldn't live without her and would summon her to Brussels … Her heart clenched with misery and she felt a sudden wave of homesickness overwhelm her. Eeyore's dark cloud, which had temporarily stopped following her around, settled over her head once more.

CHAPTER 6

The night of the Burning of the Canes was fast approaching. Thommo had called Rose with instructions, thanking her again for coming to their rescue. She'd managed to catch Mark between homework and bathtime and he'd agreed, somewhat reluctantly, that she could help out. She wasn't sure why she was throwing herself into it with such enthusiasm, though she admitted to herself she was a tiny bit excited about the prospect of getting into a proper, commercial kitchen again.

First thing Friday morning she reported for duty, having driven the few kilometres across the valley to Windsong on a glorious, crisp, sunny day, all the while singing tunelessly at the top of her voice. As she drew up at the winery, a flock of white cockatoos scattered from the nearby stand of tall gum trees, wheeling high overhead and cackling raucously. Thommo – or was it Charlie? Rose couldn't be completely sure – appeared at the doorway of a large timber-and-brick shed.

'Rose, sweetheart, great to see you. Come on in and meet everyone.'

Rose followed him into the cavernous shed, her eyes taking a while to adjust to the dim light. Inside, large hooped barrels were stacked high against each wall, while trestle tables ran the length of the room. Rose breathed in the yeasty, pungent smell.

'We've cleared out the barrel hall; this is where dinner will be. Out the back is where all the action is at the moment,' he said. She followed him to the end of the room and through a door at the rear into a spacious kitchen. Four women of varying ages and sizes stopped their activity and looked up as they entered. 'G'day, ladies, this is Rose. She's come to help you bludgers out.'

Four pairs of eyes assessed her. A round, twinkly-eyed woman introduced herself as Betty and welcomed Rose in, handing her an apron and a hairnet. 'Thanks, Charlie. We're flat out.'

Charlie winked at Rose and then made to leave, saying he'd be back later to check how they were all getting on.

'Now, love, I've heard all about you from Brenda,' said the woman kindly. 'You're the new English au pair, aren't you?'

'Brenda?' asked Rose.

'Brenda Butters. The housekeeper up at Kalkari. Well, she was until she did her back in.'

'Oh, Mrs B,' said Rose.

'Yes. There was a right old to-do there earlier this year when the lady of the house ran off with that Spanish bloke. We were all gobsmacked. Those poor little tackers! Luisa not even turned two. Disgraceful, I call it. Mind you, Brenda said that Mark was almost never there. Too wrapped up in his wines to pay much attention. I don't think she was ever really happy here in the valley,' Betty tutted to herself as she deftly peeled potatoes. Barely pausing to draw breath, she continued, 'Now, Brenda tells me you're a dab hand in the kitchen. Tonight we've got pork rillettes, sugar-cured salmon, pickled cucumber and an olive tapenade. Then there's rib of beef, roasted root veggies and we're finishing up with apple and rhubarb pies and cheeses from the Shingle Dairy. We're expecting close to a hundred for dinner, but there'll be more here for the bonfire before dinner as well, and they'll have hot soup and bread.'

Rose mentally high-fived herself for agreeing to help out. Surely with such a blabbermouth in charge of the kitchen, she'd manage to dig up some useful intel for Henry. 'Sounds delicious,' said Rose, her mouth watering. 'What would you like me to do?'

'Can you start on the fruit for the pies? The apples are over there, and the rhubarb needs washing and chopping,' said Betty, handing her a peeler and a bucket.

Ah, the glamorous jobs. Rose found a stool and grabbed an apple.

Taking a break only for a hurried lunch of sandwiches washed down with mugs of builder's tea, Rose and the other women worked steadily throughout the day. Betty clearly ran the show and kept everyone amused with her constant stream of well-intentioned gossip and sly comment, all the while managing to make short work of the mountain of fruit and veg that needed preparing.

It was a weary Rose who drove home along the valley road as the sun was setting pinkly on the horizon. As she motored along, her thoughts returned to Giles. The familiar ache in her heart was matched only by the ache of her hands from so much chopping and peeling.

One day stood out in her mind. It must have been only a few months before they broke up. Rose had a rare Sunday off – she was usually rostered on at weekends – and they had gone to Hampstead, to the heath for a walk. It was a blustery spring day; apple blossom was strewn like confetti in the streets. As they stood at the top of Parliament Hill, the wind kept blowing her scarf from around her neck, which made her laugh as she batted it away from her face. Giles stopped her and grasped both ends of it, tying them tightly together before brushing away the hair from her temples and pulling her face down to his to kiss her. He'd told her he loved her.

Lying bastard.

Despite the hard work the previous day, Rose was up again at dawn and at Windsong before breakfast, joining the local ladies as they rolled out pastry, ground up olives and herbs, and sliced sides of salmon paper-thin.

Returning to Kalkari late that afternoon, Rose found Leo excited at having taught Barnsie to sit, and Luisa chasing Maggie and Nigella back into their palatial chicken coop. There was an air of anticipation about the place; both kids were looking forward to the night's bonfire.

Leo asked Rose if she'd seen it. 'Is it taller than me?' he asked.

'It's as big as the Tower of London,' she replied, watching Leo's eyes grow round.

'Towa!' shrieked Luisa, jumping up and down.

'Cool,' said Leo. 'Will it burn really, really hot?'

'You know, I think it just might. Better be careful we don't melt away like candle wax, hey?' said Rose, teasing him gently. He really was a sweet boy.

Astrid was bringing the kids to see the lighting of the bonfire and then would take them home. Mark would stay on for the dinner. Rose would be helping in the kitchen, but she'd have time to watch a bit of the bonfire.

She arrived just as the sun was setting. After being directed into a nearby paddock that had been set aside for parking, she made her way up the lane towards the Windsong winery. Vine cuttings – the 'canes' – had been gathered into a huge pile a safe distance from the buildings; it towered above her head.

She caught sight of Astrid and the kids. Leo was craning his neck upwards to get a better look. 'Just like Guy Fawkes' Night at home,' said Rose, as she caught up with them. Astrid looked puzzled, but Rose didn't get time to explain, as Mark arrived with a cup of soup for Leo and a smaller one for Luisa. He blew on the cups to cool them down before passing them to the children and vanishing into the sea of people standing around the bonfire pile.

He returned, however, when it came time for the fire to be lit. He hoisted Luisa onto his shoulders, and they all watched as a burning cane was tossed onto the top of the pile.

Whoosh!

The fire quickly spread through the dry cuttings, crackling loudly and lending a glow to the faces of those watching. Heat radiated from the burning branches. Everyone gazed, spellbound, as the fire glowed and flickered.

As the canes continued to burn, Rose slipped away to the kitchen. Walking through the enormous barrel hall, now warmed by an army of large mobile heaters, she marvelled at the transformation. The long tables that had been clothed in crisp white linen and decorated with fairy lights threaded among cane cuttings. It looked like something from a movie set.

She reached the kitchen to find the cooks, now joined by a team of servers, all in a state of controlled panic. 'If they don't come in soon, the beef'll be overdone,' wailed Betty, peering into one of the industrial-sized ovens.

'Don't worry, Bet,' one of the other women replied, 'I've sent Thommo out to round everyone up. We'll be able to serve up any minute now.'

Sure enough, the barrel room was soon echoing with the sound of boots on the stone floor and the buzz of laughter and chatter as the guests started to file in.

As she delivered heavy platters of salmon and pots of

rillettes at intervals along the tables, Rose noticed Mark seated with a pretty blonde to his left and a redhead on his right. He was leaning in to listen to something the blonde was saying, looking intently into her eyes.

'They'll be swarming all over him tonight,' said Charlie, who'd materialised beside behind her. 'Quite the local catch he is, now Isabella's out of the picture. The blonde is Amanda Davis, she lives in the city, but her folks own Bellbirds, the boutique hotel across the valley. She's been up here a lot recently, funnily enough.' He winked at Rose. 'The other sheila is Ben Hamlett's widow, Sadie, and a merry one she is too. Word is she's inherited a fortune and isn't afraid to splash it around.'

Rose blinked. She understood that, despite his bad temper, Mark was attractive in a kind of older guy way, but she'd not really seen him in that light herself. Truth be told, she'd not seen him in much light at all; apart from the time he was with the kids every afternoon, he spent his waking hours at the winery.

'Could be just what Mark needs,' added Charlie.

'Oh?'

'Not really my place to say, but everyone knows he's been doing it tough for more than a while. Running the place on the smell of an oily rag. Word is the bank has been making life very difficult for him lately.'

Charlie moved on, filling up the legions of glasses on the table with pale gold and ruby wines that glowed in the candlelight. Rose tucked the snippet of information away to relay to Henry when she got the chance.

She went back to the kitchen, where Betty was hauling great trays of beef out of the ovens. The rest of the evening was a blur, as Rose helped serve enormous platters of beef and roasted vegetables, slice pies and collect plates and glasses. So many glasses. At least the kitchen was equipped with a cavernous glass washer.

After dinner, a bush band struck up and space was cleared in the barrel room for a dance floor. It wasn't long before most of the diners were on their feet, dancing enthusiastically to the fiddle, banjo and harmonica, narrowly missing taking each other out as they flung themselves around. It was clear that the generously poured glasses of wine had washed away the inhibitions of plenty of the guests. Everyone seemed to be having a rollicking good time.

Rose realised that it was ages since she'd enjoyed herself so much, and she loved being part of something the whole neighbourhood was involved in. She was exhausted though. It had been a tiring few days, and she was ready to drop. She was sneaking down the side of the hall, on her way to the paddock to collect her car, when she bumped into Mark.

'Oh hey, sorry, I, er—' Rose stumbled over her words. 'Hi, Mark. I was just leaving.'

His response surprised her. 'Don't suppose I could grab a ride? Astrid took our car back and I've had too much to drink to borrow one of the boys' utes,' he said.

'Sure, of course. Just give me a sec, I think I left my scarf in the kitchen,' said Rose, fumbling with her coat. She looked up and spotted the blonde from dinner heading towards them.

'Give me your keys and I'll meet you at the car,' said Mark.

'But you don't know where it's parked.' Rose was confused why he was in such a hurry.

'I'm sure I won't be able to miss it. It's yellow, right?' he said, the corners of his mouth twitching.

'Yeah, right, it is.' She hadn't even realised he'd noticed. 'Here you go.' Rose handed over her keys, and Mark strode out of the room before the blonde had time to catch him.

She found her scarf and said goodbye to Brenda and Betty, who were sitting with their feet up, enjoying a glass of wine. As she passed the bonfire, she saw that it had burned down to its embers now. When she arrived at the car, she found Mark was sitting with the passenger seat tilted way back, eyes closed.

He opened one eye as she got in and looked sideways at her. 'Sorry about that. Needed to make a quick getaway. Awful Amanda was headed our way.'

'Is she really that bad?'

'Oh, probably not,' he said with a sigh, 'but I'm just not interested in dancing to her tune – or anyone else's, as a matter of fact.'

'Oh right. Okay, well, let's get going,' she said, embarrassed to continue the conversation any further.

As she turned the key in the ignition, Mark closed his eyes again and slept, or pretended to, for the rest of the drive home. Rose stole an occasional glance at him, observing his face in the darkness and thinking how much softer and gentler his expression was when he was relaxed.

CHAPTER 7

The next morning, Rose was sweeping the front porch, nursing a headache from the noise of the night before and trying to ignore the added throbbing of a burgeoning zit just above her left eyebrow. She heard a car and looked up to see a ute, with a rust-and-white cattle dog riding in the open tray at the back, pulling up. Barnsie came out with her and started barking excitedly at the strangers.

'Quiet, you silly mutt,' she mock-scolded him, picking up the over-enthusiastic puppy and cradling him in her arms.

Charlie emerged from the ute, carrying a huge bunch of lilies and pink roses. 'These are for you, sweetheart: a thank you for all your help with the dinner last night. Those pies were bloody awesome and Betty says they were all your doing. Didn't get the chance to say so last night – you took off faster than a bride's nightie.'

Rose blushed at the attention, and let go of the squirming Barnsie to take the flowers. She was really touched – even Giles at his best had never shown up with a bouquet as gobsmackingly gorgeous as this. 'Really, it was nothing. I was glad to help out. Everything looked so magical. Such a big event to put on – everyone did a wonderful job.' She meant it. She'd had a great time, had loved the energy of everyone involved and had relished seeing it all run smoothly.

Barnsie was jumping up at the ute and barking at Charlie's dog, despite the fact that he was a quarter of its size. 'Quiet, Barnsie. Get down,' she scolded him again.

Just at that moment, Mark came down the path from the winery. 'Not-so-secret admirer, huh, Rose?' he asked, raising an eyebrow at the flowers she was holding, before going over to shake Charlie's hand. 'Great job, last night. Very impressive. Really liked your new shiraz, too.'

'Cheers, mate. Yeah, it's coming along nicely. We'll see how it does at Melbourne.'

'Melbourne?' asked Rose.

'Melbourne Wine Show. Home of the Jimmy Watson. Trophy for the best one- or two-year-old red. Most prestigious wine award in the country,' Mark explained.

'Oh.' Rose went inside to look for a vase. Coming back outside again a few minutes later, she saw Charlie drive away, a cloud of dust following his ute.

'Have you got a minute, Rose? No-one's properly shown you around and explained what we do here, have they?' Mark looked surprisingly chipper given his tired state the night before, and seemed, somewhat miraculously, to be in a good mood for the first time since she'd met him.

Excellent. She might find out something to report to Henry.

'Sure, okay, why not?' she replied, trying to sound casual.

Mark led her along the path to the cellar door: it was still shut up, just as it had been when she'd first arrived.

'We've had the cellar door closed over winter; we get a bit of business at the weekends, but not enough to justify staffing it year-round,' Mark explained as he fished a large iron key from his pocket and put it in the lock.

As they stepped inside the cool, dark space, Rose could see that a thick layer of dust had gathered on the rows of miniature glasses above the serving area. An enormous slab of varnished timber was balanced on top of a couple of old barrels at which she guessed the wines were poured for tasting, and silver buckets were balanced on stands at each end of the room. She looked inquiringly at Mark.

'Spittoons.'

'Ah.'

'Makes sense when you're tasting anything up to a dozen wines. Not everyone spits though.' Rose saw a brief smile flicker across his face. 'We've got a few different vintages that we open for tasting, and we make a chardonnay, a cab shiraz blend, a single vineyard shiraz – Assignation – from a block at the far edge of Kalkari, and then I've been experimenting with some Spanish varieties: a tempranillo and an albarino. The majority of our wines are made from estate-grown fruit, though we do take some from other growers in the valley. It gives me more control over the whole process.'

Having shown her the cellar door, they headed outside and took the path that led towards the big corrugated iron shed of the winery itself. As soon as they entered the vast space, with its rough concrete floor and towering stainless steel vats, Rose noticed the same yeasty aroma that the barrel room at Windsong had, and she breathed it in, loving the warm, almost alive scent.

'God, I love that smell. Reminds me of a bakery.'

He gave her a wide grin. 'Being here every day, you become pretty immune to it, but if I've been away for a while it certainly smells like home as soon as I walk back in here.'

Mark began to show her around, explaining what everything was and how it worked. 'We ferment all the parcels separately, only using wild yeasts, put them through malo in the barrel and then blend them together to get the finished result.' Rose nodded, not understanding everything Mark was saying but fascinated nonetheless.

He led her to the small office space and introduced her to Dan, the assistant winemaker. She'd seen Dan's car coming and going, but this was the first time she'd seen him close up. He was a crusty-looking old bloke, streaks of grey threaded through his thick brown hair, a bushranger beard that was more salt than pepper, and a checked shirt stretched tightly across his large frame, heavy boots on his feet.

He looked up from his laptop and waved a cheery hello. 'Just checking on the weather, boss. Looks like we could be in for some rain in the next week or so.'

Something clicked in Rose's brain. 'You've got internet access in here?'

'Yeah, but it's pretty slow, and not exactly reliable,' Dan answered. 'One of the delights of working in the country.'

'Ah,' said Rose, dejectedly. 'I guess I'll have to keep relying on Sacred Grounds then. Anyway, nice to meet you, Dan.'

She followed him out of the small winery office and up a set of metal stairs to a gantry catwalk that wound around the edge of the building. It was terrifyingly high and narrow. Rose was not a fan of heights but she followed him up the stairs, trying to stop her legs from shaking as she did so. They gazed down on the steel tanks, some large square concrete tanks towards the back, and a pyramid of small oak barrels in the far corner of the winery.

'French oak,' said Mark, pointing to the barrels. 'Limousin and Vosges. Bloody expensive, but the best there is.'

As they climbed down the stairs, Mark walked over to the barrels and pulled out a long curved glass tube. It looked to Rose a bit like an elongated turkey baster, and she watched as he pulled out the rubber bung from a barrel and sucked up some of the wine. 'A barrel thief,' he said.

'Are you referring to the baster, or yourself?' she asked, risking a cheeky grin.

He raised one eyebrow in response.

Putting a thumb over the end to stopper the baster, he then released it and let the wine slosh into two small glasses that he had in his other hand. 'Here, have a taste of this. It's our 2014 shiraz, the Assignation,' he said, offering her a glass. 'Here, this is how to taste it,' said Mark. He showed her how to hold the glass by its stem and swirl the liquid, poke her nose into the glass and take a deep sniff and then slurp some of the wine over her tongue all the way to the back of her throat before swallowing. Rose knew how to taste wine from spending time with Henry, but she let Mark demonstrate and followed his instructions. She didn't want him to find out that she knew more about wine than she was letting on.

'Whaddya reckon?'

Rose could taste rich fruit and spices – almost like her grandma's Christmas cake. The wine was smooth and supple on her palate, and the flavour seemed to go on forever. Despite the early hour, it was so delicious that she certainly didn't want to spit it out.

'Blimey, that's good. I can just imagine it with filet mignon or Chateaubriand.'

'Or a big, juicy Aussie steak?' he suggested, teasing her. 'Yeah, I'm pretty happy with this vintage. We'll see how well it does at Melbourne. It's just about ready for bottling, I reckon.'

'Is that the Johnny Watson thing that you and Charlie were talking about?'

'Jimmy Watson,' said Mark. 'Anyway, we'd better get on. I've kept you away from the house for too long and I've got a heap of things to do here.'

Rose knew when she was being dismissed. 'Sure. Thanks for showing me around, Mark. It was fascinating, really, it was.' Rose wasn't even lying. It *had* been surprisingly interesting to see something of the secret business that went on inside a winery. Even though she'd learnt a bit about French wines as part of her *Diplôme de Cuisine*, and of course Henry had been involved with wine for as long as she could remember, she'd never actually set foot in a winery until now.

And now she knew where the office was. It was probably her best bet for finding out what Henry needed: she'd had time to figure out that Mark almost certainly didn't keep any business papers in the house. She just had to choose a time when she was sure no-one was around and she wouldn't be caught.

Oh, and there was the small matter of getting her hands on the keys, which she'd seen hanging up in the winery office earlier. She'd have to wait for her opportunity – Mark was bound to leave them somewhere when he locked up for the night.

budburst

noun

the emergence of new leaves on plants such as grapevines
at the beginning of the growing season

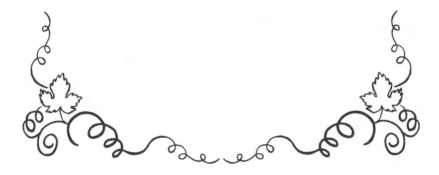

CHAPTER 8

As she jogged along Shingle Road, through the clearing early morning mist, Rose noticed that a bright green fuzz had appeared over the valley, formerly brown, dormant hillsides spiked with new growth. Green shoots thrust from the wizened vines and bright golden wattle shone on roadside bushes. The air wasn't nearly as punishingly cold as it had been a few weeks ago, and she was able to ditch the gloves and beanie Astrid had lent her and soak up the sun as it rose over the distant hills.

She stopped to survey the landscape, and a strange feeling welled up within her. For a moment she didn't recognise it. Then it came to her: she was happy. She was really, truly happy. The Shingle Valley was beginning to take root and grow in her heart.

Oh Christ, that's all I need.

The sunshine, however, was short-lived; thick grey clouds blanketed the valley for the next few days, holding the promise of rain but not delivering.

One morning, Astrid had taken Leo to school and Luisa to play with some friends, and the house was unnaturally quiet. Mark was out visiting a grower at the far end of the valley, so Rose finally had a chance to explore the winery. She knew Dan would be there, but she could use the offer of a freshly baked carrot cake as an excuse to nose around. She still hadn't found out anything specific about the financial state of Kalkari, just rumours, and her brother would want something concrete soon, she knew.

Inside the winery, she popped her head around the office door, proffering the sweet treat.

Dan looked up and smiled at her. 'Hey, Rose, how are you going? Is that for me? Don't mind if I do. Ta.' For a large man, Dan moved surprisingly gracefully. He slid from his chair and moved over to a small countertop that was fitted with a sink. 'Let me put the kettle on. Will you stop and have a cuppa?'

'Sure, I'd love one.'

'How're you getting on up at the house?'

'Oh, it's all pretty good; although now I've got everything shipshape, I have to confess I've got a bit of time on my hands.'

'Ah, that's bloody gorgeous,' said Dan as he bit into the still-warm cake, savouring the rich sweetness and licking his lips, which were smeared with icing. 'How did you know I had a sweet tooth?'

Rose grinned at him. 'Lucky guess.'

'Well, if you're bored, you could always make more of these ripper cakes … actually, you know, what we need around here is someone to take the cellar door in hand. Clean it up and start offering tastings again. I think your cakes'd be a hit too, judging by this one. Hey, there's a bit of a CWA competition coming up next week. My missus always does well there, but I reckon you'd give even her a run for her money.'

Rose looked at him in surprise. She wasn't sure what Mark would have to say about her taking on the cellar door as a project, but as she turned the idea over in her mind, it did seem to have definite possibilities. She might be a bit more involved in everything, rather than always stuck at the house. It could also be a good way to get her hands on a set of keys. 'But I don't know anything about wine – well, apart from how to serve it, of course,' she said doubtfully. She didn't want to let on that she had some knowledge. 'I've no idea how to talk to people about it, describe how it was made and so on.' That much, at least, was true. 'And what's a CWA competition?'

'I could give you some tasting notes, get you up to speed on the wine lingo, no trouble,' Dan said as he handed her a mug of tea. 'You'd be a natural. And the CWA is the Country Women's Association. They hold an annual baking competition in Eumeralla. Be good for you to go and ruffle the feathers of a few of those old birds. Some of them think they rule the roost around here.' He guffawed at his own joke.

'Oh, yeah, Mrs B mentioned something about that,' she said noncommittally. 'But I think perhaps I should check with Mark about it first. About the cellar door, that is.'

'You're probably right. He doesn't take kindly to people interfering without his say-so, or doing things without him knowing. We haven't really had anyone here who could take on the job of managing it – not since the lady of the house upped and left, that is. Mind you, she didn't care to lower herself to serving customers. Just floated about the place, giving orders to everyone else. About as useless as tits on a bull she was.'

Rose spluttered into her tea. She'd never heard the expression before, but it certainly conveyed its meaning clearly enough.

'She was all high-falutin', hoity-toity. What do they call it? High maintenance. Yep, that's it. High maintenance. Eeessabella.' Dan drew out the syllables of her name in an exaggerated Spanish accent. He looked suddenly guilty. 'I shouldn't be talking out of school, but she thought she was too good for the likes of us. She knows all about wine alright, and she's certainly a looker. Things were okay in the beginning, but I reckon the grind of it got her down. There's never been more than two beans to rub together round here, and any money we do make Mark spends on French oak or new rootstock. I don't think we were glamorous enough for her in the end. She was always escaping to Sydney, leaving the little mites on their own with Brenda for days on end.' Dan shook his head at the memory and slurped another mouthful of tea.

Rose was intrigued to hear more about the absent Isabella and especially interested to have confirmation of the state of Kalkari's finances. She knew Henry was only interested in businesses that were on the brink of bankruptcy. That way he could swoop in and snap them up for a bargain-basement price. 'So things are still pretty tough around here?' she asked.

'Yep. Reckon this vintage will either make or break us. Mark's a brilliant winemaker, has great knowledge, an amazing palate, but what he's really got that puts him head and shoulders above anyone else is the feel.'

'The feel?'

'Yeah, a gut instinct for making exceptional wine. That's a rare thing. You can have all the knowledge, but it's got to be in your blood as well. But then that doesn't add up to enough without a great vintage — an outstanding vintage, actually — and an understanding bank manager …' Dan's voice trailed off and he laughed hollowly. 'Not asking much really, are we?'

Rose was surprised. She'd gathered things weren't all wine and roses, to use an appropriate cliché, from Charlie's comments at the Burning of the Canes, but she hadn't known just what a knife-edge Kalkari was operating on. This was clearly why Henry was snooping, but she still wasn't sure why he'd be so interested in a winery on the other side of the world — it was all just a bit far away. There must be something else she didn't know — why else would he have sent her here?

She was in an agony of indecision. Despite her best efforts and her initial impressions of the place, she'd been feeling a small but growing sense of loyalty and affection for Kalkari and the Shingle Valley, and especially towards the kids, who, bless them, were adorable. Even Mark had warmed up a tiny bit and wasn't as irritable as he had been when she first arrived. It was also clear how hard he worked and how passionate he was about the place. She was torn between loyalty to her brother and her growing feelings for Kalkari. She decided to put off thinking about exactly what to tell Henry for a few more days. In any case, he'd most likely be after more concrete information. Facts and figures, that's what Henry dealt in, not airy-fairy emotional stuff.

CHAPTER 9

A few days later, Mrs B bustled into the kitchen, taking Rose by surprise.

'Oh, hello, dear. Sorry to startle you. I forget that I don't work here anymore. I'm so used to letting myself in. Thought I'd come and see how the kiddies are doing. I miss them. And how are you getting on? Everyone treating you okay?'

Rose smiled at the nosy ex-housekeeper, 'Yep, all good, thanks. How are you feeling?'

'Right as rain, love, right as rain. Any chance of a cuppa?' The old lady didn't wait for an answer, but picked up the large kettle that sat on the range and filled it from the sink. 'So, how do you fancy throwing your hat in the ring for the CWA competition? Lord knows, we could do with some new blood. Dan's missus mentioned you might be interested.'

'Well, I'm not quite sure how she got that impression as I've never even met her, but okay, what's it all about?' said Rose.

'Well, if you are interested, I've got a couple of basic recipes for you here somewhere, and an entry form,' she said, fossicking around in her handbag and retrieving a couple of dog-eared pieces of paper. 'Here you go: there's a fruit cake and a lumberjack cake recipe there if you need them, or you can use your own. Can't go wrong with those. Just deliver them to the town hall next Tuesday.'

Mrs B wasn't someone Rose could easily refuse. In any case, baking was what Rose did best. How hard could this competition really be? She was Cordon Bleu–trained after all. Perhaps she could show the women of the valley a thing or two.

'Oh, and you'll need to pay the entry fee. It's a dollar per cake.'

Rose laughed. 'I think I can manage that.' Who knew? It might even be a bit of fun.

But she didn't have much fun when, on Sunday afternoon, she attempted the first of the cakes. She went with the recipe given to her by Mrs B. It looked simple enough, but in fact it was so simple that a great deal of detail – at what temperature and for how long to bake each cake, for example – had been left out. Detail that Rose could really have done with, she realised as she read it through more carefully. She'd just have to wing it.

'Oh no, sweet pea, don't add any more sugar, I've measured it exactly.' Luisa had thudded into the kitchen just as Rose was weighing out the ingredients for the lumberjack cake.

Why's it called that anyway? If you bake this cake, will a lumberjack show up and whisk you off to the woodshed and show you his axe?

She gazed out the window, lost in a fantasy about a strong and silent, check-shirted man who was good with his hands ...

'Luisa!' Rose was brought back to reality. 'Please, sweetie, don't touch. I need that for the next cake,' she said, exasperated.

Luisa was waving the packet of sugar around in an arc and pouring it all over the floor.

Christ – where's Astrid when I need her?

It was just Rose's luck that Mark chose that moment to come into the kitchen. He frowned, puzzled, as his feet crunched on the sugar scattered all over the floor. 'Everything alright in here?'

Rose tucked a stray strand of hair behind her ear. 'Super, thanks,' she said brightly. 'We're just doing a bit of baking.'

Mark raised an eyebrow. 'Really?'

'Dada, we cooking,' said Luisa, beaming at him.

'So I can see.'

Mark came closer to Rose and brushed her cheek with his hand. Rose was startled at the unexpected intimacy of his touch. 'What?'

'Flour,' he replied, holding up his index finger.

'Oh, right. Thanks.' Blushing, she hid her face, gazing intently at the mixing bowl in front of her, silently cursing her flaming cheeks, where she could still feel the touch of his hand. She was taken aback by her reaction – was she really so desperate that just a touch from a man, any man, could turn her into a blithering idiot? She reminded herself that it was Giles she missed. She did miss talking to him about her day, the solid feel of him next to her in bed at night, even the irritating way he whistled Moves Like Jagger when he was happy about something …

Rose shook her head and, with some effort, brought her mind back to the job at hand. Mark, thankfully, had left her and Luisa to finish their baking without further distractions, but by the time she had swept up all the debris from the floor and wiped down a very sticky Luisa, it was getting late and there weren't enough ingredients remaining to make the fruit cake. Mrs B would just have to be satisfied with the lumberjack cake. Despite Luisa's best efforts and the lack of baking instructions, it actually looked halfway decent. She'd decided to make a couple of versions, using a slightly longer cooking time for one, and then cut the least successful of the two up for afternoon tea. Just as well, as the little girl was desperate to taste it, and even Leo had been lured into the kitchen by the buttery smell wafting through the window.

'You'll want to put that over there, love,' a kindly voice instructed. 'I'll take your entry form. Money in the tin. And here's a number to tape to your plate.'

Rose had driven to Eumeralla, the cake balanced precariously on the passenger seat of the car, and arrived at the town hall just as several other women were ferrying their baking to the judging tables. The hall was fragrant with the sweet aromas of butter, lemon, brandy, chocolate and spice – and barely veiled ambition.

Lord! The Great British Bake Off's *got nothing on this*, she thought in astonishment as she took in the rows of near-identical perfectly risen sponges and luscious iced fancy cakes. She deposited her effort next to several others on a table that bore a folded cardboard sign that read 'Lumberjack', stuck the assigned number on it and dropped her dollar in the tin.

She was just on her way out the door when she bumped into Mrs B.

'Hello, love, how'd you get on?'

'Not too bad, but Luisa wanted to get in on the action too, so it was a joint effort, if you know what I mean,' replied Rose.

Mrs B laughed, her belly shaking with mirth. 'You and Astrid have got your hands full there now, haven't you?'

'Sure do. So when is the judging?' asked Rose, curious.

'They bring in a judge from New Bridgeton – that's the region's nearest big town – and only the CWA's Shingle Valley president knows in advance who it's going to be. That way there's no carry-on about an unfair result, and no-one can try and nobble the judge.'

Rose looked astonished. 'Really? They'd try to do that?'

'Oh, you'd better believe it,' said Mrs B, looking darkly around the hall. 'Trust no-one.'

Rose laughed at Mrs B's cloak-and-dagger expression.

'The judging is tomorrow; then there's a bit of a fundraiser tea at the end of the week, where everyone gets to sample the entries and the results are announced.'

As Astrid, Rose and Luisa trooped up the stairs to the Eumeralla town hall later that week, they were assaulted by the noise of some fifty-odd women, all of whom seemed to be talking at once, the sound of their voices amplified by the room's high ceilings.

Despite her earlier nonchalance, Rose couldn't wait to find out how she'd done. She'd seen two magpies hopping around outside that morning, and was feeling buoyed up.

'Come on. Luisa, let's go and get a drink, shall we?' suggested Astrid, bearing the little girl towards a table at the far end of the hall, where three enormous enamelled teapots were being hoisted aloft by several strong-armed women.

Peering between the press of bodies, Rose spied the cakes, laid out on tables that ran the length of the room. She fought her way over to the section where the lumberjack cakes were – there were eleven of them – and was astonished to see that number five bore a rosette. That was hers!

'Well done, love!' Turning around, Rose saw that the voice belonged to Betty, one of the cooks from the Canes night. 'Merle Stubbins took out the gong. She's won the gold rosette for best lumberjack cake for the last nine years. But you got a creditable third place. You should be really pleased with that. Some of these women have been baking for more than forty years.'

Rose might have been beaten into third place, but she had to admit the two cakes judged better than hers were pretty damn impressive-looking. 'That's not bad, hey?' she said.

'Rose!' It was Mrs B. 'Rose, there you are!' she bustled over to Rose's side. 'How about that? A third place in your first competition. That's terrific. You even beat Maggie, and she'll be none too pleased about that.'

'Maggie?'

'Dan's wife.'

'Oh.' Rose wasn't sure if that was necessarily a good thing, but she allowed herself to be a tiny bit chuffed at the rosette, regardless of whom she'd outplaced.

Later that day, as Rose was putting the finishing touches to a shepherd's pie – Leo's request – for dinner, forking the mashed potato down over the mince mixture, Mark appeared in the kitchen.

'Oh, hi,' she said, flustered at seeing him unexpectedly. *For goodness sake*, she told herself, *stop acting like a silly school-girl*. Mark still intimidated her a bit, and she didn't know quite what to make of him. Once minute he was distant and aloof, the next friendly. She never knew what to expect.

'Guess what?'

'What?' Mark's tone was curt and she almost lost her nerve.

'That cake Luisa and I made, well, it won third place at the Eumeralla CWA competition. Look.' Rose pointed to the rosette, which she'd stuck to the fridge door. 'Twenty dollar prize too!' she said, unable to keep the pride from her voice.

'Well, that will have set the old dears talking,' Mark replied dryly.

Rose was a bit deflated by his response. He might have congratulated her.

'Actually, Rose, I was wondering if you might be able to rustle up some tucker for a few guests we've got coming next week. There's a couple of distributor bigwigs in the country from the UK, plus the wine buyer from Channings, one of the biggest supermarkets; you'd have heard of them, right? Anyway, they're coming to have a look at our char-donnay and the cab shiraz, and I reckon we should give them some lunch as well.' Mark's voice sounded deliberately casual, but Rose had picked up enough since arriving at Kalkari to realise that this visit was a pretty big deal.

Her first thought was that she wasn't up to it. It had been a long time since she'd cooked anything more than very basic dishes. 'Of course,' she was surprised to find herself saying. 'What type of food were you thinking of?'

'Oh, I don't know. Something simple. Hearty. Nothing fancy. Just good country cooking. I'm sure you'll do a fine job if what you've been doing so far is anything to go by. There'll be eight of us. I'll get Dan to drop the wines over so you can taste them and get an idea of what might work flavour-wise.'

Rose's heart beat faster. He was putting a lot of faith in her, and she really didn't want to mess this up. After he had left the kitchen, she turned to the tattered copy of *Gourmet Traveller* that lived on the dresser, but it was a summer issue and so didn't offer much inspiration. *Hmm.* She mentally sorted through the classic French dishes she'd mastered at Le Cordon Bleu. Nothing too fancy. Hearty. Well, that ruled most of them out then. She'd need to make a trip into Eumeralla for provisions too. Next Thursday, he'd said. It was Tuesday today, so that gave her just over a week.

She went to bed that night with ideas swirling around in her head but feeling frustrated that her cookbook access was limited to a couple of old grease-spattered tomes she'd unearthed in the kitchen and that had been published sometime in the last century. What in the hell was she going to cook?

CHAPTER 10

'Bugger!' Rose exclaimed to herself, hitching up her jeans for the ninety-ninth time that day.

She had just finished making the kids' beds and was giving the ancient vacuum cleaner a thorough workout, though she suspected it was merely moving the dust around from one place to another rather than actually sucking it up. As she worked, she kept having to stop and put the vacuum down to hitch her jeans up. It was seriously giving her the shits. They were down somewhere below her hips and she was showing a good deal of plumber's crack. Now that Rose's diet was heavy on fruit and fresh veggies and considerably lighter on midnight pie leftovers and raw cookie dough, and now that she was exercising almost every morning, there was plenty of room in her pants, to the point where she really needed to replace them with something that actually fitted. Even her belt was on the tightest hole and really needed a couple more punched in it. With that thought in her head, she went in search of Astrid. Perhaps she'd like a shopping trip too?

Rose found Astrid and Luisa in the small sitting room, Luisa having emptied the contents of a toybox onto the floor. The little dark-haired cherub was searching through the rubble, singing softly to herself.

'Hey, girls, what's up?' asked Rose.

Astrid wasn't her usual pink-cheeked self; she looked wan and rather fragile.

'We're just sorting out the toys. Or at least that's what I was trying to do.' Astrid rolled her eyes and smiled weakly at Rose.

'Are you okay? You look really pale.'

'Oh, sure, just feeling a bit yuck. Must be something I ate.'

'Nothing I made, I hope?' asked Rose.

'Oh no, I don't think so. Everyone else is fine. Maybe it's something I had for lunch yesterday in town, or I might have picked up a bug of the tummy,' Astrid reassured her.

'That doesn't sound much fun. You poor thing. I came to see if you felt like some retail therapy, but if you're not up to it, maybe another time. I've *got* to get some new trousers,' said Rose, pulling the waistband of her jeans away from her now nearly flat stomach.

'You do look a bit different than when you first arrived,' Astrid said. 'Not so much jelly wobble.' She laughed at Rose.

'Thanks. I think,' replied Rose, not especially offended. 'Anyway, it's ridiculous. These just keep falling down.'

'Nice problem for you to have. I think your cooking has had the opposite effect on me. I can hardly do my jeans up anymore,' Astrid grimaced and turned even whiter.

'If you're not feeling well, why don't you go upstairs and have a lie-down? It must nearly be time for Luisa's nap too, yeah?'

'It'd be great if you could settle her for me. There's some milk for her here and she likes to be sung to.'

Astrid walked gingerly up the stairs. Rose went to get the milk, then bent down and picked Luisa up in her arms. 'Come on, my little turnip, let's go and have a lovely nap, shall we?'

Luisa clung onto Rose and snuggled into her shoulder. Rose breathed in the fragrant toddler scent of her, loving the smoothness of her skin, the pillowy-soft cheeks and the spun-silk hair.

Rose struggled to recall any childhood songs, and was only able to come up with a tuneless rendition of 'Twinkle Twinkle'. Singing was definitely not her strong point, but Luisa seemed satisfied, drinking her milk and then closing her eyes.

Rose kissed her softly, shut the door gently and tiptoed down the hallway to check on Astrid.

'You okay? Can I get you anything?' asked Rose, standing outside the door. She thought she heard a sob, so she pushed the door open tentatively. The floor of the room was scattered with possibly even more clothes, magazines and make-up than it had been the first time she'd seen it. Astrid lay on her bed, curled up in a ball.

'What's up?'

'Oh, Rose, what have I done?' Astrid wailed. Gone was the bubbly girl Rose had come to know. In her place was someone who looked like they'd just heard the worst news in the world. 'You can't tell a soul; you must swear you won't.'

'Cross my heart,' said Rose solemnly, wondering what on earth was up.

'I think I might be pregnant,' said Astrid in a small voice.

'Oh my God.' Rose was shocked. 'Really? Are you sure?'

'Well, my period is a week late, and I just feel so sick all of the time, and these,' Astrid cupped her breasts, 'are like rocks.'

'Have you told Thommo?'

'Noooo,' wailed Astrid. 'I can't.' She sobbed even harder.

'Why not?'

'But I thought you and Thommo …?'

'No, it was just a mad moment, that night after the pub; it didn't mean anything. A hook-up … is that how you say it? What am I going to do? *Gott in Himmel*, I can't believe I'm such an idiot!'

Rose sat down next to her on the bed. She was lost for words, particularly words of advice, and could only pat Astrid on the shoulder in a vain attempt to make her feel better. Had the silly girl not heard of contraception? 'Perhaps the first thing to do would be to take a test, just to be sure?' she suggested gently. 'I'm going to head into New Bridgeton tomorrow to see if I can find some trousers that

won't fall down around my knees. Why don't I get a pregnancy test for you then?'

'*Ja*,' said Astrid through her tears. 'Thank you. That
would be good, I suppose. But please, don't say anything to
anyone about this, okay?'

'Of course.'

Astrid looked at her uncertainly.

'Swear on my granny's grave, okay? I'll not tell a soul.'

'Thank you, Rose. Again.'

CHAPTER 11

The next morning, leaving a peaky-looking Astrid to get Leo organised for school and Luisa ready for her weekly playgroup, Rose set off for New Bridgeton and the shopping centre, which, according to Astrid, promised at least one jeans emporium as well as a couple of chain stores and a few boutiques. As she whizzed past the now green vines that marched in obedient rows across almost every square metre of the valley, she couldn't help think how different it looked from the bleak scene of her arrival. It really was terribly pretty now, and just as the tendrils of the vines were curling along the wire trellises, so the valley was stealing its way into her heart.

She also couldn't help think about the quandary Astrid was in. Rose's own love life was far from perfect – well, in actual fact, it was pretty much nonexistent – but at least she wasn't in that kind of a jam. If Astrid was pregnant, what would she decide to do? Would she – could she – keep the baby? Either way, she had a tough road ahead of her, that much was certain.

Rose drove through the outskirts of New Bridgeton, following the signs to the town centre. Parking the car, she hopped out and began to investigate. Jean Jeanious was easy to spot, right in the middle. Unsure of the Aussie sizing, she grabbed a few of pairs of each. There wasn't a full-length mirror in the barn, so Rose hadn't seen herself properly for a couple of months.

She got quite a shock when she zipped up the first pair. The jeans gaped at the waist and bagged around her bum. She pulled them off and tried on another, much smaller pair. These ones moulded to every inch of her thighs and backside. She turned around to check how she looked in the mirror.

Holy shrinking arses! Is this really me?

For one of the few times in her life, Rose was thrilled by what she saw in the mirror. On a good day, she could imagine a resemblance to Anne Hathaway. On a bad day – and there had been plenty of those recently – she felt more like Kirstie Alley. Before Jenny Craig. Today, it seemed, was a rare good day. Her rounded belly and muffin top were nowhere to be seen, and her legs were lean and toned.

She wasn't quite so thrilled by her tangled mass of dark hair, which was in dire need of a good cut, but the sparkle in her eyes and her clear, glowing skin were testament to her growing happiness; the smile was the result of seeing herself looking like she'd never dared to even imagine she could look. She couldn't stop staring at herself. If only Giles could see her now – she'd bet a hundred quid he wouldn't even recognise her. Hell, she hardly even recognised herself.

Her thoughts were interrupted as the shop assistant poked her head around the curtain to check if she needed any help. Rose handed back the sizes that were far too big for her and pulled her old, very baggy, pants back on.

She also tried on a couple of t-shirts that she found clung to her in all the right places, and a pair of shorts, and decided she needed those too. The mornings and nights were still chilly, but in the middle of the day it was starting to be deliciously warm outside.

Being stuck out at Kalkari most of the time meant there was very little there for her to spend her money on, so she handed over several fifty-dollar notes without too much concern. Swinging her shopping bags from one hand, she strolled out of the store with a spring in her step, looking up and down the mall for more boutiques to scope out.

Less than an hour later, a scarf, new running tights and a pair of delicate turquoise and silver earrings were also hers. Sitting over a coffee, with her bags corralled at her feet, Rose basked in the glow of a successful shopping trip. Where was the sad, chubby cook now? She felt grateful after all for Henry pushing her onto an airplane. She really ought to repay him by spilling all she'd found out about Kalkari, but that meant betraying Mark and the kids. She was completely torn. Rose knew she couldn't stay at Kalkari forever, but right now she was enjoying existing in a bubble such a long way from her old life.

Don't overthink it, she told herself firmly. *And enough with the worrying.*

When Rose arrived home, she dumped the bags of new clothes on her bed and then raced over to the main house in search of Astrid, the pregnancy tests she'd purchased at the mall in her hand. She ran slap-bang into Mark just as she was coming around the corner, and he had to steady her to stop her falling over him. She dropped the tests on the ground and hurriedly tried to reach them before he saw. But Mark was too quick for her, and bent down to retrieve them.

'Steady, Rose. Here you go,' he said, handing the package to her.

Thank goodness they'd been wrapped in a paper bag. Rose, relieved at the close call, muttered her thanks and continued on her way to find Astrid.

'Phew, there you are,' she said, finding her playing on the back verandah with Luisa and Leo. They were attempting to teach Barnsie a new trick. The chooks were keeping a safe distance from the yapping puppy. 'I wasn't sure which would be best, so I got three different types. I just bumped into Mark, so thank goodness the chemist wrapped them up.' She handed over the bag.

'Thanks so much, Rose. I'm feeling a bit better now,

actually. I think whatever I had has settled down,' Astrid said, glancing at the kids and shooting Rose a warning look not to say more in front of them.

'Right, who's going to help me fold these dry clothes?' Rose asked, eyeing off the dark clouds on the horizon and looking pointedly at Leo and Luisa as she marched to the overloaded line.

'Not me,' said Leo, 'I'm training Barnsie.'

'And you're doing a great job with him. He only barked the house down for ten minutes this morning,' she said dryly. 'Luisa?'

'I hep you, Wosie?' said Luisa

'Thanks, honey, I'd love that.'

Rose unpegged the stiff, dry clothes from the line, snapping them straight and folding them with an efficient flick of the wrist before depositing them in the laundry basket, where Luisa tried to help by removing them and attempting to fold them again. Rose was still wearing her old jeans, and as she reached up to the furthest rail to unpeg the last sheet she felt them slide down past her bum.

Oh Christ!

She looked down to see her trousers concertinaed around her knees and Leo cracking up with laughter.

'Rose, your pants!' he said, doubling up with mirth.

'Wosie got pink undies!' chimed in Luisa, giggling at her.

'Ha ha, guys, pretty funny, huh?' Rose bent over to haul up the baggy jeans. 'Okay, show's over. We're all done here. Nothing more to see.'

'Come on, let's head inside,' said Astrid, who had been laughing along with the kids at Rose's predicament. They both looked up at the darkening sky.

'Yep, I think it's about to hammer down at any minute,' Rose agreed.

It rained for the rest of that day, and all of the next. The rain sluiced down as if someone had tipped a giant bucket of water over the valley. The chooks huddled miserably in their hen house, Leo's scooter and Luisa's trike lay abandoned on the back verandah, and puddles formed in the yard, turning it into a quagmire.

On Friday, Leo's school had a pupil-free day, which also coincided with Astrid's day off, so Rose was left to entertain two fractious kids and one over-active puppy, in addition to trying to plan the menu for the following week's VIP lunch. She started off with a game of hide-and-seek, but Luisa's squeals soon gave her away and Leo proved such a good hider that it took them forever to find him. Rose's patience was seriously tested. The rain eased off a little after lunch and she found raincoats and wellies – 'gumboots', Leo corrected her – and buttoned everyone up for a walk. Barnsie delighted in nosing into the muddy water, drinking from the puddles and trotting along the lanes, before finally rolling around in a puddle so big he could almost swim to the other side of it. By the time they returned to the house, his coat was filthy with mud.

'I think he needs a bath, don't you?' said Rose.

'Oh, can we help?' asked Leo.

'Sure can!'

Rose lifted the dog up under its belly to prevent muddy

footprints on the hall floor, and she and the kids trooped upstairs to the bathroom, where she ran a deep, warm bath and deposited Barnsie in it. They giggled as he yelped and snapped at the water, trying to swim. Using an old hair-brush, they scraped away at his coat until the puppy's white patches returned, flicking plenty of mud on themselves in the process. After a rinse-off and a brisk towel-down, he was clean and relatively dry, but the kids were wetter than when they had been outside, and needed a good wash themselves. *Well, it's one way to while away an afternoon*, thought Rose.

She had just got them bathed and into their pyjamas and popped all three of them in front of *Frozen* when Mark came in.

'Guess what, Daddy! Wosie got pink undies,' announced Luisa.

Leo looked up and giggled, paying no attention to the stern look Rose shot him.

'Does she now?' replied Mark, raising an eyebrow at a blushing Rose. Not attempting to explain, she escaped to the kitchen to prepare dinner.

She was in the depths of the pantry when she heard Luisa calling for her. Putting down the rice she was holding, she headed back to the sitting room.

Leo and Barnsie were snuggled up on the sofa together, the pup with his snout resting on Leo's leg. Luisa and Mark were on the floor at their feet, Luisa sitting on a cushion, leaning against her daddy. The family made a touching sight, thought Rose.

'Wosie! Wosieeee!' the little girl called out.

'What's up, Lulu?'

'Love you, Wosie,' said Luisa, looking up at her. 'Don't go.'

Seeing Luisa's dark eyes and sober expression, Rose felt a knot of guilt twisting in her stomach. She swallowed. 'Oh sweetie, I love you too, and don't worry, I'm not going anywhere, I'm just in the kitchen.'

Satisfied, Luisa turned back to the screen. Elsa had just begun to belt out 'Let it Go', and Barnsie howled along with gusto.

CHAPTER 12

The morning of the VIP lunch dawned bright and cold, with a fresh spring wind rustling through the tall eucalypts, tossing their olive-green leaves like a giant bowl of salad. Rose cleared her head with a quick jog alongside the vineyards. She noticed the pale, shiny vine leaves and curling tendrils were beginning to unfurl along the rows.

She'd scoured the glossy food magazines at Sacred Grounds earlier in the week, and Bevan had lent her a copy of a book by Maggie Beer. The conversation with him had enlightened her about the chooks' names: of course she'd heard of Nigella, but not of Stephanie Alexander or Maggie Beer. Mrs B must have had a hand in the naming, she thought. Bevan assured her that Maggie and Stephanie were a couple of Australia's foremost cooks, and queens of honest, down-to-earth food. Just what Mark had ordered. She'd found some new-season broad beans at the previous week-end's farmers' market, and planned to serve them in a salad with shards of crispy prosciutto and fresh curd cheese; the salty, creamy flavours would contrast well with the albarino and the Kalkari chardonnay. Then she'd serve fresh ravioli stuffed with slow-roasted beef cheeks and wild mushrooms and a demi-glace to go with the Kalkari reds, and she planned to finish with a blood orange and custard tart.

She'd prepared the stuffing for the ravioli the previous day, and the tart was cooling on the counter in the kitchen. She just had to make the ravioli pasta (she sent a mental thanks to Mrs B, who'd come to the rescue with a machine that was now firmly bolted to one end of the kitchen table), and prep the salad. There was a new moon in Venus, Rose had turned around seven times in the kitchen before she started cooking, and she was wearing her lucky knickers. She wasn't taking any chances.

Astrid had taken Luisa out, and Leo was at school, so there were no distractions. In fact, Rose was sure Astrid had been avoiding her ever since she'd given her the pregnancy tests, and Rose hadn't had the chance to ask her, without the children being around, what the result had been. She supposed it could have been a false alarm – Astrid certainly looked a bit brighter than she had done previously. Anyway, she didn't have time to worry about that now: there was work to be done.

A few days earlier, Rose had persuaded Mark to give her the key to the cellar door, and she'd dusted and polished everything until it sparkled. The glassware shone in the shafts of sunlight streaming through the windows. Next to the cellar door tasting room she'd discovered a large dining area, furnished with a heavy-legged table and upholstered dining chairs. She'd raided the linen cupboard, and starched white damask now clothed the table, with small glass pots of spring flowers dotted along the centre. Dan had helpfully shown her how many glasses they would need and instructed her how to line them up next to each place setting.

She was double-checking everything was perfect when Mark came through the door.

'Oh. Rose, there you are. Hey, it looks great,' he said as he glanced around the room. He was carrying a case of wines that he'd brought over from the winery and began to arrange them on a side table, placing bottles of white into a large pewter trough that Rose had already filled with ice.

'It's all under control from my end,' she said, doing her best to reassure him. From her conversations with Dan, she knew how much this visit meant to Mark: the way Dan made it sound, the entire future of Kalkari was at stake. 'You might want to get yourself back to the house and put on a clean shirt.' Rose was nervous about ordering him around, especially as he seemed so tense.

Mark looked down at the worn sweater and muddy jeans that were his usual winery finery, and then glanced at his watch. 'Yes. Right. Of course. Good call,' he said somewhat distractedly. 'Actually, I've got something for you. Hang on a sec and I'll go and grab it.'

Rose was mystified, but waited while he loped back to the winery.

'Reckon this should fit you.' Mark returned, holding up a navy polo shirt with the Kalkari logo embroidered on the pocket. 'You're one of the team now,' he said, handing it to her.

Rose felt an enormous pang of guilt. He wouldn't think she was one of the team if he found out her real reasons for being there.

As she was leaving the cellar door, Rose ran into Dan, who was also looking anxious.

'Place is absolutely spotless,' he said. 'It's been hard yakka, but we couldn't make it look any better than it does now. Fit for a bloody princess, I tell ya.'

As she looked around, Rose saw that the grass had been freshly mown, its normally unruly edges neatly trimmed, and the gravel drive had been levelled out. 'It looks great, Dan. Anyway, it's the wines they're here for, and you know they're good.'

'I'm a bit worried about the albarino. It's just been bottled and is a bit flat.'

Rose looked at him blankly, not understanding what he was saying.

'Bottle shock. Bottling day is one of the most stressful days in a winemaker's year. Wine's a temperamental mistress,' Dan explained. 'You've got to treat her with care, and she doesn't always like the transition to bottle. Takes her a while to settle down. Bit like a woman, really,' he guffawed at his own joke and stomped off to the winery.

An hour or so later, and Rose had the ravioli filled and the salad waiting to be assembled. She peered out of the kitchen window and saw a telltale plume of dust from the road leading up to Kalkari. A white minivan was making its way up the long drive, headed for the winery. Nervousness clutched at her stomach – not for the lunch, which she was fairly confident would be fine now she had it all under control, but for what the visitors might think and what decisions they might make. This was a red-letter day for Kalkari. But why was she so bothered about the outcome? She had to keep reminding herself that she was only going to be at Kalkari for a short time; she really shouldn't care so much. After all, she was only here because Henry had insisted.

She lost herself in a daydream, remembering the last time she'd cooked the ravioli. Giles had said it was one of the best things he'd ever tasted. Her heart sank. Despite everything, she hadn't stopped missing him. She still caught herself hoping that eventually he might change his mind and realise that he couldn't live without her.

She was disturbed from her thoughts by the unmistakable smell of burning. *Oh holy crap!* Thick smoke was billowing from the grill. Without thinking, she grabbed a pair of oven gloves and ran out of the front door, holding the tray aloft and blowing fruitlessly on the flickering flames.

Of course, just at that moment, Mark chose to walk over from the winery.

'Nothing to see here.' Rose was scarlet with mortification. 'Really. It's. All. Under. Control.' She attempted to hide the tray behind her back.

'Rose, why is there smoke coming from behind you?'

'It's all part of the cooking process,' she said airily. 'I'm smoking the, er, prosciutto.'

'Oh really?' said Mark disbelievingly.

'Yes, it's fine. Honest.' At least the flames had now gone out and the smoke had been blown away on the breeze. 'Best be getting on, then. See you later.' And she fled back to the kitchen, bearing the tray like a trophy.

At least she had more prosciutto in the fridge. 'Keep your mind on the job this time, Rose,' she warned herself as she carefully laid the remaining strips on a clean tray.

Mark had instructed her to serve lunch right on one, so at ten to the hour she carried the salad over to the cellar door, planning to plate it at one of the side tables. The visitors were already there, gathered at one end, each holding a glass of wine daintily by the stem. They paid little attention to Rose, but Mark noticed her and suggested they take their seats as she arranged the salad on plates and placed them at each setting.

There was a hum of conversation from the guests and the mood seemed to be friendly – well, as far as Rose could tell. Five of the visitors were men – two in suits and the others in jeans, jackets and open-necked shirts – and there was a lone female wearing a loudly checked tweed jacket and skirt, a silk shirt with the collar turned up and a chunky pearl necklace. From the woman's accent, Rose guessed she must be the buyer from Channings.

She hurried back to the kitchen to poach the ravioli and warm the sauce through. She'd reckoned that the cellar door was just close enough to plate everything in the kitchen and walk it across. But as she was ferrying it over, she tripped, stumbled and dropped two of the three plates she was carrying onto the dusty ground. Of course they landed face-down in the gravel.

Bollocks. Bugger. Bum. How the bloody hell could she be so clumsy?

She was furious with herself. Could she screw it up any more if she tried?

She collected herself, scraped the gritty ravioli back onto the plates and limped back to the kitchen. One thing was clear: she was not cut out to be a waitress.

There were plenty of ravioli on the kitchen bench, but no sauce left, and she'd already plated up the other servings. Trying not to panic, she heard the voice of her old Cordon Bleu teacher, Guillaume Chapeau – Monsieur Asshat, they'd nicknamed him – berating her. 'Rose, *c'est incroyable*, you really can do better than this,' he used to say, with the corners of his mouth turned down in a disgusted frown. 'Use your imagination, eh?'

Imagination ... she dashed to the pantry and pulled out a can of crushed tomatoes, wrenched open the lid, spooned the contents into a bowl and put it in the microwave. Once the tomatoes were warm, she spooned them over two new plates of ravioli and walked – carefully this time – back to the cellar door. 'Allergies,' she mumbled as she placed the extra plates with the tomatoes in front of Mark and Dan. Mark raised an eyebrow as he looked at the plate, but made no comment. Rose breathed a sigh of relief. Perhaps it would be alright after all. Before anyone could ask her any questions, she made a swift exit.

Returning with the orange and custard tart some time later, she was gratified to see that all the plates were clean, with not a skerrick of ravioli or sauce left on them. The noise level in the room had also risen, and there were empty wine bottles lined up along the sideboard. A couple of the men complimented Rose on the lunch, one of them giving her an appreciative wink. Mark smiled tightly, giving nothing away, and once she'd cleared the table and served the tart, she returned to the kitchen and the washing up, remembering to leave packages of prettily wrapped homemade shortbread for each of the visitors, together with a folder of tasting notes on each of the wines that Dan had compiled, on the bench at the cellar door.

It was more than an hour later when she saw the visitors' van trundle back down the drive. She returned to the cellar door to clear the glasses and put everything back in order. There was no sign of Mark or Dan. How had the visit gone? Despite herself, Rose found herself hoping it had gone well.

CHAPTER 13

Once she'd fed the kids some of the leftover ravioli with the tomato sauce, and then cleared up, Rose settled down on the barn sofa with a couple of slices of cheese on toast. She was worn out from the day's effort and felt unexpectedly flat. It would have been nice to share the aftermath of the event with Dan at least. She hoped the near-disaster with the main course hadn't been too obvious. Astrid had asked how it had all gone but had been too absorbed with helping Luisa feed herself without throwing food on the floor to listen to a blow-by-blow account.

Rose didn't have much of an appetite, but the warm melted cheese would be comforting. Just as she was about to take a bite, there was a rap on the door. She opened it to find Mark leaning against the frame, a bottle and two glasses in his hand.

'Didn't get the chance to thank you for lunch this afternoon,' he said, swaying slightly.

'Oh, sure, come in.' Rose felt a little awkward inviting her boss into his own property, but she stood back and ushered him in.

'Thought you might fancy a glass.' He held up a bottle of red. 'Lunch was excellent, truly excellent, by the way. I couldn't have asked for better, really. Everyone loved the ravioli – those flavours made the reds positively sing. Even the tomatoes. And you were right about the smoky aromas in the salad.' He had a twinkle in his eye.

Rose grimaced. 'Sorry about that. I nearly stuffed it up, didn't I? And then I tripped … and, well, two plates ended up in the dirt. God, I'm such a muppet sometimes. I was just waiting for the third thing to go wrong.'

'Third thing?'

'You know: bad luck comes in threes.'

'That's superstitious nonsense, you know,' he said. But his voice was gentle and he swayed again, slurring on the word superstitious.

'Anyway, I hope it wasn't too obvious.'

Mark put her out of her misery, 'They were all fairly well lubricated by then; it didn't matter at all. Just as well it was only two of the plates, hey?'

'Oh yes, thank goodness. I wouldn't want you to think I'm totally incompetent.'

'That lunch was far from incompetent, Rose, and you know it. Don't sell yourself short just because you can't carry a couple of plates. Anyway, between you and me and

116

the food and the wine, I think we managed to knock their socks off.' Mark was smiling at her, his grin reaching from ear to ear.

Oh, he's gorgeous when he smiles. Rose felt suddenly warm all over. *Stop it, Rose!* she scolded herself.

She realised he was still standing.

'Please, sit down.'

Mark plonked down heavily on one of the sofas and Rose perched on the far end of it, twisting to face him as she tucked her long legs underneath her.

'Does this mean you think they'll place an order?'

'Well, it's hard to tell, but Alicia seemed really impressed with the albarino and the tempranillo, and she certainly slurped down a lot of the chardonnay.'

'That's good, isn't it?'

Mark nodded. 'Said she preferred it to a lot of the Spanish stuff she'd tasted. We just need to be able to supply enough, and at the right price. The Trevelyn sisters have got a couple of blocks of tempranillo just coming on board, but I'm not sure if they've tied up their contracts yet, and I can't really put my hand up for it if I'm not going to get the order.'

'When will you know?'

'She said she'd be back in the UK in a couple of weeks' time and be looking at it sometime after that.'

'And how about the distributors?'

'They've supported Kalkari since the beginning; we've been really lucky. They reckon the Spanish varietals'll go really well in the metro markets, both on premise and off.'

'On premise?'

'Restaurants, clubs, bars. Off-premise is your bottle-os, drive-throughs.'

Mark poured them each an enormous glass of wine and turned to face her. 'You have a real talent, Rose. That was a superb meal.' He looked at her as if he was seeing her for the first time. Rose chewed her lip and tried to mentally quell the rising warmth she could feel creeping up from her breastbone. Nope. No luck. She felt her cheeks redden under his scrutiny. 'I really hope you can stay here for a while. You're a big hit with Luisa. She adores you – she told me so tonight.'

'Oh, she's a darling. Gorgeous Lulu. Such a sweetie.'

'It hasn't been easy. For any of us. I expect someone's filled you in on what happened.' Mark paused, as if deciding how much to tell her. 'I'm probably partly to blame. I realise that now. Too bloody wrapped up in the winery to see that the wheels were falling off at home. I had no idea Isabella was that unhappy. You know, I don't think she ever really settled here … I still don't understand how she could leave the kids behind though. Me, yes, but not Luisa and Leo. Luisa's too young to remember much, but Leo misses his mum so much. He keeps asking when she's coming back. I'm glad she didn't take them though. I'd be lost without them.' Mark sighed and took another gulp of wine.

Rose had never seen him with his guard down before: he was a different person.

'Anyway, that's enough about me and my misery. Tell me some more about you. D'you mind if I have a piece of this?' Mark indicated the cheesy toast.

'Oh, please do. I'm not really that hungry anyway,' said

Rose. As he crunched through both pieces, scattering crumbs on the sofa, she continued. 'There's not much to tell. Lost my job and my boyfriend both on the same day. Pretty careless, huh?' she glanced up at him from under her eyelashes. 'There wasn't much to keep me in London, and I'd always wanted to see Australia. My big brother told me about the job here and practically escorted me onto the plane. I spent a few days in Sydney, and now, well, here I am.' Rose hoped this didn't sound too sketchy and that he wouldn't delve deeper.

He leaned towards her and she caught the tang of citrus, leather and spice.

She tried, but failed, not to breathe in deeply.

Divine.

She mentally kicked herself for reacting to him. What was she thinking, lusting after her boss, for God's sake?

'Tell me what you love about cooking,' he said.

'I can't remember ever *not* cooking – as a little girl I'd mix up awful potions of herbs and Tabasco and whatever else was in the cupboard,' Rose laughed at the memory. 'My mum was never much interested in being in the kitchen, so as I grew up I gradually took over the cooking, especially for holidays and celebrations. My nanna was a good cook though – she taught me a lot of the basics. Mostly, I love how food brings people together, how recipes can knit together generations of memories, and how cooking for someone lets them know you care about them ...' Rose trailed off. 'Sounds kind of silly, really.'

'Not at all,' said Mark. 'That's an admirable philosophy.'

He kicked off his shoes and they chatted some more: about Mark's plans for the winery and why he had started Kalkari. As the wine snaked its way into her veins, Rose felt herself relaxing and, she noticed with surprise, enjoying Mark's company. He'd clearly had quite a lot to drink, but as he talked about his love for the valley, for its soil and its people, she could hear in his words an echo of her own growing feelings for the place. But after a while, her head began to nod back against the upholstery and she felt her eyelids beginning to flutter. It had been a long day.

'Oh, look at you, you're exhausted, and here am I boring the pants off you,' Mark said. 'I'll leave you to get some rest.' He rose unsteadily from the sofa and looked down at her.

Rose made to get up.

'No, don't worry, I'll see myself out.'

'Okay, goodnight then,' she said sleepily.

'Goodnight, Rose,' he said softly as he reached the door. It closed gently behind him.

With Mark's departure, the air in the room seemed less charged. Despite her tiredness, Rose was left wishing he'd stayed longer.

The first thought in Rose's head, when she woke early the next morning, was of the previous night. She smiled to herself as she remembered. She'd seen a new side to Mark, one that was vulnerable and gentle, not grumpy and dismissive. She blushed at the memory of his lean, muscular thighs and broad shoulders under his check shirt. She had to admit he was pretty hot – well, for an older guy. She lost herself in a little daydream of him looking deeply into her eyes and wrapping an arm around her waist, pulling her towards him for a sweet, delicious kiss … telling her he'd been waiting for her for a long time … that she was the woman he dreamed about …

Sweet Jesus, Rose. What are you thinking? Every time a member of the opposite sex does something remotely kind, you start to behave like a puppy dog.

She gave herself a mental shake and told herself crossly not to be such a romantic fool. *Mark is your boss, and you've got instructions to spy on him. You do not need to fall for him, and that is an order.*

Mark Cameron was definitely off-limits. She was here to get the inside dirt on whether Kalkari was ripe for an easy takeover by her brother – and that was it. There was no scope for anything else.

She figured that a run would be just the thing to chase away such nonsensical thoughts, so she hauled herself out of bed and pulled on running tights, top, shoes and a cap and headed out along the vineyard path that led to the Trevelyn sisters' land. The early morning air was crisp and fragrant with the smell of spring flowers and freshly turned earth, and the dew soaked through her trainers almost immediately. The sun was streaking its way across the sky, colouring everything pale gold.

Pausing to catch her breath at the top of a rise, she looked back down the valley, drinking in the picture-perfect view of serried rows of vines, a couple of glittering triangular dams and the honey-coloured stone of Kalkari.

She was surprised to see a dark-haired figure making its way towards her, clad in a pair of faded blue shorts and a t-shirt with almost more holes than material. As the figure got closer, she saw that it was Mark.

As he reached her, puffing and blowing, he gasped, 'Overdid it last night – thought it was about time I got fit again.' He doubled over, hands on his knees, recovering from the effort. He didn't meet her eyes. 'Mind if I join you?'

'Okay,' said Rose, trying not to sound as surprised as she felt by his unexpected appearance and attire. 'I usually head over this hill and down to the boundary with the Trevelyn sisters' property and then loop back around to the house. Generally takes me about forty minutes. Think you can manage that?'

'Lead the way,' he said, having only just caught his breath.

The route downhill was easier, and by the time they reached the bottom they were running in unison, though Mark wasn't capable of coherent conversation and she could tell it was only through pride and determination that he kept pace with her. Rose snuck a glance at him as he ran, discreetly checking him out. *Not bad*, she thought as her eyes travelled upwards. The solid, muscular legs she'd noticed last night. Check. Lean torso. Check. Broad shoulders and biceps. Check. Inscrutable expression. *Oops!* Mark caught her looking at him and she quickly turned her head away.

'Glorious, hey?'

'Mmm,' said Rose noncommittally. Presumably he was referring to the countryside, but at that moment she had other things on her mind.

'Sorry about last night, Rose. I've a feeling I got a bit carried away. Apologies if I bored you.' Mark's mouth was set in a firm line.

'Not at all. Nothing of the sort.'

'Good.'

They jogged on but Rose was caught unawares as Mark called out, 'Race you to the gate!' He sped away, giving her no chance to catch him over the final hundred metres to the Kalkari front gate.

Not happy at having been outwitted and outrun by Mark at the last moment, Rose vowed to pay more attention next time.

CHAPTER 14

'Look,' Astrid said to Rose, thrusting the white plastic sticks at her after the kids had gone to bed. Sure enough, each of them had telltale blue or pink lines on them. 'What am I going to do?' she wailed. 'My parents will never forgive me. Papa will have an attack of the heart, I just know it. It was bad enough me for a year to travel so far away, but to have a baby like this will be more than he can bear.'

Rose tried her best to calm her down, but wasn't able to suggest much in the way of help. 'Look, it might not be as bad as you think. You need to talk to Thommo.'

'I know I do,' wailed Astrid. 'But he's in France for their vintage at the moment. I suppose I could send him a text, but I don't want to tell him while he's so far away, and not over the phone. He's due back at the end of the month.'

'Yeah, it might be better to wait till he gets back and

do it face to face,' Rose agreed, looking at her with concern. She felt increasingly like Astrid's big sister, somehow responsible for her. The poor girl was still so young and was clearly going to have to do a lot of growing up in the next few weeks.

Thommo wasn't the only one going to be away from the valley for a while. One morning the following week, as Rose and Mark were catching their breath after a morning run, he mentioned that he was leaving that Friday.

'I'm off to your part of the world, in fact,' he said casually. 'London via San Francisco.'

Rose's eyes widened in surprise but she said nothing.

'Catching up with a couple of Yank distributors and then the people from Channings again. We've been after a break into the US market for a while now, and I really need to go and see our British distributors too, show them some love.'

'Oh, I see. How long will you be gone for?'

'Just under three weeks. I'll be buggered by the end of it.' Mark grimaced. 'You'll have to give me some tips for London. I've one free day there I think, and I'd love to know what you think I should see.'

For a split second Rose imagined Mark in London, running into Henry ... but she quickly assured herself that was a ridiculous notion. So what if it was the same big city. *What are the chances?*, thought Rose. *Well, it's a* very *small industry*, murmured a voice in her head.

'Sure,' said Rose. 'I'll make a list for you.'

'Anything you've been missing that I can bring back for you?'

Rose thought of home, realising with a bit of a shock that she'd not thought about Giles for days. That was a first. 'Nope, not really.'

Later that day, Rose was singing along to the radio – with more enthusiasm than tunefulness, it had to be said – when Leo came rushing into the kitchen.

'Rose, there's someone coming,' he said excitedly, hopping from foot to foot. 'They've got surfboards!'

Rose hadn't heard a car approaching, but then again, the radio had been up at full volume.

Surfboards? What's someone doing with surfboards in the middle of the valley?

She paused to wipe her hands on a dishcloth, turned down the radio and walked outside.

Heading up the drive was the distinctive breadbox shape of an old Kombi van, its Fanta-orange sides streaked with dust, and sure enough, a raft of surfboards strapped to the roof. As the van approached, a thumping bass could be heard coming from inside and Rose could see two streaked blond heads in the front.

She felt her heart thudding in her chest. She knew just who it was. Thrilled, she hurled herself at the taller of the blonds as he clambered out of the van.

Barnsie, too, was excited to see visitors. Weaving in and out of their legs, he yapped and barked and chased his tail.

'*Alors!*' cried Philippe. 'What a welcome!' He pulled back and took in Rose's new shape appreciatively. 'What has happened to you, eh? *Oh la la!* You look *incroyable*, Rose!'

Rose had first met Philippe on a Cordon Bleu exchange in Paris, and they'd stayed in touch ever since. She'd been thrilled to discover he'd moved to Sydney six months earlier, and he had gallantly picked her up from the airport and let her crash at his place in Bondi when she first arrived.

The other occupant of the van came over and wrapped her in a big bear hug. Philippe's mate Frostie had taken a bit of a shine to her when she was staying in Bondi, but Rose had not been ready for anything back then. Evidently he still fancied his chances, as he was just planting an enthusiastic kiss on her when Mark wandered over from the winery. Pulling away, she could see that Frostie's t-shirt bore the brash slogan 'Wanna Ride My Longboard?' Her lips twitched.

'Oh, Mark, hi, these are my friends from Sydney – well, Paris and Sydney actually,' she said, moving out of Frostie's arms and catching her breath.

'So I see,' he said, looking the boys up and down. With their wild, sun-bleached hair, wifebeater singlets, boardies and worn-down thongs, they couldn't have looked more incongruous in the lush vineyard setting.

'We're on our way up the coast, bit of a surf safari. Livin' the dream, man. Thought we'd cruise by to see how Rosie's getting on,' said Frostie, holding out his hand to Mark.

'Also, we were wondering if there was the chance of a bed for the night?' Philippe grinned cheekily at Rose. 'Or we can sleep in the Kombi.'

Rose looked towards Mark. 'Sorry, I didn't know they were coming. It's a complete surprise to me, or I would have mentioned it.' She was nervous about Mark's reaction, though she wasn't sure why.

'Living the dream, eh?' Mark's tone was curt as he shook Frostie's hand. 'There's plenty of extra room in the barn; Rose will look after you, I'm sure. Please excuse me, I've some packing to do.' Mark stalked off to the house.

'So, Rosie, fill us in: who's this?' Philippe said, ignoring the cool reception and bending down to greet Barnsie and Leo.

Once they'd stretched their legs and played with the dog, she showed the two boys over to the barn and they immediately slumped onto the worn sofas, sucking thirstily on a couple of cold beers that Rose had brought over from the house.

'I'd better go and get dinner started, but come over in an hour or so and you can meet Astrid and Luisa.'

'More babes?' asked Frostie with a wicked glint in his eye.

'Luisa's two and Astrid's the nanny,' said Rose tartly.

'Oooh, I love nannies!' said Frostie.

'Behave yourself! I work here, you know,' Rose mock-scolded him as she left.

Reaching the house, she bumped into Mark again: he had a suitcase in each hand and a leather laptop satchel slung across his chest.

'Oh, you're going already,' said Rose, feeling a little deflated.

'Driving to Sydney tonight and staying with a mate before an early flight tomorrow.'

'Oh, okay. Well, take care and have a good trip. We'll miss you.'

I'll miss you, she added silently, suddenly realising just how much she would.

'I've said my goodbyes to the kids, but they don't know where I'm going, so keep it on the downlow – if Leo knew I was going anywhere remotely near Tottenham and not taking him, I'd never be forgiven,' he said with a wry smile.

They stood in front of each other, awkwardly. Then, surprising her, Mark leant down and kissed Rose briefly on the cheek. A faint aroma of spice and soap tantalised her senses, making her dizzy. It was over before she could properly react, but the memory of his lips on her skin continued to arc across her brain as he moved away. She had to stop herself from putting her fingers to the spot where his lips had been.

Mark loaded his cases into the boot of his car, which was parked next to the Kombi. As he headed off down the drive, he stuck a hand out of the car window in a goodbye salute. Rose waved back with an enthusiasm she didn't really feel. She was suddenly overcome by a hollow feeling in her stomach.

Bloody hell, get a grip girl. He's your boss, he's mainly a grumpy bugger and, most of all, he's married. Well, sort of. Not to mention that you're still supposed to be heartbroken over Giles.

Luisa toddled out to wave off her dad. 'Daddy go on a hairy plane?' she asked Rose.

'Yes, honey, but he'll be back soon, and I'm sure he'll bring presents too.'

Confused by her emotions, Rose picked Luisa up, settled her on one hip and turned away from the sight of the car disappearing into the distance. She headed back to the kitchen to rustle up enough food for a posse of hungry adults – Astrid had quickly gotten over her sickness and was now eating for Austria – and two little tackers.

CHAPTER 15

L ater that night, as they lingered over the remains of
roast chicken, and having demolished a couple of
bottles of wine, Frostie and Philippe regaled Astrid
with stories of Rose's antics when she'd stayed with
them in Bondi, making Rose laugh as their descriptions
grew more and more outrageous. 'That's so not fair!' she
protested as they recounted her asking for a cup of hot tea
on the beach. 'I'd only just arrived: it wasn't my fault that I
didn't know that you don't take tea to the beach!'

Astrid's face was flushed, and her hair glowed in the
candlelight. It was nice to see her looking better than she
had in a while, Rose thought. She'd clearly enjoyed the boys'
company over dinner; perhaps it had taken her mind off her
predicament, even if only for an evening.

'Well, I don't know about everyone else, but I'm ready
to hit the hay,' said Rose, yawning theatrically and getting

up to clear the table. She tried not to meet Frostie's eye, though she could tell he was looking directly at her. Philippe hung back to chat with Astrid, as Frostie said he'd join Rose in heading for the barn.

A thousand stars twinkled in the clear night air as they walked to the barn, and Rose glanced up at them, briefly wondering if Mark had reached Sydney safely. She turned to Frostie, who had taken her hand in his warm one.

'What's up, babe?' he asked.

'Look, I don't think we can ever be more than friends ...'

There was a brief pause and then Frostie replied, 'Hey, that's cool. I'm cool. No dramas, babe, if that's how it is. Can't blame a bloke for trying, you know.' He let go of her hand.

Rose was thankful for his unruffled attitude. The only waves Frostie liked making were out on the ocean, it seemed.

'I'm glad you understand. I'm really not up for anything more from anyone right now, and I love having you and Philippe as friends – I don't have too many of them in Australia.'

'No worries, babe.' His clear blue eyes lingered on hers. 'Though you might want to warn that boss of yours too – any idiot can see from the way he looks at you that he's pretty keen.'

'Don't be ridiculous.' Rose protested. 'He's married, even if his wife is nowhere to be seen, and anyway he's a grumpy old git most of the time.'

Does Frostie really think Mark likes me? How could that be?

'Just sayin' what I'm seein',' he said, shrugging.

As they reached the barn, Frostie walked over to the room he was sharing with Philippe.

'Sweet dreams. Don't let the bugs bite,' said Rose. She really was very fond of both of them, and dead chuffed that they'd come to see her, but their presence didn't make up for the hollow feeling in her stomach now that Mark had left and was going to be gone for so long.

After a fitful night's sleep, plagued by dreams of Mark driving off and never coming back, Rose crept out early to roam the vineyards and take out her tumult of confused emotions on her run. She pounded up the big hill at the back of Kalkari in record time. It was the best way to blow the cobwebs away. Her fitness was returning, after all the years of fried foods and sloth and she now craved the early morning exercise. Despite the cool morning air, her skin was beaded with sweat by the time she returned to the house, and she felt calmer and cleansed of most of her worries.

She went to knock on the boys' door. 'Breakfast in thirty!' There was an answering groan and she hurried over to the main house and got started on pancake batter.

Leo was in heaven. Rose usually only made pancakes on weekends, and today was a school day. He was rewarded with the first stack of pancakes and slurped the syrup from his knife as Astrid tried to get him to mind his table manners.

'Have a good night?' Astrid winked at her.

'Nothing doing there. Tell you later,' replied Rose, just as Philippe and Frostie walked into the kitchen.

'Maaate.' Frostie drew out the one-syllable word in appreciative emphasis. 'Could smell this all the way out the door. Forgotten how good your cooking is, Rosie. Should never have let you leave Bondi,' he said, mock-mournfully.

The boys hoed in to plates piled high with pancakes, syrup and bacon, barely pausing to speak. Leo stared wide-eyed at them, too shy to ask many questions, while Luisa chattered away, banging the end of her fork on the table for more food.

Suddenly, Frostie looked up. 'What this needs to wash it down is a decent cup of coffee.'

'Sorry,' said Rose apologetically, 'not a latte to be had around here, I'm afraid. You're closest bet is in Eumeralla. Sacred Grounds. Tell Bevan I sent you.'

'Actually,' said Philippe with a secretive look on his face. 'We're going to change that. Come and see.'

Rose was puzzled, but followed him out to the Kombi, Leo and Barnsie bringing up the rear. 'What is it, Rose?' asked Leo excitedly.

'I don't have a clue, sweetie, but let's find out, shall we?'

As Philippe slid back the door of the van, he reached inside and motioned for Rose to take a look. There, nestled among threadbare towels and wrapped in a sleeping bag, was a La Marzocco three-group machine in cornflower blue.

'What a beauty!' exclaimed Rose, marvelling at it. 'Where did you get it?'

'Upgraded.' When he wasn't on a surf safari, Philippe

was managing a cafe on the beachfront at Bondi. 'Didn't need this one anymore,' Philippe said. 'It's all yours if you want it.'

'You're kidding, right?'

'*Non*, I not kid you, Rose,' replied Philippe seriously.

'But these things are freakin' expensive. And you're just giving it away?'

'All for a good cause,' he winked at her. 'Anyway, the owners were going to chuck it out – crazy, I know – and I couldn't let that happen. It had seized up, but Frostie had a look at it, polished it up, and she's good as gold now. Runs like a dream. You've got to look after her, but I know you will; there's not much to it.'

Rose was astonished that anyone would want to throw something so beautiful away, but she knew immediately what she would do with it. 'You'll have to show me how to use it,' she said, running her hands over the gleaming metal. 'I can't believe you thought I'd need this. How did you know?'

'Ah, you only mentioned in your emails about a million times that you were desperate for a decent coffee more than once or twice a week,' he replied sarcastically. 'So, your wish is our command.'

'Oh, thank you! I've already got plans for this little baby,' said Rose, beaming at him.

In no time at all, Philippe had got the machine set up in the cellar door, Rose having sweet-talked Dan into lending her the key again to get in.

'I still don't know why you want this in here, not the kitchen,' said Philippe.

'I'm going to open up the cellar door again and offer

tastings, but also coffee, cake and scones. There's nowhere close by where you can get a decent coffee, and I reckon there'll be a market for it, especially in summer.'

'I like your thinking, Little Miss Starbucks,' he teased.

'Get out of here, you!' Rose expertly flicked a tea towel at him. 'Starbucks my arse!'

Philippe had also brought her a five-kilo bag of freshly roasted beans and a grinder, and promised to keep her supplied with more once they returned to Bondi if she needed. He gave her a crash course in how to make the different types of coffee she was likely to be asked for, from macchiato and ristretto to the more familiar latte and cappuccino, and then demonstrated how to clean and look after the machine. Frothing the milk without scalding it took a little time to master, but by the end of the morning Rose had proved to Philippe that she could make a half-decent cup.

'You're all set,' he said, looking proudly at her and patting the machine. 'I am very glad she's found a good home.'

The boys were keen to be on their way before much more of the day disappeared, and Rose made them several rounds of sandwiches to sustain them on the rest of their journey. 'It's a very small thank you for the coffee machine. I still can't believe you lugged it all this way just for me.'

She was sorry to see them go, as she was very fond of both of them. She hugged each of them tight, promising to stay in touch and insisting they call back in on their return in a few weeks' time.

As she watched their Kombi trundle down the drive, she felt suddenly alone. Kalkari was very quiet again.

CHAPTER 16

The delivery of the coffee machine, combined with Mark's absence, galvanised Rose into action. The housekeeping account was running very low, and she and Astrid hadn't been paid since before Mark went to London. With a long weekend coming up, Rose saw an opportunity to inject some funds into the winery's diminished coffers. She raided the cupboards for a mismatched selection of dainty teacups and side plates, but still came up short. A chance conversation with Mrs B, who'd called in to see the kids, led her to the Eumeralla op shop, the incongruously named Thrifty Orange, where she found a crate of unused commercial-grade china, perfect for her needs. She also grabbed a handful of old teaspoons and tarnished silver cake forks that she could polish up. Not wanting to be in debt to Mark for a venture she had yet to discuss with him, and knowing how tight Kalkari's funds were, she paid for these out of her own pocket. She also stocked up on flour, sugar, butter and milk, keeping careful record of her purchases.

Calling in to Sacred Grounds, she casually mentioned to Bevan that she was thinking of opening up the cellar door again and serving coffee, tea, pies and cakes there.

'So, we'll be in competition then,' he said. His tone told her he didn't mind too much.

While she was there, she sent a quick email to her brother, letting him know that Mark was on his way to London, and gave him Mark's hotel details just in case Henry wanted to engineer a meeting with Mark himself. She also spent some time going over her favourite baking recipes, deciding on fruit muffins, chocolate and hazelnut biscuits, and chewy date bars. The pies she could almost make in her sleep, after her years at The Pine Box.

The monthly farmers market was on again that weekend, and she hauled home several kilos of apples, lemons and oranges. Bevan had also suggested that she drop in to the town's visitor information centre and chat with them about her plans; she added that to her growing to-do list.

The name of the new venture came from Dan. She'd wandered over to the winery for a chat, bringing a test batch of lemon curd tartines for him to try. He was enthusiastic about the cellar door reopening, and had promised to drill her in some basic wine-tasting patter.

'Well, it's got to be something wine-related, I reckon,' he said as he ran a hand over his beard thoughtfully. 'What do you think of Ferment?'

Rose loved it. 'Oh, that's perfect! Thanks, Dan,' she said, dropping a kiss on the top of his head.

'Get away with you now,' he muttered, embarrassed by her show of affection. Rose could have sworn he was blushing under his bushy beard.

Despite the almost impossibly short timeframe, Rose planned a big opening for the following Saturday – the first day of a long weekend, as she'd heard from Mrs B that the valley would be buzzing with visitors on the wine-tasting trail. Earlier in the week, Astrid had helped her with some fliers as well as a sign for the end of the drive, copying the curlicued Kalkari wine label logo and showing a flair for design that Rose hadn't known she possessed. With Luisa in tow, they distributed them to the visitor information centre, and a few shops in Eumeralla also taped them up on their windows. The information centre seemed excited at the prospect of something new happening in the valley, and they promised to give it top billing in their weekly email newsletter, which, fortuitously, was due to go out the following day. Rose hoped it would be enough to entice the crowds.

On Saturday morning she got up even earlier than usual and was greeted by the beginnings of a bright sunny day with just a few clouds scudding across the Wedgwood-blue sky. She still hadn't become used to the piercing brightness of the Australian light, and shielded her eyes as she looked down the drive, wondering what the day would bring and trying to ignore the nerves clenching her stomach.

The cellar door dining room was set up and, with fingers crossed for fine weather, she'd also asked Dan to help her shift a couple of old wine barrels and an offcut of timber to form a long makeshift table under the she-oak just outside the cellar door, so that people could enjoy their coffee and cake in the sunshine if they wanted to. Astrid and Leo had made some multicoloured bunting and strung it up across the front of the building, giving it a festive look.

'Looks like you're all set,' Dan came up behind her as she was setting out a freshly baked rhubarb pie on the counter next to the gleaming coffee machine. 'Care to serve your first customer? A macchiato would be great. And one of those muffins, too, if you can spare it.'

'Coming right up!' Rose beamed at him.

Even though it was his day off, Dan had volunteered to help out with the tastings, and Mrs B had also been persuaded to lend a hand later. Dan had run through a few pointers on the wines with Rose, giving her notes on how they were made, as well as showing her how to taste and spit, and advising her to practise with water in the shower. She planned on paying close attention to how he worked behind the tastings bench.

Astrid, Leo and Luisa – accompanied by a madly yapping Barnsie – wandered across from the house to check them out.

'Looks wonderful!' exclaimed Astrid. 'Save me one of

those banana muffins if you've any left at the end of the day!'

'Can we have something now, Rose?' pleaded Leo.

'What, and leave nothing for our customers?' Rose teased. 'Okay, then, just one muffin each. Banana, caramel and walnut? Or raspberry and white choc-chip?' The kids helped themselves and headed outside to devour the buttery cakes. Barnsie lay panting next to them, keeping a close watch for stray crumbs.

At only a few minutes past ten, the first car turned up the drive, and from then on there was a steady stream of visitors for coffee, cakes and tastings. By three o'clock they'd sold out of muffins and cookies, and there was just one lonely slice of pie left. Rose was tired, but elated. Her plan, it seemed, had worked, and she carefully counted up the day's takings, showing them gleefully to Dan.

'It's not a fortune, but it's a good start,' she said.

'Actually, we've also had the best day's wine sales that I can remember too,' said Dan, polishing a wine glass. 'Looks like you got the word out!'

'Well, the information centre certainly must have!' laughed Rose.

She was glad she'd had the foresight to bake in advance and that she'd filled the freezer with enough baked goods to see them through the rest of the long weekend. If today was anything to go by, they were going to need everything she'd prepared and more. She glanced down at her arms, which had turned rosy from so much to-ing and fro-ing in the hot sun. 'Your face looks a bit pink too,' said Dan. 'Best get some sunscreen before tomorrow.'

'Best get some rest before tomorrow as well,' said Rose, piling up used coffee cups and wiping down the table.

Sunday proved to be an even busier day than Saturday, with the spring sunshine bringing out the crowds in full force, and by the end of Monday Rose's feet bore more than a few puffy blisters and she'd had to make an emergency trip to Sacred Grounds in Eumeralla for more coffee beans. Bevan joked that she'd lured away half his customers, but as there as also a throng of people in the cafe she doubted he was serious.

Rose was putting away the last of the glasses when her eyes came to rest on the cellar door keys hanging on a chain behind the door. Dan had left them with her, asking her to return them to the winery at the end of the day. She'd lay bets that the key chain also included a key to the winery office.

In her last email to Henry, despite feeling that her loyalties had become compromised, she'd told him the little she'd managed to find out. 'He's on his uppers,' she'd typed. 'And by that, I don't mean taking controlled substances.'

'Yes, sis, but it's leverage I need. Get me some hard info. Something that I can use to tighten the screws when the time comes,' he'd replied. 'But knowing that he's in London might be helpful.'

Why Kalkari? It had been puzzling Rose for some time now. In her distracted state when Henry had first put the plan to her, she'd never asked why he was targeting this particular winery, especially as it was on the other side of the world. It seemed a stretch, even for his far-reaching plans.

Unable to figure out an answer, she brought her mind back to the present. Grabbing the chain and turning the keys over in her hand, Rose knew this was her chance to do the sleuthing Henry was demanding. She felt sick to her stomach. Did she really have to do this? But blood was thicker than water, after all ...

All of the winery accounts were in the office, and last time she'd been talking to Dan, she'd seen the computer login details scribbled on a bit of paper next to it, so she didn't think it was going to be that difficult.

She walked over to the winery, glancing about to check that there was no-one else around. All the visitors were long gone and Astrid was in the house with the kids. There was no sign of Dan. This was her chance. Rose's heart pounded as she stepped into the paper-strewn office.

Remember your promise to Henry. Just see what you can find. In any case, it might not be very much.

All it took was the press of a few keys and she easily located the winery's accounts on the computer's desktop. She'd helped out in the office at The Pine Box from time to time, so she knew her way around a spreadsheet. Tabbing through the sets of monthly figures, it was immediately obvious that everything she'd heard was true. In fact, if anything, things were even worse than she'd imagined. Kalkari was in the red by a frightening amount. On a tray on a shelf next to the computer was a thick pile of unpaid bills, weighed down with a horseshoe. Flicking through them, she came across a bank loan application to remortgage Kalkari House. It was dated the previous month. No wonder Mark was so stressed.

What was she going to do? Could she really pass this on to Henry? He'd always been vague about the exact nature of the information he'd wanted her to dig up – 'just have a poke around and see what you can find out' he'd urged – but she knew this was probably gold as far as he was concerned. Her brother would waste no time moving in quicker than a school of great whites when he thought the time was right, that much she was sure of.

She was just shutting the computer down when she heard a step behind her and she whirled around, her heart thudding at ninety kilometres an hour.

'Is that you, Rose?'

It was Dan.

'Um, er, yes.' She thought on her feet. 'I was just putting the day's takings in a safe place.'

He looked at her suspiciously. 'Well, the boss doesn't like anyone in here, I'm afraid, so you'd better find another place for them.'

Rose played the innocent. 'Oh, gosh, sorry. I didn't realise. I'll take them over to the barn instead.' Rose's back was to the computer. She prayed that the computer had shut down in time. She didn't dare risk a look.

'That'd be a good idea. Off you go. I'll lock up in here.'

She couldn't meet his eyes. 'Sure, okay, Dan.'

CHAPTER 17

The following weekend, though not as busy as the first, brought plenty of visitors to the cellar door, including some locals, who'd heard the buzz about Rose's cakes and pies. Rose had been flat out restocking, baking and clearing up, not to mention keeping the house in order and Astrid, herself and the kids fed, but she had managed to get Astrid on her own after dinner one night and find out what was going on.

'Have you decided what to do?' Rose asked.

Astrid nodded. 'I saw the doctor in Eumeralla last week and he did some tests. He says I am now about twelve weeks pregnant.'

'Okay, well you're leaving it a bit on the late side for a termination, if that's what you decide. How are you feeling?'

'Not so sick any more, just a little in the mornings.'

Astrid looked subdued. 'I'm just so scared. I think I'm going to keep it, but I don't know what Thommo is going to say.'

'Wow, that's very brave.' Rose was surprised at Astrid's decision, but tried not to show it. 'I'll be here for you, whatever happens,' she said, trying to comfort her. *What was she thinking? She hadn't planned on sticking around at Kalkari.*

'Thanks.' Astrid gave her a grateful smile. 'I might need your support.'

Mark had left his schedule in the kitchen, and Leo was counting down the days until he was due back. His flight was set to land early the next morning, and he'd promised to be home in time for dinner with the kids, after stopping to call on his distributors in Sydney before driving back to the valley.

Rose had spent that morning putting the house to rights, gathering up abandoned toys and teddies from all corners of the house, and slow-cooking a shoulder of lamb with rosemary, garlic and red wine (she'd been careful to check the label this time) for the homecoming dinner the next day.

Astrid returned with Luisa around noon. 'Hey, Rose, do you think you could give her lunch for me? I really need a lie-down.'

Rose nodded her assent; Astrid did look tired.

'Thanks, just want to rest for a bit.'

Astrid might have been tired, but Luisa certainly

wasn't, and it took all of Rose's powers of persuasion to get her into bed for a nap after lunch. Eventually, Rose lay down with her, read a couple of stories and cuddled the little girl until her dark eyelashes fluttered shut.

Rose woke with a start. Something – a loud bang from downstairs – had disturbed her, and she blinked, the coloured elephants that decorated Luisa's room coming into focus as she remembered where she was. Luisa lay beside her, breathing softly, cheeks flushed and full lips parted in sleep. Rose's eyes flicked to the door as it slowly opened. A tall, dark figure stood in the doorway. *Mark!* Her heart leapt at the sight of him.

Mark raised a finger to his lips.

Rose looked dazedly at him. She noticed purple shadows under his eyes and stubble covering his jaw. His gaze softened as he looked at first Luisa and then Rose; then he was gone as suddenly as he'd appeared.

Still dozy from sleep, Rose eased her arm out from under Luisa, stretching her fingers as pins and needles fizzed through them, and crept out of the room and down to the kitchen.

'You're back early!' Rose rubbed a hand across her bleary eyes and drank in the tall, dark sight of Mark, larger than life. Even rumpled from travel, he looked pretty hot. Why hadn't she noticed all this when they'd first met? The broad set of his shoulders; the dark hair that curled into his collar; the deep green eyes on a level with hers.

Busying herself by needlessly tidying the already well-ordered kitchen, she forced herself not to look at him, lest she be caught staring.

'Yeah, wound up my meetings, changed my flight and got in a day earlier. Couldn't wait to see you all,' he grinned at Rose. 'How have you been?'

Rose found herself inexplicably shy. 'Oh, you know … pretty good. Anyway, how was it? Was my home country good to you?'

'Yeah, it was full-on, but I think we've made some headway and there's a few promising prospects there. Your countrymen really know how to turn it on – a lot of red wine was drunk. Right now though, all I could really do with is a long, hot shower.'

Rose reddened at the thought of Mark naked in the shower, involuntarily imagining herself there too, and turned away so he couldn't see her blushing. What on earth had gotten into her? She was behaving like a love-struck teenager. This was ridiculous. She clearly needed to get out more.

She heard Astrid coming down the stairs. 'Feeling better?' she asked.

'Much, thanks. Oh, Mark, you're back!' Astrid said. 'Welcome home!'

'Thanks, Astrid. How are the kids?' Mark kissed her, European-style, on both cheeks. Even though she knew she was being silly, Rose felt immediately jealous. He hadn't kissed *her* hello. 'I've missed their cheeky faces. Can't wait to see them.'

'I'm just on my way to pick up Leo from school. Rose, is Luisa still asleep?'

'Yes, but it's probably about time for her to wake up. Why don't you go in and surprise her, Mark? She'd be thrilled.'

Mark didn't need further encouragement; he bounded out of the kitchen and up the stairs. Pretty soon Rose could hear Luisa's shrieks of laughter echoing through the house.

Bang. Bang. Bang.

With a start, Rose sat up from her position slumped on the couch in the barn. She'd been browsing a few food magazines, looking for inspiration for recipes for Ferment. Getting to her feet and lifting the latch, she was confronted by a very pissed-off-looking Mark.

Oh fuck. He must have found out I've been snooping at the winery. Dan must have said something. Rose's heart sank. It was, without doubt, a sackable offence.

'What's this I hear about you starting up a cafe? I've just had a word with Dan. I hear you've gone and started your own business behind my back – and at the Kalkari cellar door to boot. Funny, but I thought you were employed by me to help Astrid look after the kids and to keep the house running smoothly.' He glowered at her, his hands clenched into fists by his side and his dark eyebrows knitted together in outrage. 'Using my premises, trading on the name of the winery ... and just where did you get the coffee machine from? Did you think I wouldn't find out? Do you take me for a fool? Just how long was this little operation going to continue? Did you bother to find out if it was even legal? I could be sued, for God's sake!'

Rose breathed a tiny sigh of relief. He didn't know about her logging into the winery accounts. But she'd had no idea he'd blow his top about the cafe. She'd stupidly thought he might be pleased at her showing some initiative. 'I – I was just trying to help. I thought it would bring people to the cellar door and give them another reason to visit here. I'm sorry for not telling you, but Philippe gave me the coffee machine and that started the whole ball rolling. I'm a qualified chef! I wouldn't poison people. I've kept a record of everything I've spent, and, look—' She strode over to the windowsill where the jar containing the cash from Ferment had been sitting. 'We had to use a bit of the money for groceries, but the rest is here. The credit card and EFTPOS takings are over at the cellar door. It's all for you.' Rose thrust the jar at him, eyes flashing with her own anger now. 'I only wanted to help; I know how tough things are at the moment.'

'Well, I certainly don't need your charity, nor your help.' Mark ignored the proffered money. 'I'll thank you not to go behind my back in the future, nor to interfere where you're not wanted.' He stormed out of the barn, slamming the door behind him.

Rose sank onto the sofa, miserable and bewildered.

Arrogant sod.

Hot tears sprang to her eyes and she rubbed them savagely away.

So much for thinking he'd be pleased with me for helping

out. How could I have been so stupid as to think he liked me, even a little bit?

What a fool she felt for her silly schoolgirl crush now. It would have been fair enough if he'd been angry at her going through the accounts, but for this?

If Mark was going to be such a complete arse, she may as well spill everything to Henry after all and let him do what he wanted with the information.

It took all Rose's nerve to go back to the house to prepare dinner. Mark was nowhere to be seen, thankfully, and the kids didn't notice her subdued manner as she served them.

Astrid looked at her questioningly. 'Are you okay?' she mouthed over the top of Leo's head.

Rose nodded and managed a weak smile, but she knew it wasn't terribly convincing. As soon as the meal was over, Rose retreated to the barn, collapsed onto the sofa, curled her legs under her and numbly hugged a cushion to her chest.

What on earth had she been thinking, imagining a future for herself in the Shingle Valley? What a complete fool. Why did she always act without thinking things through? Her impulsiveness had got her into trouble again. When would she ever learn?

She heard scratching at the door, then a whine. Heaving herself off the sofa, she went to see what it was. As she opened the door, the dog leapt up at her, licking the tears from her face.

'Oh, Barnsie,' she sobbed. 'At least *you* like me.'

She walked back to the sofa and he jumped up next to her, burying his muzzle in her lap. Feeling utterly miserable and desperately alone, Rose stroked his head as she stared blankly at the wall.

CHAPTER 18

The next morning, as Rose pulled on her running gear, the memory of Mark's anger surfaced. Her heart sank as she recalled the humiliating confrontation, and she closed her eyes, as if that could make it all disappear. She didn't want to leave the barn, but knew she couldn't hide in there forever. Summoning her courage, she resolved to face whatever the day might bring.

As she pounded up the curving path that wound over the hill towards the Trevelyn sisters' property, Rose decided she didn't feel much like heading back to Kalkari quite yet and instead carried on, crossing the Trevelyn vineyards, skirting the dry soil between the vines and keeping to the grassy edges. Before long, she reached the back of a small stone cottage and spotted a bent-over figure in the vegetable garden that butted up against the house.

'Hallooo!' the old lady called out.

Damn. Now she'd have to stop.

The old lady raised her hand in a wave. Rose came closer, noticing the ropy muscles and age-spotted skin of the woman's arms as she pulled at the weeds among the cabbages.

'Hi there. It's Miss Trevelyn, isn't it? I'm Rose,' she said, pausing to catch her breath. 'I'm working over at Kalkari, for Mark. I've seen you in the pub and at the markets.'

'Yes, love, I know who you are. And call me Violet, please. A pleasure to meet you, dear. How are you getting on over there?'

'Well, if you really want to know, not so good at the moment.' Unexpectedly, Rose found tears forming in her eyes and she brushed them away roughly. 'Things have all gone a bit pear-shaped. I think I've well and truly put my foot in it, and I don't know how to put it right.' She felt a tumult of emotions: sadness, anger and loneliness hit her like a punch to the stomach.

'Why don't you come on inside and you can tell me all about it over a nice cuppa?' The old lady looked at her with kindness. There was something about the old woman that made Rose want to confide.

'That'd be nice, thank you,' Rose sniffed.

As her eyes adjusted to the dim interior, she saw that it was neat as a pin, and cosy, with a rag rug on the flagstoned floor and a round table at the kitchen window. Motioning for her to sit, Violet retrieved milk from the fridge and heaped loose leaves into a pot.

'So. Where did it all start?'

Rose felt comforted by the old lady's concern. 'Well, I don't know if you heard, but I opened up the cellar door on the long weekend and ran a bit of a cafe, offering coffee and cakes. I thought Mark would appreciate even the little bit of money we made, and to be honest, it gave me something to do. I had no idea he'd react the way he did. He totally flew off the handle when he found out. I know I should have told him about it before I went ahead with it, but, well, he was away and I thought it'd be a really nice surprise for him to come back to. But now it seems like the worst thing I could have done.'

'Come on now, love, I'm sure it's not as bad as all that. He always was a proud one, that one. I've known him since he was a boy, since his parents ran Lilybells,' Violet replied.

'But that's the biggest winery in the valley! I didn't know Mark had grown up there; he's never said.' Rose was taken by surprise. 'Why isn't he still there? What happened?'

'His dad was a brilliant winemaker but not such a brilliant businessman, and the finances got on top of them. They sold up just after Mark finished high school. They didn't tell him until he got back from spending a year away in France. I don't think he's ever forgiven them for it.'

Suddenly a lot of things made sense to Rose. No wonder Mark didn't like things happening behind his back and was so touchy about anything to do with money.

'That must have been really hard on him. Now I know why he loves this place so much. It's in his blood.'

'He left the valley and didn't come back for years. His parents moved away too. Went to the coast to run a hotel, I think.'

'What brought him back here?'

'I'm not too sure really. Kalkari had been up for sale for quite a while, but there weren't any takers. It was just so run-down, the vines were a mess, even the house was in a state. He came back here with his bride, Isabella, rebuilt the winery and replanted many of the old vineyards. They're just coming into their own now. Mark my words, Kalkari will be one to watch before too long. A shame, though, that Isabella took off the way she did. Haven't seen him smile much since she left. That also might explain him flying off the handle; he's probably a bit sensitive at the moment.'

'Hmm, maybe,' said Rose. 'How long have you lived here?' she asked, curious as to how Violet knew so much about the goings on in the valley.

'Vera and I are valley born and bred. Our parents farmed this land, and when they passed on, they left it to us. There've been grapes grown here for more than seventy years. We're just the midwives to the grapes. This land doesn't so much belong to Vera and me, as we do to it. I think you might find you belong here too, Rose,' she said. 'I've seen you out and around early in the mornings, and from what Brenda tells me, those kids are pretty fond of you as well.' There was a look in her eyes that was as old and all-seeing as time.

Rose took a big gulp of tea. She wasn't sure what to make of Violet's comment. It was nice to hear that Mrs B approved of her, but how could the old woman possibly know where she belonged?

'Did you never marry?' Rose regretted the blunt

question almost as soon as she'd asked it, but Violet didn't seem to mind.

'There was someone once …' Violet's voice trailed off. 'Didn't amount to anything. And so here we are; two old birds still flapping around.' She cackled to herself. 'More tea, love?' She picked up the pot and waved it in Rose's direction.

Rose glanced at her watch. 'Oh heavens, I really should get back. Thanks so much for everything – for listening, and, well, you know.'

'Any time, love. It's nice to have a bit of company, and don't you worry about Mark. He'll see sense soon enough. You've done nothing that's very wrong from what I can tell.'

Rose got to her feet, remembering ruefully that she had actually done something very wrong by agreeing to spy for her brother in the first place. Feeling comforted by her chat with Violet, but reminded of her torn loyalties again, she headed off on the path back to Kalkari.

Rose ran into Astrid on her return. 'Any news?'

'Thommo's due back next week – earlier than I'd expected.' Astrid bit her lip, looking worried.

'What are you going to do? Are you going to tell him everything?'

'I guess. I'm scared, Rose.' Astrid unconsciously cradled the almost imperceptible swell of her belly protectively.

'I know, honey, but sometimes things don't turn out as badly as you think they will,' Rose said, hoping to reassure her. 'Hey, you'll never guess who I met this morning,' she said changing the subject.

'Who?'

'Violet Trevelyn.'

'That witch lady from down the valley?'

'Hey, she's not a witch!'

'Yes, she is – she and her sister are strange, don't you think? They remind me of the three crones from *Macbeth* – well, except that there are only two of them of course.' Astrid gave a snort of laughter.

'If you say so, but she was sweet to me.'

'Did she give you a potion to put Mark in a better mood? What's going on there, anyway? I heard his voice coming from the barn last night, and when he came back into the house he looked so angry … By the way, he took the kids out in the car earlier and said he wouldn't be back for dinner. That's not like him at all, especially as he's been away so long. I thought he'd be straight over to the winery, not off on a day out.'

'Oh God, Astrid, he found out about me opening up the cellar door again, and he was furious. I know I should have checked with him first, but I really didn't think he'd be this cross.'

'Oh, so that's what it was. What are you going to do?'

'Dunno. I think I might be looking for a new job soon.'

'Don't be silly! The kids love you and the place is running like it's a train on the rails. It'll all blow up, don't worry too much.'

'I think you mean blow over,' said Rose. 'And I'm not so sure it will.'

Rose didn't have long to wait before running into Mark again. Late that evening, she heard the front door slam and the clatter of footsteps in the stone hallway. She looked up as she heard him come into the kitchen. He looked shattered. He was obviously still jet lagged.

'Hey, Rose.' Mark looked at her uncomfortably.

'Hello,' she said, trying to keep the hurt out of her voice.

'Look, I'm sorry about going off at you last night. I understand now that you were trying to do the right thing. Dan filled me in and said that he'd been the one to suggest it in the first place. I completely overreacted. I'm sorry. I'm tired and, well, look, there's a lot of other stuff going on that's nothing to do with you – not that that's your problem or fault.'

'Uh, sure, okay. I'm glad it's all been cleared up.' Rose turned back to the range, where she'd been attempting to scrub off years of accumulated grot, taking her frustration and anger out on the steel wool. 'I really was trying to help.'

'I know that now, and I appreciate it, really I do. Things are a bit tough at the moment.' He paused. 'I had a call from Isabella last night. I wasn't expecting it. She's back in Sydney, and she wanted to see the kids. That's where we were today. It's been really hard for them, especially Leo. He didn't say a word in the car all the way home. I'm worried about him.'

Rose hid her shock. She had thought Isabella was in Spain. 'Oh, poor Leo. What about Luisa? How long is Isabella staying for? Is she coming back here?' Rose wasn't sure she wanted to meet Isabella, not if everything Astrid and Mrs B had said was true.

'I'm not sure.' Mark poured himself a glass of wine from a bottle on the sideboard and slumped in a chair. 'Luisa's okay. It's terrible, but I don't think she really remembers her mum; she was so little when Isabella left. She was all over them today and I think it was a bit much for both kids. They've each got reasons to be wary of her: Luisa because she doesn't really know her, and Leo because he does remember and can't understand her leaving, nor forgive her for it. It devastated him. I wish I knew what to do. Oh Christ, it's such a goddamn mess.'

Rose was surprised that Mark was opening up to her, especially after the way he'd yelled at her the night before, but she guessed he didn't have too many people he could unburden himself to.

She didn't get a chance to talk further with Mark, as Astrid and two tired kids trooped into the kitchen in search of bedtime drinks.

Rose's mind was whirling. She had to admit to a ridiculous jealousy that Isabella might be back in Mark's life. Ridiculous. She had no right nor reason to be jealous at all. But for the second time in as many days, she felt that her job and happy existence at Kalkari were under threat.

While Mark had been overseas, she'd been enjoying a small – desperately illogical, she knew – fantasy of him returning and telling her how much he'd missed her, with visions of him sweeping her into his arms, and this had kept her spirits high while she'd cooked and cleaned, frothed cappuccinos and wiped up cake crumbs. She was left feeling like a complete idiot for entertaining such romantic imaginings. They clearly had no basis in reality, especially when he'd been so awful to her almost as soon as he'd returned.

At what age does a person stop having stupid crushes? she wondered glumly. *You'd think I'd have grown out of such things.*

flower

verb

to produce flowers or blossom, as a plant; to come into full
bloom

CHAPTER 19

A few days later, Mark joined Rose on her morning run. The air was cool, but held the promise of a warm day to come. Everywhere she looked, green leaves were curling and unfurling, bringing the gnarled old vines to life. It was hard to be miserable for long in such beautiful surroundings. 'Finally over the jet lag then?' she gasped.

'Yep, slept like a log last night. I definitely need to get back in shape though – can't have you getting too far ahead of me.'

'As if,' retorted Rose, secretly liking the thought of being able to outpace Mark.

As they jogged back to the house, Mark surprised her further. 'I've got to go back to the city next week. My distributors have lined up a few meetings and there's a dinner on Saturday night. Would you like to come? I reckon you need a break; you've worked hard around here, and I'd also like to properly apologise for tearing a strip off you the other day.'

'Oh.' Rose shrugged. She wasn't sure she'd entirely forgiven him. 'Well, you did upset me. And as I said, I was only trying to do the right thing.' Rose mentally crossed her fingers behind her back. She really *had* been trying to do the right thing in this instance.

'I know, Rose, and I'm truly sorry.' Mark looked at her with such a sorrowful gaze that Rose's remaining hurt melted away. Guilt crept in to take its place.

'Okay, yes, I'd love to. That's a very kind offer. It'd be great to visit Sydney again.' Rose smiled, then thought of something. 'What should I wear to the dinner?'

'A dress of some sort should do,' Mark said dryly. 'I'm sure you'll be fine, whatever you wear. It's at Oceania, right on the water. I think you'll like it.'

Excited at the prospect of a trip away and a posh meal out, Rose beamed. Much as she had grown fond of the valley, she wouldn't mind a change of scene.

Their jog over, she sprinted to the barn to change before getting started on breakfast.

Leo was still very quiet; he ate his toast with great concentration. But Luisa burbled away, asking when her mummy was coming back. Leo flinched every time he heard his sister say 'Mama'.

'Don't worry sweetie, she'll be back to see you before you know it,' said Mark distractedly, as he scarfed down a bowl of cereal. His hasty breakfast over, he grabbed a mug of tea and headed out to check on the vines, which were at the crucial point of flowering.

When Mark had left, Rose filled Astrid in on his invitation.

'Oh, you are lucky! I'd love to go away for a few days. So what are you going to wear?'

'I don't know. I didn't exactly stow a ballgown in my backpack, did I?'

'Don't worry about that. I've got something you can borrow. Now you're so skinny, it'll fit like the glove – no chance of it going near me anytime soon.' Astrid looked down at the gentle curve of her stomach.

'Pull the other one, I'm twice the size of you,' protested Rose.

'Which other one? You kid me, no? Have you looked at the mirror lately?' said Astrid.

Sure enough, when Rose slipped the dress over her head, it fitted perfectly. It looked pretty good, she had to admit, even with bare feet, a make-up-free face and scraped-back hair.

The following Friday, after an early start, Mark and Rose arrived at their hotel. Promising to collect her later that evening, Mark left her to settle in as he headed off to meet his Sydney distributors. Rose kicked off her shoes and twirled around the immaculate room before collapsing on the bed and burying herself in the soft pillows. She pulled back the gauzy floor-length curtains and looked out to a sparkling forty-fifth-floor view. The Opera House, its white sails glowing in the searing light, was way below her, and on her left the steel arches of the Harbour Bridge. In between was a wide expanse of sparkling blue water. What heaven!

Hanging up the dress that Astrid had lent her, she caught sight of herself in the mirror. It was definitely time to do something about her hair, which had grown wild and untamed in the months she'd been in the valley and now snaked down her back in a straggly, unkempt mess. A quick call to the concierge fixed her up with an appointment at a nearby salon later that afternoon.

She had a few other things to sort out first though. She might now be the same dress size as Astrid, but unfortunately her feet were far larger. She'd decided to treat herself to a new pair of shoes, even if she couldn't foresee a time when she'd need to wear them again. The concierge pointed her in the direction of Pitt Street Mall, and she headed off to look around. No doubt about it, new shoes were guaranteed to make a girl feel good.

When she was relaxing at the hairdresser later, Mark called and confirmed that he'd meet her in the hotel lobby at six o'clock sharp.

At the appointed hour, she walked to the elevator, aware of a fluttering feeling in her stomach like the beating of a pair of butterfly wings. She steadied herself, but as the elevator pinged and the doors opened, Rose gasped. She almost didn't recognise herself: the elevator's full-length mirror reflected a tall, willowy beauty. Astrid's swirling sea-green dress floated like gossamer over her shoulders before clinging to her hips and running-honed rear. She turned around to check out the view from the back.

Pippa Middleton, eat your heart out!

Astrid was quite a few inches shorter than Rose, and the dress, which must have been knee-length on her, barely made it to mid-thigh on Rose. The new sandals had delicate diamante straps and made her legs look endless. Her hair, tamed into a sweep of glossy waves, cascaded over her shoulders. If only Giles could see her now, he'd think twice about buggering off to Brussels, she was sure. She wasn't sure even Henry would recognise her for that matter.

Her brother had always teased her for never bothering to make the most of herself, telling her that she spent far too much time in chef's whites with her hair tucked away. Seeing herself like this – as she'd only ever thought girls who were born to be elegant looked – she had to restrain herself from taking a selfie and messaging it to him there and then.

As she walked through the lobby, trying not to trip in the heels she was so unaccustomed to, she caught sight of Mark. He was deep in conversation with a rather portly man who had thinning strands of grey hair combed over a balding crown. Both were wearing dinner jackets and black bowties.

'Hello, Mark,' she said shyly as she approached. Mark did almost the same double-take that she'd done in the mirror earlier, widening his eyes as he took her in.

'Look at the legs on that,' boomed the portly man, giving a low whistle.

Mark recovered himself, 'Rose, I'd like you to meet Angus. Angus McGilligot is probably Australia's most important wine writer.' Mark's tone was jovial, but Rose thought she could detect a faint undercurrent of sarcasm, not something that someone who didn't know him well would have picked up on, but she'd heard it before, at home when he was teasing Luisa.

'Less of the probably, old man!' boomed Angus. Up close, Rose could see he had a network of red veins in his cheeks, and an alarmingly bulbous nose that sat on his face like a squidge of poorly placed playdough.

'My mistake, Angus, gotta keep you humble,' Mark laughed and slapped him on the back, 'Gus is sharing a cab to the restaurant with us.'

'Pleased to meet you, Angus.'

'Pleasure's all mine,' said Angus looking at her legs again before diving in to plant a wet kiss on her cheek. 'Bonza dress.' Rose wasn't sure she liked being assessed quite so blatantly, but she was a bit miffed that Mark hadn't bothered to comment on her appearance. He might at least have said something nice about the way she looked – she'd made a special effort and he could at least have noticed.

CHAPTER 20

The restaurant was already buzzing when they arrived, and the air of anticipation was palpable as they walked up to the bar. Rose noticed several guests interrupt their conversations when they recognised Mark. She found a flute of bubbles pressed into her hand as Mark slipped one arm gently around her and leant in to whisper in her ear. 'Don't feel that you're being abandoned, but there'll be a lot of people after my time tonight. You'll be okay, won't you?' Rose, acutely aware of the warmth of his touch, nodded her assent, although she didn't feel that confident as she looked out at the growing sea of unfamiliar people. Mark's arm left her back and she shivered at its absence.

'Don't worry Mark, I'll look after her,' said Angus. 'Come with me, Rosie darling.'

Rose took a deep breath and allowed herself to be led over to a group of suited men and their wives.

'This little sweetheart is Mark's guest,' Angus said knowingly, with emphasis on the word 'guest'. Rose didn't much care for the implication in his tone of voice, but decided to ignore it and be pleasant as she was introduced to the men and women gathered around the wine writer.

Several glasses of champagne later and having listened to a long-winded but, she had to admit, amusing anecdote from Angus that involved a tractor and a pump and several gallons of grape juice, she saw that people were moving towards the snowy-clothed tables. Rose couldn't wait to try the food. It had been so long since she'd eaten out anywhere smart, and she was looking forward to seeing if Sydney fine dining was all it was reputed to be.

Sitting diagonally across from Mark, at a long table, and thankfully some distance from the leering Angus, she leant back as the waiter theatrically unfurled starched a white napkin over her lap.

The first course, tiny petals of pearl meat and beads of caviar surrounded by foaming green sauce, didn't disappoint.

Oh, this is going to be good.

The accompanying Kalkari chardonnay was a perfect match for the rich but delicate dish, its light oak and stone fruit flavours in balance with the seafood. She almost moaned aloud with pleasure as she took a first bite, oblivious to the conversation going on around her. She closed her eyes for a moment, surrendering to the textures and tastes. As her eyelids fluttered open, she caught Mark watching her, the corners of his mouth twitching with amusement. She found herself grinning back at him, fluttering one eyelid in the faintest of winks, knowing her pleasure in the dish was evident.

As the dinner flew by, each course offering new sensations and flavours, Rose found herself relaxing and enjoying herself, chatting happily to her neighbours and sipping on the delicious wines.

Before she knew it, coffee was being served, and Mark was called upon to speak. She and the rest of the dinner guests listened, spellbound, as Mark described the wines, the different vintages, and what he was aiming to achieve in the vineyard this year. She'd seen flashes of his passion when they'd chatted in the barn, but it was something else to see him, dressed in a suit that would put James Bond to shame, standing in front of a crowd as they hung on his every word. As he finished speaking, she wanted to stand up and cheer. And then drag him away to a room with just her and a king-size bed ... The wine had loosened her inhibitions, and in a flash, she suddenly realised that she had fallen head over heels in lust with her boss.

Oh Christ, that's all I need.

Amid a sea of clapping hands, Mark made his way down from the podium. He walked around the tables, stopping to chat and share stories. As he neared Rose's side, she had to restrain herself from leaping up, hugging him and recklessly kissing him full on the lips.

'That was wonderful, Mark.'

'What? The food, the wine, or me?' he asked cheekily, all traces of the grumpy boss she was used to nowhere to be seen.

She blushed.

'Just kidding, Rose. I could see how much you enjoyed the food. We can head off now though, if you like. We had an early start this morning and I'm pretty beat.'

Feeling elated by the evening: the food, the wine and the surprisingly congenial company – Angus hadn't turned out to be as lecherous as she'd initially feared – Rose could have danced on the tables all night, but agreed that they probably should get going. She wanted to get away from everyone, to have Mark all to herself, to loosen his tie, slide her fingers through his shirt, undo his buttons, put her hand over his heart and feel it beating faster …

'If we're quick, we'll miss old Gus there.' Mark nodded towards the wine writer, who was holding court over several bottles of Assignation.

Rose snapped out of her reverie. 'Yes, of course. Let's go then.'

They said a quick farewell to Mark's distributor and thank you to the maitre'd, and then slipped quickly into a waiting cab. The ride back to the hotel was mercifully short. She could feel a rising tension in the car, but there was also a closeness that did away with the need for words. At that moment, anything seemed possible.

'Care for a nightcap?' Mark asked casually, as they walked through the lobby of the hotel.

'Love one.' She didn't want the evening to end.

As they headed towards the bar, Rose ducked off to the bathroom. She saw a flushed, sparkling stranger in the mirror, eyes glittering from the wine she'd drunk earlier.

Be careful. This is dangerous. Really not a good idea at all. Don't go doing something stupid that you'll regret in the morning.

But there was a glint in her eyes that told a different story. She wasn't ready to listen to the voice in her head, the one that told her to be careful, to be cautious, to stay away from trouble. She preferred the message her heart was thrumming out.

She found Mark lounging on a low sofa in front of the fire. In front of him were two cut crystal glasses, each filled with a generous measure of rusty-looking liqueur. 'My guilty pleasure,' he said, no hint of apology in his voice.

Rose began to imagine other guilty pleasures too, and felt a warmth spreading through her that wasn't just from the whisky. She sat down next to him, clinking her glass against his. 'Thanks for a wonderful evening. I really enjoyed it.'

'Even with Gus McGilligot eyeing you up and down?'

Rose laughed. 'He's a pussycat.'

'Oh really?' Mark raised one eyebrow. 'I hope you know that he can make or break a winery with just a few column inches. He's not a man to take lightly.'

'Neither are you, Mark,' she said recklessly.

How had her mouth just run away with her like that? Rose was quietly horrified and thrilled, all at the same time. She was obviously far too relaxed from the wine and good food.

'I'm glad you think so,' Mark looked at her, amused, holding her gaze. Rose found she couldn't tear her eyes away. She felt the colour mounting in her cheeks and a warm flush rise through her directly from her groin. Warning bells sounded far away in her brain. She knew that what would surely happen next was going to be a mistake whichever way she looked at it, but she was powerless to stop as Mark leaned forward and gently touched his lips to hers. Time stood still. All she could hear was the thudding of her blood in her veins. All she could feel were Mark's lips on hers. She moved towards him, circling the back of his neck with her arm, feeling his hair, unexpectedly soft to the touch, and pulling him towards her for a long, hungry kiss.

He broke away, and Rose caught her breath.

Oh dear God. The man could kiss for Australia.

'You looked stunning tonight by the way,' he murmured and, with a finger on her chin, tilted her lips towards his again. She surrendered to the insistency of his lips …

SMASH!

They jumped away from each other as if they'd been scalded.

The barman had dropped a tumbler on the glass countertop, causing it to shatter into hundreds of glistening diamonds. The sound sobered them both and Rose found she couldn't meet Mark's eyes. She felt suddenly clear-headed again. And scared. Scared of what might happen if she let it.

'Thanks for the drink and everything. I'd really better go now,' she stammered, gathering up her bag and turning towards the lobby. She didn't give Mark a chance to stop her.

Back in her room, Rose eased off the sparkly shoes and unzipped her dress, letting it fall in a puddle on the carpet. She pulled on an old t-shirt, wound her hair up into a knot and fell back onto the bed, staring up at the ceiling. Her sensible side knew she'd made a lucky escape. For once she hadn't acted on impulse. So why did she feel so god-damn miserable?

CHAPTER 21

Rose watched Astrid as she wriggled back and
forth and then sighed with frustration. They
were in Astrid's bedroom, Rose having cleared a
space for Astrid to lie on the bed as she tried in
vain to do up the zip on her jeans.

'There's no denying it. You're starting to show, sweetheart,' said Rose.

'Oof,' Astrid grunted as the zip refused to budge. 'I
can't believe how bloated I feel. But I am not sick in the
mornings anymore – quite the opposite in fact. I'm starving
all the time.'

'Well, at least you've got the pregnancy glow – I'd kill
for your skin,' said Rose, hoping to boost her mood.

Giving up on the struggle, Astrid grabbed an elastic
band from among the clutter on her dresser and looped one
end through the rivet and the other through the buttonhole

and then back on to the rivet. 'There,' she said triumphantly, 'that will have to do until I can get to New Bridgeton for some larger trousers.'

'Are you sure about keeping it?' asked Rose, broaching the subject that was on her mind.

'Don't be silly. Of course I will.' Astrid was adamant. 'It is too late for an abortion, and I cannot give it up for adoption, I just can't.'

'Well, it's good that you know your own mind. But what about Thommo? He's been back in the valley for a couple of days now. When are you going to see him?'

'He rang me as soon as he landed, but I panicked and let it go to voicemail. I didn't know what to say to him. He left a message – he wants to catch up.'

'Best grab the bull by the horns, so to speak,' advised Rose. 'Tell him before someone else does – you know what gossip is like in this place.'

'But no-one else knows about this except us,' Astrid said, looking worried.

'I know, and I'm sworn to secrecy, you can trust me on that, but nevertheless, I'd speak to him as soon as you can,' Rose warned.

'Yes, I know you're right. I'll call him later today.' Astrid looked at her watch. 'I'd better go and see if Luisa's woken up from her nap.'

Ever since they'd come back from the visit with their mother, the kids had been unsettled. Luisa was playing up, refusing to cooperate and throwing more than her usual share of tantrums. Leo was closed off again, retreating to his room, spending hours on his iPod, tuning out the world. Even Barnsie was feeling neglected, as Leo had stopped playing with him; the pup slunk around the verandah instead, looking for a patch of sun to lie in. Leo only came to life when Mark appeared, but his father had been largely absent lately, spending all his waking hours in the vineyards, checking on his precious vines.

'Honestly, I feel like a parent already, being a stand-in mum to Leo and Luisa. How much more trouble could a baby of my own be?' said Astrid.

'Well, you've got a point there, but what about the night feeds?'

Astrid made a face. 'Ugh, I do like my sleeps.'

'You'll do just fine. I know you will,' Rose reassured her. She knew that Astrid needed someone in her corner at the moment – and also in the months to come.

The sun was setting and the birds were heading home to roost as the girls drove along the narrow Eumeralla Road. The vines on either side of the road were swathed in netting like brides on their wedding day. Turning down the volume on the car radio, Rose asked, 'So what are you going to tell him? How do you think you'll break the news? A pair of baby booties?'

'Oh, don't tease me,' Astrid wailed. 'I'm nervous enough as it is.'

'I know, sweetheart. Just trying to lighten the mood.

You never know, it might not be as bad as you expect.'

'Humph.' Astrid didn't sound convinced.

The pub was packed, which was not unusual for a Thursday night at the end of the month, but Rose soon spotted Thommo, Charlie, Deano, Mick and Angie sitting at a corner table. She waved in their direction as she and Astrid headed first to the bar.

Thommo rose from his chair and followed Astrid: arriving at her side, he slid his arms around her waist. 'Astrid, gorgeous girl!' He aimed a kiss at her cheek as she turned her head towards him. 'I've missed you … Whoa! What's that you got there, a bun in the oven?' Thommo's hands had encountered her belly, blooming out over the top of her jeans.

Tears sprang up in Astrid's eyes. 'How can you know this?' she asked, shocked.

Rose looked on speechless as Astrid wrenched herself from his grasp and fled out the door. Thommo glanced at Rose questioningly, then rushed after her. Rose hastened after them.

As Thommo flung the pub door open, he called out to Astrid. 'Hey, I was just kidding! Don't get upset! You know me, always putting my foot in it. I didn't mean to offend you. I was kidding, really.'

Halfway to the car already, Astrid whirled round to face him. 'Actually, you've not put a foot in it. I really am pregnant. And guess who's going to be a father?'

Rose hovered behind them, uncertain if she should step in.

Seconds ticked by. Comprehension dawned on Thommo's face.

'Whaat? What are you saying? I don't believe you. How can that be? I've been away for months. And anyway it was only once,' he spluttered. 'It's just not possible.'

'Well, I am afraid it is possible. It's not like I had planned it. Completely stuffs everything for me too, if you care to know.' Astrid strode towards the car, visibly upset. 'Can we go Rose, please?' she pleaded.

'Okay, if that's what you want.' Rose unlocked the car door. 'Sorry, mate,' she said to Thommo, 'Best give her a bit of breathing space, hey? She wasn't quite expecting to break the news to you like this, I'm afraid.'

Astrid climbed in and slammed her door, and Rose quickly started the engine. As they drove away, Rose caught sight of Thommo in the rear-view mirror, standing in the carpark with his hands hanging loosely at his sides, a look of absolute bewilderment on his face.

'I remember when I was a girl, you just settled down with the first boy who took your fancy, or who was nice enough to ask you to take a turn with him. Clean shoes, neat haircut. Those were the marks of a good sort. Not like these days. Too many shenanigans going on now.'

Rose was sitting in the sunshine with Violet at Trevelyn Cottage. She'd got into the habit of popping over in the late afternoon, just as the ladies were finishing up for the day. News travelled fast in the small Shingle Valley community, and Violet and Rose were discussing Astrid and Thommo's reunion in the pub the week before.

Rose didn't mention her trip away to the city with Mark. She still hadn't made sense of it in her own head, and in any case Mark had kept his distance since they'd returned to Kalkari. If she was honest with herself, she would have said she was deliberately avoiding him too. He'd tried to apologise as they drove home from the city, and she'd pretended airily that she was completely cool with it. 'Look, it was just a drunken moment. Don't even think about it. I know I won't.'

That was a complete lie.

She still couldn't get the memory of his warm, insistent lips out of her head, the feel of his strong arms encircling her, the way her legs had turned to jelly when he kissed her. When she couldn't sleep at night, she brought out the memory like a treat to be savoured, reliving it over and over again, until she finally dropped off.

'Life doesn't always turn out the way you plan it,' Violet said cryptically.

'Tell me about it,' Rose agreed.

'Well, girl, just hang on for the ride and don't fall off, I say,' Violet cackled.

The back door banged, and Vera trudged in, 'Bloody hot out there,' she grumbled. 'That pot still going?'

Rose poured the dregs from the pot into a chipped china mug. 'Just enough, if you don't mind it stewed.'

'I'll take it any way it comes, darl. As long as it's warm and wet.'

'How are the grapes looking?' Rose was genuinely interested.

'Well, it's hotter than it's ever been round these parts for this time of year.' Vera heaved a thick leather-bound journal off the sideboard, and flicked through the pages. She showed Rose the spidery script, scrawled across pages dating back thirty years. 'There's a page for every day, with a line for every year, and then we make a note of the weather, the health of the vines, the canopy, what the grapes are looking and tasting like, what we're up to, and so on,' Vera explained.

'Wow, that's amazing. It's good that it's getting warmer, no?'

'Actually, it's not. We need long, cool growing conditions for the grapes that do well here. Makes our job even harder now. Bloody global warming.' Vera stomped off down the corridor to the front of the cottage.

'Don't mind her, Rose,' said Violet. 'Her bark's worse than her bite. She's just stressed about this year's vintage. Happens every time. Now, back to Astrid – do you reckon she'll be able to knock some sense into Thommo – get him to do the right thing?'

'Well, she's certainly a determined girl. I rather think she's prepared to go it alone.'

'You wouldn't have got away with that in my day – you'd have been carted off straight to the unmarried mother's home and then had the baby whipped away from you before you'd so much as looked at it,' Violet said sadly. 'Wouldn't have been allowed to give her a name or anything …'

Rose looked at the old lady. It sounded like she might have been speaking from experience.

184

CHAPTER 22

The phone rang in the hallway and Rose raced out of the kitchen to get to it. There was a pause on the line, and then she heard an English accent.

'Hello. May I speak to Mark Cameron, please?'

'I'm sorry, this is the house. He's at the winery right now. Do you have the number there?'

'Oh right-o, I thought that was where I'd rung.'

There was a click: the woman calling had hung up abruptly.

She looked up to see Astrid and Luisa coming down the stairs.

'Who was that?' asked Astrid.

'Don't know. She was English and I could have sworn I'd heard that voice before, but I can't place it. She sounded a bit like my mum. Actually, for a minute I thought it was her. She was looking for Mark.'

Luisa piped up. 'Mum?'

'No, not your mummy, darling. I was talking about my mummy.'

'You don't have a mummy, do you?'

'Actually I do, sweetheart, but she lives a long way away, just like your mummy.'

'Oh.' Apparently satisfied with this explanation, Luisa trotted out of the kitchen, dragging her bunny by its floppy ears as she went.

Rose finished off the preparations for dinner, making a salsa verde with herbs from Kalkari's garden, which had miraculously sprung back to life after the winter cold. She scattered crumble mixture over sliced apples and cinnamon, set it aside on the counter, and then headed over to the winery.

The phone call had reminded her that she needed to speak to her brother. Henry had been away for a few weeks, so she'd managed to stall him, saying she needed more time to find out what was really going on. With every day that passed – with her unlikely but growing friendship with Violet Trevelyn, and then the feelings that had been stirred up by her late-night, alcohol-fuelled kiss with Mark – Rose felt herself being drawn in to the valley, becoming knit into the fabric of the place. She woke every morning with anticipation of what the day might bring, and went about her chores with a spring in her step. The idea of betraying the people to whom she was becoming so close was an unpleasant one and the subterfuge was starting to make her feel very uneasy.

'Hey there, Rose. How's it going, love?' Dan was in the office, sitting at the computer. 'How's everything at the house?'

'The kids are doing okay, I think. Luisa's being a bit tricky and Leo was pretty upset at his mum leaving again, but I think things will settle down soon.'

'And how are you?' Dan's gaze penetrated a bit too deeply for Rose's liking. She felt like he could see right through to the turmoil inside her. Either that or he was starting to be suspicious. He certainly didn't miss much.

'Oh, you know, keeping busy. I miss Ferment though, despite all the hard work.'

'Yeah, well, he did spit the dummy on that one, hey? But just between you and me and the wine,' Dan angled his head to where the dozens of oak barriques lay on their sides in serried rows, 'I've been working on the boss. We'll see if we can't change his mind. Watch this space.'

Rose's eyes lit up. 'Oh, do you think he might? We could even find out where to hire an inflatable castle for the kids. Keep them happy while their parents taste.'

'Fair dinkum. We're not Disneyland here, you know,' said Dan with a chuckle. 'I'm not so sure Mark'll go for it; that might be a bridge too far.'

'Oh, I know, but it'd be a bit of fun, don't you think?' Rose teased.

'Well, it's not up to me now, is it?' he said, 'But give me some time and I'll see what I can do.'

'Oh. I almost forgot. Did you get a phone call earlier? Someone with an English accent rang the house, wanting to speak to Mark.'

'Yeah, that was Olivia, from Channings.'

'Alicia, you mean?' Rose remembered the tweedy woman from the lunch she'd cooked a few months previously. That was where she'd heard the voice before.

'That's right. Alicia.'

'Oooh, exciting! What did she want?'

'Not sure, really. I told her she'd get Mark on his mobile. He's been out in the vineyard all day.'

'Oh, well, I was just making sure she'd rung back. Thanks, Dan. I'd better go and keep an eye on dinner.'

'No worries, Rose, and I'll work on the boss about reopening the cellar door, especially now the weather's warming up. The valley gets heaps of visitors in spring and summer, up from the big smoke for some fresh air, good food and plenty of wine. You should see how some of them knock it back. Hens' parties are the worst.' He shook his head ruefully.

It was dark by the time Mark came in. Rose heard him shucking off his boots outside the back door and looked up as he entered the kitchen, acutely aware of his solid frame filling the room. He looked tired again, she thought, noticing the deepening network of fine lines around his eyes. She couldn't help it: her heart went out to him; he had so much on his shoulders and no-one to share it with.

He had a couple of bottles of red tucked under his arm. Rose could just see a glimpse of mildewed labels. Cobwebs hung off the necks. She wondered if they were more from his family's old vineyard. Mark carefully uncorked one of the bottles and she watched as it glugged into a decanter he'd retrieved from the sideboard.

It was Astrid's evening off – she'd gone to the cinema in New Bridgeton with Angie from Lilybells – so it was just the two of them for dinner. Mark had finished up earlier than usual, and asked if they could eat with the kids. Leo and Luisa hung off their dad, Luisa pretending to whisper in his ear and Leo showing him his homework.

'Look, Dad, it's a drawing of a boa constrictor,' Leo said proudly.

Mark ruffled the boy's hair. 'Quite the artist, aren't you, mate?'

'Dinner's going to be a little while longer, guys. You can go and watch TV until it's ready, if you like.' Rose wanted to seize the opportunity to have a chat with Mark. They'd not been alone together since they returned from Sydney, and the drive back had been a tense one, each of them lost in their own thoughts.

The kids scampered off, leaving them alone.

'Here, Rose, try this,' Mark said as he handed over a glass of the deep purple wine he'd decanted.

She sniffed in a sweet, heady perfume and then took a sip. Liquid like velvet and the taste of ripe blackberries flooded her palate, lingering there. It was like nothing she'd ever tasted. 'Holy shit. I could bathe in that!' Rose was mesmerised by the flavours and sensation of the wine as it hit her palate. 'What is it?'

'Chateau Margaux 1982,' Mark said. 'One of the best vintages in recent times.'

Rose had heard of the wine – it was one of Henry's favourites – but she'd never tasted it before. She was surprised they were drinking it on an ordinary Friday night at home. 'Bloody hell, Mark, I'm not sure that bangers and mash will do this justice. What are we celebrating?'

'I had a call from the UK earlier on. So, actually, "bangers" as you call them, will be the perfect thing tonight.'

Rose wasn't sure if Mark was making fun of her or not. She often didn't know how to read him: his moods were so changeable. 'Oh yes, they rang here first. Dan said it was Alicia from Channings and that she was going to try you on your mobile. What did she want?'

'Only 30,000 cases of tempranillo.' Mark shook his head in wonder. 'That kind of order should really turn things around. If we can get hold of enough fruit from the valley in this vintage, that is. Plantings are a bit thin on the ground, and it'll all depend on yields. That and being able to twist the arms of some of the valley's best growers, Trevelyn's among them. Most of the grape contracts are locked in years in advance, but we might have a bit of leeway.'

'Well, that's great, right?'

'Well, it is if we can fill the order.'

'Oh, that's wonderful news, Mark, really it is. It'll work out. You'll see.'

'Yes, it's a good news day. And we're celebrating. That's why I pulled the Margaux out. God knows it's been a while since there was something worth making a song

and dance about around here. This was a wedding present.'
He laughed bitterly.

'Oh.' Rose didn't know what to say.

'Look, Rose, I'm sorry again for what happened in Sydney. I got carried away. I was completely out of line. You work here, and I shouldn't be taking unfair advantage.' Mark looked uncomfortable. 'Things are a bit of a mess for me right now, and it's not fair to complicate your life with my problems. Someone as fresh and lovely as you deserves someone far less battered and jaded than me. In any case, I'm far too old for you.'

Fresh and lovely, he called me fresh and lovely ... the words sang in her head.

She took a gulp of wine for courage. 'You're wrong,' she insisted. 'You're not in the slightest bit battered or jaded, and you're not exactly headed for the knackers' yard yet. But okay, yes, I get it. Really, I do.' She was proud of herself for being so rational, for holding it together and not giving anything away, but the reality was if he'd swept her up in his arms again she wouldn't have protested at all. Oh God, it was all so frustrating.

'Rose, I know you've not been here long, but I've come to think of you as part of the family: you and Astrid. I honestly don't think I could cope without either of you at the moment. I hope you know how much I appreciate you both. It's been a really ordinary few months and I don't know what I'd do without you.'

Rose felt her heart break for him as she looked into his troubled green eyes. She took a deep breath. *Strike while the iron is hot*. She also needed to change the subject. If he kept on talking about her like that she might be tempted to throw all caution to the wind and pull him towards her, ignoring the fact that he was her employer, ignoring the children in the room next door ...

'Mark ... do you think you might reconsider opening the cellar door? Just at the weekends? It won't be any extra bother for you. I'll do all the baking, and Astrid said she'd help me serve, and Dan's offered to run the tastings. I think we can bring in quite a bit of cash too ...'

'Dan's been on at me about this as well. Are you two ganging up on me?' he asked, but his words held no censure this time. 'Look, as it gets warmer, we'll certainly get more visitors. As long as it's not too much extra work for you. I don't want you to feel taken advantage of. In any way.'

Rose couldn't suppress a grin. She wouldn't mind being taken advantage of in another way. 'I loved doing it last time. I really do want to do this, Mark. I've got the time. It won't interfere with the rest of my work.'

'Alright, well, there's no reason why you can't start again in a couple of weeks' time – will that give you enough notice? And how about we split the cafe takings? That way I won't feel so guilty about you working so hard.'

'Super! Oh thank you, Mark!' Rose had just the excuse she needed to lean over and gave him a quick kiss on the cheek.

'Daaad!' A voice called from the hallway, interrupting them. 'Luisa's hurting meeee!'

Mark glanced towards the door, 'I'd better go and sort them out before they strangle each other.'

Rose sighed and went over to check on the dinner.

They'd cleared the air and she'd got what she wanted, so why did she still feel dissatisfied?

CHAPTER 23

It was the smell that first alerted her. Rose was out on her early morning run and had just reached the rise in the hill that overlooked the valley. She paused, hands on her hips, taking in the view as the sun came up over the horizon, colouring the sky rosy pink and purple. The morning air was cool. She sniffed the wind – and that was when she caught an unmistakable aroma, bitter and acrid. She looked around but couldn't see anything out of the ordinary. It was, however, strangely quiet this morning, she thought. No birdsong, no roosters crowing at the dawn.

Acting on impulse, she decided to head down the hill towards Trevelyns, a sixth sense guiding her footsteps there. As she approached, she saw wisps of smoke curling out from under the cottage's back door.

Oh God! Her breath caught in her throat. *Vera and Vi are in there!*

She raced over to the window, peering in to the dark, smoke-filled kitchen. She could hear a crackling and cracking sound coming from within. 'Violet!' she screamed. 'Vera!'

Fearful for the old ladies' safety, she cast around, looking for something – anything – to help her. She'd seen too many inferno movies to want to risk trying to open the door, and in any case the handle was metal and would probably sear the skin on her palm right off. If only she had her phone with her – she could have called for help. She spied a garden hose lying to one side of the cottage, and rushed over to see if it was attached to something useful like a water supply.

Oh, thank Christ for that.

She wrenched the rusty tap on to full volume – as far as it would go – and dragged the hose around to the back, aiming the gushing water at the gap under the door.

She was vaguely aware of the sound of sirens in the distance, but the roar of the fire coming from inside the cottage still dominated. Gasping, she called out again, 'Vera! Violet! Are you there?' She had no idea if they were still in the cottage, and was terrified the smoke, which was billowing from an open window, might have overcome them. Rose felt the smoke stinging her eyes and making her cough, but she carried on aiming the hose at the house.

After what seemed an eternity, the fire engine sirens grew louder and she turned her head to see a truck coming up the drive, lights flashing. Screeching to a halt at the front door, the brigade climbed down and swiftly got to work.

Strong fingers prised her hands off the hose and gently led her to a safe distance from the cottage. Rose suddenly felt her legs give way from under her and she collapsed on her knees in the veggie patch, her fingernails digging into the dirt, coughing violently, her lungs scoured by the smoke.

Two of the firemen went in through the front door. They returned swiftly, carrying Violet and Vera, respectively, cradled in their arm. The old ladies must have still been in their beds, as they were in their nightdresses.

Rose heard the wail of an ambulance siren approaching, and soon other cars pulled up at the front of the house. Rubbing her eyes and getting up on unsteady legs, she watched as Vera and Violet were loaded into an ambulance. They didn't appear to be conscious.

'Are they going to be okay?' she asked one of the firemen, coughing again at the effort of talking.

'I hope so. They've inhaled a bit of smoke and likely had a very nasty fright, but they're tough old birds, those two, known them all my life,' he said as he raised his helmet and wiped sweat off his face. 'Looks like it started in the kitchen. It's under control now and the damage won't be too bad. Lucky for them you came along when you did, and that you found the hose. This old place is like a tinderbox; it'd have gone up in minutes.'

As Rose was talking to the fireman, she heard a familiar voice behind her. 'Rose, what are you doing here? What on earth's happened? I saw the fireys and heard the sirens and followed them. Are you okay?'

Rose's legs suddenly turned to jelly. 'Oh, Mark,' she

sobbed, falling into his arms. 'I was so scared; there was just so much smoke and they couldn't hear me. They just couldn't hear me,' she repeated. 'They might have died in there.' Rose went into a paroxysm of coughing, unable to stop.

Mark pulled her tightly to him, rubbing his hand across her back to soothe her. 'There, Rose, it's all right. Hush now. You're in shock. Try and take some slow breaths.' His gentle tone calmed her, and she clung to him, finding she couldn't let go, feeling the roughness of his unshaven cheek against her forehead and breathing in the comforting, familiar spicy scent of him. His arms, strong as oak, wrapped around her, steadying her.

Mark held her until her coughing stopped and her breathing slowed, seemingly in no hurry to let her go. 'How did you end up here at this hour though?' he said, eventually releasing her. Rose wished he hadn't; she'd quite liked the feeling of his arms around hers.

'I woke up early and went for a run. I was at the top of the hill and smelled smoke. Once I got closer to the cottage, I could see it coming out from under the back door, the one to the kitchen. I ran as fast as I could and grabbed the garden hose,' she blurted.

'She did a great job,' the firey said to Mark. 'Her quick thinking probably saved their lives. It kept the kitchen fire from spreading further.'

'Now, love,' said one of the paramedics, who had come over. 'I heard that coughing. I reckon we need to get you checked out as well.'

Rose tried to protest that she was okay, but he insisted

197

that she accompany him to hospital. Mark backed him up.
'I'll be there later to see how you're going. Don't worry,
they'll take good care of you.'

Rose found that she was grateful, after all, for the rest in the
New Bridgeton hospital – they sedated her to stop her
coughing, and she quickly found herself dozing off.

When she came to, Mark, Leo, Luisa and Astrid were
standing around her bed. Her eyelids felt as heavy as lead
and she could barely flutter them open. She felt Mark brush
back a strand of hair from her forehead and lean down and
gently kiss her cheek. She immediately recognised the delicious, familiar scent of spice and citrus soap.

'Oh, Rose, I'm so sorry. I promised I'd keep you safe,'
he whispered to her.

Rose was woozy from the drugs and his words floated
over her, making no sense at all. She was only aware of the
warmth of his hand in hers and the sense of comfort that
overtook her in his presence.

'Is Wosey okay, Daddy?' asked Luisa.

'Yes, darling, she'll be fine,' said Mark. 'I hope you don't
mind, Rose – Leo and Luisa were asking after you. They
really wanted to see you.'

'S'fine,' she mumbled, stirring.

'Do you mind if I check on Vera and Vi? I'll come back
to you in a bit.'

''Course.' Rose sank back against the pillow.

The Trevelyn sisters were at the far end of the ward. Mark left her side and the kids followed. He tiptoed over to Violet's bed and took the old lady's hand.

'Hello, Vi, how are you feeling?' Rose heard him say.

'Not too bad, love,' Violet rasped. 'Bit of a sore throat though. Drier than a dead dingo's donger. Got a cold beer on you by any chance?'

Leo giggled.

Rose watched as Violet raised herself up in bed. 'Hello young feller, it's nice to see you.'

'Hello, Violet. I'm sorry your house caught on fire,' Leo said. 'We brought you some lollies.'

'Don't worry, mate, it'll all get sorted. Just gotta get out of this place first.'

'We also brought you a few other things – nightgowns and toothbrushes. We thought you wouldn't have anything with you,' Astrid said.

'That's very kind of you, love. It'll be good to put something on that's not backless. Been showing me arse off to the world every time I go to the dunny.' Violet cackled at herself, which set off a hacking cough.

'How long will they be keeping you in?' asked Mark when she'd stopped coughing her guts up.

'I'm not too sure, a couple of days they reckon,' said Violet. 'Then I think we'll go and stay with our cousins across the valley. Just till we get the house sorted. We've no idea how bad the damage is yet. Have you seen it?'

'Don't worry yourselves about that. I'll help you sort it all out. And don't worry about the vineyards; we'll look after them until you're back on your feet. I've got a bloke starting next week. Viticulturist, from Adelaide. Young gun, completely on board with biodynamics, so don't stress about a thing. In any case, we'll be needing all the grapes you can give us, Channings have just confirmed a big order.'

'Oh, so that's why you're here.' Rose heard a teasing note in the old woman's voice. 'You're not worried about us at all, just the grapes. I might have guessed. Seriously, that's bloody good news, Mark. About time you had something go your way. Good job the fire didn't spread to the vines then.'

'Yeah, we could do without smoke taint in the fruit, that's for sure.'

Mark looked round as Vera stirred in the next bed and gave a hoarse cough. 'Hello, Mark. How's Rose?' she asked in a whisper.

'She's fine. She's just down at the other end of the ward,' Mark said, pointing towards the door.

'They told us that she helped fend off the flames. Is she alright?'

'She'll be fine,' said Mark. 'She's only got mild smoke inhalation and the doctor says she'll be right as rain in a few days. You two gave us all a fright though.'

'Oh thank goodness. I couldn't bear it if anything had happened to her.'

'Can you hear me, Rose?' Violet asked, raising her voice.

Rose slowly lifted a hand in reply.

'I think that means she can,' said Mark, who was watching.

'Well, we're grateful to you, Rose, that's the truth,' Violet added. 'We'd have been charcoal if you hadn't turned up when you did.'

'She's one in a million, that girl, you know,' said Vera.

'I know,' said Mark, smiling at the two old ladies. 'She certainly is.'

Mark, Astrid and the kids stayed a while longer, and Mark promised to contact the insurance company and check when they could go back to the house to assess the damage. He stopped by Rose's bed on the way out and leaned down to kiss her again. 'Rest up, darling girl,' he whispered to her.

CHAPTER 24

Rose was allowed to come home after a night in hospital and, although her throat still felt tender, was back on her feet after a day in bed. Even though she made a swift recovery, Mark was solicitous with her, calling over most evenings to check on her, often staying for a chat and telling her about his day.

But the following week, after a trip to Eumeralla for groceries, she opened the door to the barn and immediately spied a large duffle bag in the middle of the room, an empty coffee mug on the table and a jacket slung over one of the sofas. At that moment, she heard the loo flush; a tall, dark stranger emerged from the bathroom. She quickly took in the long legs encased in jeans, cinched around the hips with an alligator-skin belt, and the broad expanse of tawny, muscled torso. Finally, scanning up to connect with a face, she found a wide mouth, razor-sharp cheekbones and wavy dark hair. Her mysterious visitor looked like a disturbingly attractive but slightly menacing gypsy. The only thing missing was a gold hoop in one ear. Sticking out of his mouth was the white handle of a toothbrush, and a dribble of foam was making its way down to his chin. This went some way to making him look slightly less alarming.

'G'day,' he said, having removed the toothbrush. 'You must be Rose. Jake. Jake Salmon. Just got here. Hope you don't mind me sharing your digs. Mark said you'd be cool with it.' He extended his hand, looking her up and down lazily with sleepy blue eyes so dark they were practically indigo.

Rose was uncomfortable: she felt those eyes travelling over every inch of her as she took his strong, calloused hand in hers. 'I guess not,' she said brusquely. 'Anyway, Mark's the boss. There's a spare room through there,' she said, gesturing to the door on the far side of the large living area. 'I'll show you where to get some sheets and things from the house. I see you've found a towel.'

Rose was put out by the thought of having to share the barn with a stranger, particularly someone as full of himself as Jake clearly was. Mark could have at least given her a heads up. She'd got used to having her own space since she'd been at Kalkari, and had been surprised to find that she enjoyed the solitude.

She couldn't help but notice the half-moons of dark earth under Jake's nails. 'Goes with the job,' he said. 'Can't ever seem to get them clean.'

'Oh,' said Rose, 'right.' She was embarrassed at having been caught staring.

'Okay then,' said Jake, unperturbed by her lack of effusive welcome. 'Better go and see what the boss wants me to get started on first.'

'Umm, don't you think you've forgotten something?' Rose gestured to his bare chest.

'Yeah, a shirt'd probably be a good idea, right?' Jake bent down to his bag and retrieved a pale blue tee, slipping it effortlessly over his six-pack and grinning cockily at her. 'All set. Catch ya later, babe.'

'I guess,' said Rose to his retreating back. It dawned on her that with a new roommate there'd be far less likelihood of Mark stopping by the barn in future. She'd come to look forward to their time together at the end of each day more than she realised.

The weekend rolled around. Rose had been so busy preparing to reopen Ferment, baking and freezing vanilla cupcakes, chocolate brownies and sweet lime and coconut bread late into the night that she'd hardly had time to exchange more than a few words with either Mark or her new roommate. Although Jake had certainly made his presence felt, with stray shirts left on the sofa and boots claggy with vineyard mud on the barn's doorstep, he was still asleep when she went out for her dawn run, and gone by the time she was back to cook breakfast for the kids. With immaculate timing, they managed to miss each other every morning.

At dinner, he and Mark joined Rose and Astrid, wolfing their food down and talking incomprehensibly about clones and trellising, stuck ferments, bunch rot and fruit set. Rose felt usurped from her place as Mark's confidante and it was making her cranky. She'd already snapped at Leo for leaving wet towels all over the bathroom floor. 'Honestly, Leo, could you pick up after yourself?' she'd grouched. And she'd nearly lost her temper with Luisa when she spilled her juice on the carpet, even though she'd known it was an accident. She felt irritable and out of sorts, her normal sunny good humour deserting her.

It didn't help that Henry was pressing her for more information: in his last email he'd said he'd need specifics soon so he could make a bid for Kalkari. Despite her bad mood, Rose wasn't sure anymore that she wanted him to. She wondered how she could get him to change his mind. It wouldn't be easy.

On Friday night, the two men headed into town for dinner at the pub, leaving Rose up to her elbows in flour, sugar and pears, hard at work on muffins for Ferment. After settling Leo and Luisa into bed, Astrid lay on the sofa, zoning out in front of *The Biggest Loser*. Rose could hear her occasional snorts of incredulous laughter sounding all the way though to the kitchen. Absorbed in her baking, she quickly lost track of time, but knew it was late when she heard Mark return from the pub. He poked his head inside the kitchen door, 'Still up, Rose?'

'Nearly finished,' she replied, elbowing away the hair that had fallen into her eyes.

'You've got flour on your face again,' he said, motioning to her. 'Here ... just here.' He moved towards her, placed a thumb on her cheek and gently rubbed the smudge away.

Rose shivered involuntarily.

'Well, I'd better hit the hay,' he said, giving a huge yawn.

'G'night,' she replied, 'Don't let the bugs bite.'

He grinned at her, a crooked smile spreading across his face and lighting up his eyes, but then he was gone as soon as he'd arrived.

Rose's cheeks burned as she took the last cake out of the oven, though she knew it was from the heat that Mark's touch had ignited, and not from her baking. She felt powerless to do anything about the growing feelings she had for her boss. 'It's just a silly crush; get over it,' she kept repeating whenever she found herself thinking about him, which was all too often. She sighed. She wasn't doing a very good job of convincing herself.

Finishing the washing up, she made her way over to the barn. The only sign of Jake was a thunderous snoring coming from his room.

Rose woke even earlier than usual on Saturday, excited at the prospect of reopening Ferment. She'd persuaded Mrs B to come over and serve tea, and Dan was on hand to run the tastings. As she crept out of the barn, the air was already heating up. It was going to be a warm one. Blackbirds warbled a cheery good morning to her as she headed over to the cellar door to crank up the Marzocco, savouring the prospect of a strong dose of caffeine to help her power through the day.

And she'd needed it. She'd contacted Eumeralla's visitor centre to let them know of the reopening. They said they'd been fielding inquiries about Ferment for weeks and would be happy to put the word out again. they'd done their job well. People came in droves. She and Mrs B were rushed off their feet, and they had sold out of pear and chocolate muffins and lime and coconut bread by noon. Thankfully Rose had learnt from previous experience and stocked up on several sacks of coffee beans from Sacred Grounds before the start of the weekend.

Sunday was even busier, and Rose was glad she'd risen at five to bake more muffins, despite having to be as quiet as she could manage to avoid waking the slumbering house.

Mark and Jake arrived at the cellar door in the late afternoon, just as she was collecting the last few cups from the outdoor table they'd set up in front of the cellar door.

'Hey, Rose, got any leftovers for two hungry blokes?' asked Mark. 'Looks like you've had a good day, judging from the stream of cars we saw heading up the drive this morning.'

'It's been hectic, alright. But you're in luck. I saved a couple of slices of caramel date cake. I'll just go grab them.'

'You had me at caramel,' groaned Mark theatrically. 'But don't worry, I'll fetch them,' he said, heading towards the cellar door before she could move.

Rose was left outside with Jake, who was leaning comfortably against the tree, 'You're in your element, aren't you?' he said, taking in her flushed cheeks and dishevelled hair, which had escaped from the morning's sleek ponytail. 'There's something awesome about seeing someone doing exactly what makes them happy.'

'I guess,' said Rose, unsure how to answer him. 'It's good to feel useful, and I love it here,' she admitted.

'I can see why. It's a beaut bit of land. I'm looking forward to seeing what we can do with it, though Mark's made a great start already.'

'Do you think you'll get the grapes he needs for the UK order?'

'It's all a bit early to tell. A lot depends on the vintage. And there's still a fair bit to do over at Trevelyn's. Those old girls were pretty switched on, but there's a lot of work needed to grow decent grapes.'

'They've been doing it perfectly well for years,' Rose said, feeling that she should defend the sisters.

'Yeah, but you have to admit they're getting on a bit now. And they were pretty knocked around by the fire. Anyway, they've agreed with Mark that we can oversee their vineyards as well as ours in return for first dibs on their extra fruit, so it's a win-win. We'll be continuing to grow their grapes biodynamically, and bringing that in at Kalkari too. But it's labour-intensive.'

'What's labour-intensive? Making this perfect caramel cake?' asked Mark, emerging with a slice in each hand and offering one to Jake. 'Rose, I can see why you drew the crowds today; this is bloody delicious.'

Well, at least he appreciated her baking, if not the rest of her. 'Thanks, but it might have had more to do with the fact that the Assignation shiraz was open for tasting, you know.'

'Nope. I'm sure they came for the cake,' said Mark through a mouthful of crumbs.

Later that evening, as the sun was colouring the hills golden, Astrid returned from Eumeralla bearing a tower of square cardboard boxes. 'I guessed you'd be too tired to cook, so I picked up pizza. Ham and pineapple for the kids. Gourmet for us. Salami, fetta and olives, anyone?'

'You're a lifesaver,' said Rose, sinking into a chair and easing off her boots. 'It smells like heaven.' She'd been on her feet since five that morning.

The six of them gathered around the scrubbed kitchen table, Astrid jammed a couple of candles into some empty wine bottles and lowered the lights as Mark retrieved a clutch of reds from the cellar.

'Not drinking, Astrid?" asked Jake, waving the bottle in her direction.

'Umm, no, thanks. Don't really feel like it,' replied Astrid, glancing at Rose. The Austrian girl had taken to wearing baggy tops to hide the growing evidence of her pregnancy.

Despite feeling completely knackered from her early start and the frantic day, Rose found a second wind and chugged down the wine and pizza with gusto. Even Jake was less annoying than usual and she found herself chortling with laughter at his impression of some of the valley's characters. It felt like she was becoming part of a family, albeit an unconventional one, even if she still wasn't sure exactly where her piece of the puzzle fitted.

CHAPTER 25

'Hey! Psst ... Rose.'

Rose raised a groggy head from her pillow, wincing as the sunlight hit her eyes. It took a minute before she remembered where she was and why she wasn't up with the birds, running across the vineyards. Oh yes. She'd had more than one bottle of red last night with Jack, Mark and also Thommo, who'd dropped in to see Astrid, but on finding she'd gone to bed had been persuaded to stay for a drink or two.

'Rose. Are you there?'

'Umnngh,' she groaned. 'Come in.'

Astrid poked her head around Rose's door. 'Hi, I'm glad you're up.'

'I wasn't,' protested Rose.

'Listen, I've got to go to New Bridgeton for a scan this afternoon. Can you come with me? Please?'

'You know Thommo was here last night, looking for you?'

'Oh, was he?' Astrid looked a bit taken aback. 'I don't know what to say to him. The other week didn't really go so well, did it?'

'Perhaps he wants a second chance? After all, you did kind of spring it on him,' said Rose.

'It's not like I had a choice. Is not my fault he went straight and put his arms round my waist!' Astrid protested. 'Anyway, you don't look too well this morning,' she said, changing the subject.

'One glass of wine too many for me, I reckon. I don't know how those guys do it. Don't think it helped that I'd been on my feet for more than twelve hours.'

Astrid passed her a glass of water from the side table, and threw a packet of painkillers onto the bed. 'They're already out in the vineyard. They grab a slice of toast and hop into the ute. What do you think about Jake, hey? If I wasn't already in trouble, I'd crack to him,' she said, winking at Rose.

'It's "crack on" to him, Astrid,' said Rose, having heard the expression from Angie once in the pub. 'Anyway, you're impossible! Don't you think you're already in enough trouble?' Rose threw a pillow at her.

'Okay, I was joking, honest,' replied Astrid. 'So, can you come with me? I really don't want to go by myself, and I don't think Thommo will come. The appointment is at two. Luisa has a playdate this afternoon, so we should be finished in plenty of time to pick up Leo and then her.'

'Of course. Now, can I try and sleep off this thumper of a headache?'

Rose and Astrid headed to the medical centre after lunch, Rose feeling clear-headed again after a sleep-in, painkillers and a large coffee.

'Ohhh, that's really cold!' Astrid winced at the jelly being spread on her stomach by the woman performing the ultrasound. Her fierce grip on Rose's hand betrayed her nervousness. The technician pressed a large white probe down onto her belly and on a screen above them they watched a grainy swirling mass.

'It's a bit hard to tell what's in there, isn't it?' Rose said.

The technician smiled, 'There's your baby, Astrid.' An outline of a baby came into view. 'Look, that's the heartbeat.' She pointed to a tiny pulsing movement.

Tears welled up in Astrid's eyes. 'Oh, look at that. It looks just like a little alien! Look at the size of that head!' She beamed at Rose, brushing away her tears. 'Oh God, it really is real now.'

'Sure is, sweetheart,' said Rose, squeezing her hand, feeling suddenly protective of the younger girl, but fearful for her too.

'Would you like to know the sex?' asked the technician.

Astrid and Rose looked at each other. They hadn't expected this.

'Not that it's a hundred percent sure, but we can get a pretty good idea at this stage.'

Astrid shook her head. 'I want to wait until it – I mean he or she – is born.'

After their appointment, as Rose drove her back home, Astrid pulled out the black and white print they'd given her. Rose caught her smiling as she looked at the evidence of what was growing inside her.

'Are you going to give Thommo another chance?' asked Rose.

Astrid thought for a moment. 'Well, he at least has a right to see this,' she said holding up the piece of paper.

'I'll drop you off on our way home if you like.'

'No, I've got to collect Luisa and Leo, and anyway, I'd like to give him some warning this time.'

'Yeah, you're right. Might also be an idea to talk to him in a less public place too. Someplace where the whole neighbourhood isn't looking over your shoulder. Why don't you invite him over to the barn? I'll make sure Jake isn't there.'

'Well, stone me. Good-lookin' little fella ain't he? Must take after his dad.' Thommo looked up from the piece of paper Astrid had given him, wonder in his eyes. 'I'm sorry about the other week,' he said. 'I really put my foot in it. I honestly had no idea.'

'You weren't to know that you'd hit the nail with the hammer,' said Astrid. They were sitting in the barn. At

Astrid's insistence, Rose was also there – for moral support, she assumed.

'Looks like that's something I'm good at,' Thommo joked.

'Ha ha, even *I* get that. Very funny, Thommo. This was hardly something I expected to happen. And I didn't want to tell you on the phone, or while you were so far away either.'

Thommo was still gazing at the scan. 'So, this is really him?'

'It could be a girl, you know,' said Rose, unable to stop herself from interrupting.

'They could have told me at the hospital,' explained Astrid. 'But I didn't want to find out. I hope that's okay, or do you want to know?'

'Girl, boy, I don't mind. I'm just stoked that there's a little tacker of mine on the way.'

'Are you sure? Really? It's not as if we are exactly boyfriend and girlfriend. It was just a one-night thing. And it's going to change both our lives.'

'Are you kidding? I can't wait to put him up on a tractor, kick a footy around ...'

'Or her ...' Rose reminded him again, with a smile.

'Well, it'll be a while before that happens. Can we just take it one day at a time?' said Astrid. 'But first I must tell Mark before he finds out from someone else. I don't know what he's going to say. I don't think he will be happy at his nanny getting up the spout.'

'Up the duff!' laughed Rose, relieved for Astrid's sake that Thommo's reaction had been so positive.

'I just hope I keep my job for as long as I can,' said Astrid.' After that I'm going to need some help.'

'Oh, don't worry about Mark. I'll come and see him with you if you like. He'll be fine; he's a good bloke underneath it all. And you could always move in to our place if things get sticky at here.'

'With you and Charlie? I'm not so sure about that.'

'Well, Charlie's going to be in Italy for most of next year, so there'll be plenty of space if that's what you're worried about, but in any case, he won't mind.'

'Thommo, look, a baby kind of changes everything, doesn't it? I'm not sure how I'm feeling, about whether there is a future for you and me, but I do know I'm going to try to be the best mother I can be,' said Astrid.

Thommo took her hand. 'Listen. I'm not going anywhere, and now I've had time to get used to the idea I'm thrilled. Really I am. And us? Well, let's just take that one foot at a time, hey?'

Rose's spirits lifted. Maybe, just maybe, things would work out for her friend.

'Thommo, that means a lot to me,' said Astrid. 'I've been going out of my head trying to figure it all out on my own. I've been so scared.'

'Don't worry, babe. I won't let you down,' said Thommo as he gave her a reassuring hug. He pulled away and looked at her. 'May I?'

Astrid nodded as he placed a gentle hand on her stomach.

CHAPTER 26

Early one evening, just as Rose was heading back to the barn, she ran into Mark. 'Hey there, how's it going? Not off to the bright lights of Eumeralla tonight? Isn't that where Jake's gone?'

'Nup. Feeling a bit tired actually.'

'Don't suppose you fancy a bit of a drive? I've gotta go over to the east vineyard, make one last check on the vines there. Haven't had the opportunity to get around to it till now.' Mark looked enquiringly at her.

Rose wasn't going to turn down the chance to spend a bit of time with him. She was beginning to realise how much she enjoyed his company. Mark had relaxed a lot since she'd first met him – he seemed a lot less stressed now the Channings order had been confirmed. He was almost a different person. 'Sure, okay. Just let me grab a top in case it gets colder.'

'Meet you at the car in about half an hour. I just want to check on the kids first.'

'Cool. See you then.' Rose walked nonchalantly back to the barn, though every fibre of her wanted to run.

Half an hour was long enough for a quick shower and fresh makeup. Just.

Brushing out her hair and loosely braiding it into a thick rope that fell down her back, she rubbed on a bit of blush, slicked on some lipgloss and was done. Her eyes were bright and her skin was clear, just lightly dusted with a few freckles, thanks to the long sunny days that had blessed the valley over the past few weeks. Her new jeans clung to her long, slim legs and she buttoned a clean cotton shirt over a lacy bra. Definitely worth breaking out the good underwear. *You never know.*

True to his word, half an hour later, Mark was standing waiting for her beside his mud-spattered four-wheel-drive. He was carrying a cloth-covered basket from the kitchen, and a bottle of wine. Rose raised one eyebrow at him, as she glanced at the basket.

'Thought we might have a bit of tucker while we're there. We might not make it back till after dark,' said Mark. 'In any case, the pantry's certainly well-stocked these days, thanks to you.'

A picnic? Is he for real?

Rose didn't want to read too much into the plan, but it looked pretty promising from where she stood.

A flock of white cockatoos wheeled overhead, cawing loudly as they set off. The sun tinged the vines golden as they drove down through the leafy avenue of trees that lined the long Kalkari lane. Dragonflies danced on the beaten silver surface of the dam. Rose felt a small bubble of happiness well up inside her. The beauty of the landscape and the feeling of rightness about being beside this man, the man who haunted her dreams most nights, were only marred by the remembrance of the promise she'd made to Henry, and his designs on Kalkari. Right now though, that promise seemed a lifetime ago, made by a different girl than the one who sat here, and she determinedly put it to the back of her mind, not wanting to spoil the moment and her mood. Worrying would get her nowhere.

'Here we are.' Mark spun the wheel and brought the car to a halt just off the road, parking in a lay-by. 'It's just a short walk up there.' He indicated a path that followed the line of a hill about a kilometre from where they stood.

Rose jumped out of the car as Mark grabbed the basket and bottle of wine, handing her a picnic rug. 'So what is it that you need to check on here?' she asked as they walked up the hill.

'Oh, you know, just that the fruit's set properly, whether we might need to bunch-thin later, what the leaf coverage is like.' Mark sounded vague, something Rose wasn't used to from him.

They reached the top of the rise, and Rose stopped suddenly as she saw the view laid out before them. Neat cornrows of vineyards criss-crossed the landscape, a few solitary trees dotted between them, before the land rose up to the Shingle escarpment in the distance. The fading light cast long shadows over the valley and the sky was streaked with pink and rose gold. She had to admit it: sunsets in the Shingle Valley were nothing short of spectacular. The air was clear and warm, gentle birdsong and Rose's own breathing the only sounds. The world seemed to pause for a moment, pleased with its own magnificence.

'Pretty special, huh?'

'That's an understatement.'

'It's my favourite spot in the valley. The place that started it all – the Assignation block. When times are tough, I come here to remind myself how lucky I am to be here at all,' he said, gazing at the view. 'What makes it all worth it.'

'I can see why. It's incredible.'

'Did you know that Kalkari means "to wait" in the local Aboriginal language?'

Rose shook her head.

'Pretty apt really,' he said with a dry laugh. 'Now come on, let's go and see how these vines are doing.'

They stepped off the path and along one of the leafy rows.

Rose found it hard to concentrate on what Mark was saying, as he explained what he was looking for when he inspected the tightly clustered bunches of tiny green grapes. Her mind kept returning to the fact that he'd brought her somewhere that obviously meant a lot to him. She glowed at the thought.

'. . . so that's what we mean when we talk about *terroir*, the ability for a wine to truly express the place where it was made, the soil, the climate, the geography, the growing conditions ...'

Rose zoned out, enjoying the sound of his voice and the softness of the air as they walked. She imagined walking with him always, enjoying the feeling of being by his side.

'How about we take a break? Are you hungry?' Mark's voice interrupted her daydream. They'd come to the end of a row, where there was a clearing under a large gum tree.

'You bet.' Rose could always eat.

The ground was soft with fallen sword-shaped leaves that gave off the distinctive pungent eucalypt scent.

She spread the picnic rug over the leaves, and they both sat down. Leaning their backs against the trunk of the tree, they were completely hidden from view. Not that there was a soul for miles around in any case.

Mark cracked the seal on the wine and, reaching into the basket, produced two glasses with a flourish. 'Drinking the wine from the place where the grapes grew. Nothing like it, hey?'

As the deep purple-red liquid glugged into their glasses, Rose looked up and caught him staring at her. They locked eyes and the world stood still.

Rose blinked first.

'Cheers,' he said softly, clinking his glass against hers.

'Cheers,' she echoed, and tipped her head back to sip the rich, fruity wine.

They feasted on the picnic Mark had brought: wood-fired bread, smeared with a terrine that Rose had made the previous day, ripe strawberries and a small fresh goat's cheese from the Shingle Dairy. The wine disappeared as they chatted easily, laughing about Leo's not entirely successful attempts to train Barnsie and Luisa's efforts to catch the chooks, talking about everything and nothing. The shadows lengthened over the vineyard and Rose shivered slightly as the sun's warmth began to leave them.

'Here, come closer. You're cold.'

She scooted over to Mark. It felt like the most natural thing in the world for him to put his arm around her shoulders. She breathed in the scent of him, spicy and masculine, just as she had when he'd held her after the fire at Trevelyn's. She'd never felt so utterly safe, so utterly at peace.

And then he turned, and she raised her face up to his and he kissed her, delicately at first, then deeper. He pulled her down so that he was half lying on top of her, resting an elbow on the ground, his other hand cupping her breast through the thin fabric of her shirt.

'Oh, Rose, you have no idea what you do to me,' he muttered into her hair.

She answered by pulling him tighter in, drawing his hips onto hers. She felt the hardness of him, his long muscled legs stretched out alongside hers, their boots entwining, rucking up the picnic blanket and tipping an abandoned glass on its side.

He dragged his mouth away from hers, his breath rasping as he deftly unbuttoned the front of her shirt, pulling the hem of it free from her jeans. Rose gasped as his mouth found the rosy bud of her nipple, teasing it through the lace of her bra. He gave a low groan and rolled her sideways, using his other hand to unhook the underwear, and then his mouth was on the bare flesh of her breast. He gently trailed a line of kisses along its soft underside, then down towards her taut stomach and along her hipbone. A white heat engulfed her and she was beyond coherent thought. As if of their own accord, her hands dragged his shirt off and over his head, exposing the wide brown expanse of his back and the fine pelt of hair across his chest that trailed down to his belt buckle. Rose kissed him hungrily, running her hands up and down his bare skin. It was Mark's turn to shiver at the sensation.

Rose thought she could hear music, a lilting melody that carried on the breeze. The sound grew louder. Mark groaned and rolled away from her, reaching into his back pocket and pulling out his phone. 'Dammit, I thought I'd turned this off.'

Rose raised her eyes to the heavens, seeing that the first glimmerings of the Milky Way, millions of light years above them, had emerged. She couldn't believe they'd been interrupted just as things were finally getting interesting.

Just my sodding luck. This had better be good.

Mark cleared his throat. 'Hello?'

There was silence as Mark listened to the voice on the other end of the phone. 'I see. No, you did the right thing, we'll come straight away.'

Rose looked blankly at him.

'It's Leo. He's running a temperature of over forty and Astrid says that Panadol isn't touching it.'

Rose immediately felt guilty. Poor boy. 'Right, let's get a move on then.'

'Sorry, Rose,' said Mark. Their eyes met. She could see the regret in his.

'Don't be daft. It's not your fault.'

She buttoned up her shirt and together they packed up the remains of the picnic, then dashed back to the car as fast as their legs would take them. Mark floored the engine and they spun onto the road back to Kalkari.

'How is he?' he asked as they pushed open the door to Leo's room. Astrid was sitting on the side of his bed, sponging the little boy's forehead with a cloth.

'He is still very hot. He's also very restless.'

'Dad. Rose,' Leo called them over. 'I don't feel very well.' As he finished speaking he sat up in bed and vomit sprayed out of his mouth and nose with such force that it caught Rose front-on and spattered Mark too. A sour smell immediately filled the room and Leo began to sob and choke.

'It's alright, sweetie,' soothed Astrid. 'I know, honey, it's rotten to be sick.' She looked at his pyjamas, which were soaked with vomit. 'Now, let's get these off and change the sheets too, eh?' Leo was now shivering like a dog left out in the cold. 'How about a nice warm bath?'

While Astrid and Mark took Leo to clean up, Rose opened the window as wide as it would go and began stripping the sheets. Rose dumped them in the downstairs laundry, found a clean set and set about re-making Leo's bed.

When he returned, there was a bit more colour in his cheeks and Astrid took his temperature again.

'Thirty-eight-point-seven. That's better. His temperature's coming down, thank God,' Astrid said. 'I'm sorry to have bothered you, but I was so worried when the medicine wouldn't work.'

'Don't be silly. You did exactly the right thing. I was only out in the vineyard, in any case,' said Mark.

'Daddy, can you stay?' whimpered Leo.

'Of course, mate. I'm right here.'

Rose left them alone, retreating to the barn to hose herself off. Mark was a wonderful father, that much was evident, but there was nothing like a bout of projectile vomiting to take the shine off a romantic tryst.

CHAPTER 27

'It's only the most prestigious bloody wine show in Australia,' Dan grumbled to Rose. 'Nothing to get too het up about.' She'd popped over to the winery with some morning tea and made the mistake of asking Dan what was up. It turned out that the Melbourne Wine Show was being judged that week, and Kalkari had a number of wines entered in different classes.

'Don't remind me. I'm trying my best not to think about it,' said Mark, coming over and helping himself to a large slab of sultana cake. He was noticeably on edge. 'I just want to know about the Assignation. It ought to do well, but who can tell what the judges thought on the day, or what the competition was like?'

'It's still a bloody good wine, no matter what,' Dan reassured him.

'Thanks. I know we know that, but if it gets up, it'll be

just what we need. The rest of the country will take a bit of notice of us and our little valley for once.'

It was no use telling Mark to calm down, thought Rose. He was wound tighter than a two-dollar watch. Not surprising really. Despite how much he tried not to let it show, she now realised how much this mattered to him, how much he needed it to help get the winery out of the red.

Earlier in the week Mark had received a call asking him to supply several cases of the Assignation for the wine show dinner. This was a pretty big tip-off that it had done well, but other than that they had no idea. Mark and Dan were flying to Melbourne later that afternoon, both of them last-minute invitees to the dinner, where medals and trophy winners were to be announced. The signs were promising – but there were no guarantees.

The phone call came just after nine-thirty that night. Rose had been checking her phone repeatedly since about eight, making sure it hadn't run out of charge. She and Astrid and Jake were watching TV, but none of them really paying much attention to it. They were all waiting to hear the news from Melbourne.

She could barely hear over the roar of noise in the background.

'We did it, Rose! We did it!' It was Dan. She could tell he was practically jumping for joy at the other end of the line. 'We won the bloody Jimmy Watson!'

Rose let out a whoop, as Astrid and Jake looked questioningly at her, anticipation on their faces.

'Wahooo!' she yelled down the phone. 'That's awesome! Congratulations! How's Mark?'

'He's right here. Just a minute, he wants a word.'

'Rose, we did it! The Assignation won! It was incredible, just incredible. I knew it was good, but crikey, I'm blown away. It's just bloody brilliant!' Mark was rambling, clearly over the moon.

Dan came back on the line, 'Sorry, love, but we've gotta go, they're calling Mark for interviews. We'll see you all tomorrow.'

Rose and Astrid looked at each other and beamed, then hugged each other with joy. 'Well, that should put him in a good mood until at least Christmas,' said Astrid, laughing.

'We'd better organise a party for their return. Whaddya think?' said Jake. 'Get the valley together – this win is great for them too, and I'll bet they'll want to congratulate the boss.'

'Oh, you bet! I'll call Windsong, and Lilybells, let the boys know there'll be a celebration tomorrow,' replied Astrid, heading off to find her phone.

'He likes you, you know,' said Jake.

'What do you mean?' asked Rose.

'He likes you. Mark. I can see it in the way he looks at you. He's had a rough trot by all accounts, and he's a decent bloke. Go easy on him.'

'I'm not sure what you're getting at,' said Rose. 'Anyway, he's too old for me,' she said, echoing Mark's words to her of a few months ago. 'He's my boss, and in case you'd forgotten, he is still married, you know.'

'Yeah, but it doesn't sound like she'll be back in a hurry now, does it?'

'Not even to see the kids?'

'Well, yeah, maybe that, but the local intel is that she never liked it here, never settled. And Mark's a man of this land. He belongs here. Just as you do.'

'Well, you're all up to speed on everything, aren't you? What's it to you anyway?' Rose said feeling irritated at Jake's know-it-all attitude. He'd only been here five minutes and already he was sticking his oar in, assuming he knew best.

'I like to know what's what, and I'm all for a happy workplace,' Jake said lightly. 'Anyway, we've got a party to throw. Bring it on! I hope they won't have celebrated too hard tonight, 'cause they'll get more of the same tomorrow.'

Rose and Astrid put the word out – not that they really needed to, as by the next morning the entire valley was buzzing with the news. Everyone they spoke to was thrilled for Mark and promised to be there that night.

While Astrid got Leo off to school, Rose headed into Eumeralla. She bumped into Bevan as she was on her way into the butchers.

'Heard the news. It's just amazing!' he said, hugging her.

'Yep, we're all pretty stoked about it,' said Rose, the Aussie lingo she'd picked up coming easily to her now.

'Want a hand tonight?'

'That'd be cool. I'm just getting a ton of sausages and some steaks. A few people have promised to bring salads. I've no idea exactly how many are coming though.'

'Oh, if I know the valley, it'll be practically everyone who can walk. We haven't had something as awesome as this to celebrate in a very long time. Everyone is so proud of Mark; they know how tough he's had it recently, and it might even bring a few of them round to his way of doing things,' said Bevan.

'Well, I think I'll be cleaning the butcher out then!' said Rose with a laugh.

She stopped off at Sacred Grounds to check her emails – there was one from Henry, but she deliberately left it unopened. She didn't want to think about it right then.

The weather looked set to be fine, so later that afternoon Astrid and Rose pulled out several trestle tables that they'd found at the back of the winery, lining them up under the she-oak and covering them with checked tablecloths. Leo and Luisa raced about trying to keep Barnsie under control as the hyped-up puppy snapped at balloons that festooned the cellar door and hung from the tree. Jake had helped them drag over an old tin bath so that it now sat outside the cellar door, and Bevan had promised to bring over several bags of ice to add to it for a makeshift drinks cooler.

They were just finishing setting up, as a flock of what Rose now knew to be galahs wheeled overhead, their rose-pink underbellies catching the fading light. The valley glowed in the setting sun. She was beginning to wonder what time Mark and Dan would be back from the airport, when she saw a telltale plume of dust in the distance. That must be them, she thought, and, suddenly feeling shy, raced off to clean herself up and find something more feminine than the faded t-shirt, dusty cut-off shorts and work boots she was wearing.

As she wound her long dark hair into a sleek twist and secured it with a silver butterfly pin that had been a gift from Henry, the knowledge that she should have read his email worried away at her. She was completely torn between her loyalty to him and her fondness – actually it was more than fondness – for Mark and everything at Kalkari. She reasoned that the news of the winery's success had probably already made its way to London. Winning the Jimmy Watson was a big deal, she now realised. She wasn't sure what it might mean for Henry's plans, and she found herself hoping that the winery might no longer be of interest to him, though she figured that chances were it would probably make it even more appealing. She also wasn't sure what the Jimmy Watson win might mean for her, for her place here, and for her fragile relationship with Mark, if a few brief but brilliant kisses and a bit of fooling around in the vines were anything to pin your hopes on.

She'd lied to Jake when she'd said she thought Mark was too old for her. He was older, that much was true, but she felt so in tune with him, whether they were out running together through the valley or chatting quietly in the barn.

Hell, even on that silent drive back from Sydney after the dinner she'd loved just being near him.

She pushed thoughts of her brother out of her head and concentrated instead on the much more appealing prospect of seeing Mark again soon. He'd only been away a couple of days, but she'd missed him like crazy. Applying a slick of gloss to her already rosy lips, she looked at her reflection. She saw clear eyes and sun-bronzed skin, cheekbones that had been previously hidden under a layer of chub, as well as a glow that came from the hours spent outdoors and the daily exercise she was now getting. She looked so much happier too, she thought, briefly remembering the days in London when she looked and felt permanently exhausted. A world and a lifetime ago. What a shame she was planning on partying hard tonight and writing off some of that healthy living, she thought mischievously, clicking the lid back on the lipgloss and striding over to the cellar door.

CHAPTER 28

Everyone had made a huge effort. The tables nearly bowed under the weight of three enormous glass bowls of salad, and there was a pretty array of fruity and creamy desserts covered with muslin cloths. 'Keeps the flies off,' explained Mrs B, who'd come over early to help out. A trail of cars snaked up the long drive, unloading passengers hoisting slabs of beer on their shoulders, or carrying clutches of bottles or trays of food in their hands.

Deano and Mick had ditched the polar fleece for once and were looking unusually smart in pressed cotton shirts and moleskin trousers. Hell, it looked like they'd even shined their R.M. Williams boots for the occasion. Rose was impressed. They were standing with Dan, hanging on his words as he described the previous night's events, waving his hands around with the excitement of it all. Even Dan had tamed his normally wild beard and was wearing a collared shirt. Wonders would never cease.

She almost didn't recognise Angie, who was standing near them, wearing a flouncy floral frock instead of her usual sweatshirt and jeans, though when Rose looked down she saw she was wearing the same boots as the boys, but topped by vivid pink socks.

Angie was chatting to Jake, whose hair gleamed from a recent wash. He was turning the full force of his charm on her, and Angie didn't look at all displeased to be the object of his attention.

Bevan had already fired up the barbie and was grilling meat with practised skill, a pair of tongs dangling from one hand and a beer grasped in the other.

'Anything I can do?' she asked, looking around for a sign of Mark.

'No sweat, sweetheart, it's all under control. Go and grab a drink and enjoy yourself,' he replied.

Rose remembered that she'd bought some paper napkins earlier that day and went into the house to collect them from the kitchen. As she was walking through the hall, she saw Mark's boots and long legs making their way down the stairs.

'Rose? Is that you?' his voice boomed in the hallway.

'Here, Mark.'

'Wow, you're a sight for sore eyes,' said Mark as he reached her. 'Love the outfit. Very nice.'

Rose looked down at her shiny silver dress. 'Thanks. Astrid lent it to me. It's not too short, is it?'

Mark rested one hand on his chin and pretended to give the question serious thought. 'I'm not sure. Let me just check.'

As he walked behind her she couldn't suppress a bubble of laughter that welled up inside her. 'Yeah, right, I guess it isn't. Congratulations again, by the way. You must be dead chuffed.'

'Yup. It's huge. I still don't think it's sunk in yet,' he said, 'though we certainly celebrated last night, and by the looks of things we'll be repeating that again tonight. Thanks for pulling this all together, by the way; you're amazing.'

Rose was thrilled at the unexpected compliment. 'Oh, it was nothing really. We all helped, and once the word was out the whole district wanted to come and congratulate you. Not to mention that everyone around here seems to love an excuse to have a party,' she said.

'That they do.'

Their eyes met. Rose's throat was suddenly parched and she struggled to swallow. Mark reached out to her, tucking a stray tendril of hair back into the butterfly clip and letting his hand linger on the nape of her neck. A jolt of electricity ran through her at his touch, turning her stomach to liquid and her knees weak with lust. She was absolutely certain what she wanted now. She just had to be brave, or foolish, enough to go through with it.

He must have read her mind.

Wordlessly, he pulled her to him, pressing her lips to his and kissing her like she was the sweetest nectar, neither of them caring that he was smearing her lipgloss or that her hair had come loose from the clip. She needed no further encouragement to wind her arms around him, pressing herself to him, hips meeting hips, her breasts crushed against his chest.

Once again, they lit a fire inside each other. 'Oh Rose,' he murmured in her ear. 'To hell with being sensible. You have no idea …' His voice trailed off as he resumed kissing her.

Rose felt rather than heard the hammering of both their hearts, and sank into the heat he was giving off through his thin shirt. If he hadn't been holding her up, her legs would most likely have given way beneath her. She wasn't used to compliments, and his extravagant whisperings left her breathless, not to mention the exquisite touch of his lips as they traced a trail along her collarbone that left her begging for more. She wanted him, a big bed and no interruptions.

Unfortunately, the universe wasn't listening.

But someone else was.

'Daaad.'

They leapt away from each other at the sound of Leo's voice. The boy was looking at them from the kitchen doorway.

'Dad, can we come outside for a bit?' Leo seemed unfazed to have caught his father in a clinch with Rose.

'Sure thing, mate. How about we go and get this party started, hey?' Mark shot Rose a rueful look and mouthed the word 'later' to her over Leo's head. Rose smiled back. She'd have to clamp her thighs shut a while longer. A glass of wine might help cool her jets. They headed over to the cellar door, where Jake had managed to rig up an outdoor sound system and had INXS blaring from the speakers at full volume.

The night was warm, the stars lit up the vast sky, and the mood was exuberant. Bevan had been right; almost the whole of the valley had turned up. Everyone had brought a plate or dish of something, and Harry the butcher arrived with several more kilos of sausages, so there was more than enough food to go round. As for booze, Rose couldn't believe the amount that was being thrown back. *For winemakers, they sure know how to drink beer*, she thought as she caught sight of the growing pile of empties.

As Mark and Dan walked towards the throng of guests, Rose heard the applause begin. They all but disappeared under a sea of congratulatory back slaps and man hugs. Everyone was genuinely thrilled for them.

'Reckon we oughta put the price up, hey, boss?' said Dan to Mark as they stood around later that evening.

'No way. It's a thirty-dollar red and that's the way I hope it's going to stay. I might have an argument on my hands with the distributors, though, but we'll jump off that bridge when we get to it. This puts us on the map. Kalkari. The Shingle Valley. They're up there with the greats now. It's more than I dreamed of. People will be clamouring for our wine. The best restaurants will want it on their lists. The knock-on effect on the other wines should mean we'll be out of the woods as far as money worries are concerned. We can all sleep a little easier at night, and concentrate on what we're good at – making wine, not cosying up to bank managers.'

Rose overheard them talking and couldn't help but be happy. She knew now that the last thing she wanted to do was to betray Mark, no matter what her promises and allegiances to her brother might be. She wanted only the best for him. She also knew, with a sudden realisation, that she wanted to stay, to be a part of it, to be a part of Kalkari and

237

Mark's life. As she watched the party swirl around her she knew with absolute certainty that she belonged here, that this was good and right and true. That this was the best thing that ever happened to her.

Oh shit. This wasn't supposed to happen.

Someone turned the music up and Rose found herself pulled over to dance. She shimmied to the energetic sound, feeling vibrant and free in that instant, not caring about what the future might bring, soaking up the moment in this lush valley, on a warm evening, surrounded by her friends. Jake grabbed her by the hand and twirled her around on the grass in front of the cellar door, making her dizzy, but she still didn't want to stop. She closed her eyes as the world spun before her.

'Might want to take it a little easy there, Rose.' Mark's voice interrupted her thoughts.

She snapped open her eyes as he gathered her in his arms and steadied her against him. 'Wheee …' she giggled, aware that the wine she'd knocked back earlier in the evening had gone straight to her head.

'You, my girl, look like you need to go to bed,' he said quietly in her ear.

'Oh yes, please!' She grinned cheekily at him.

'Now, Rose, you know that's not quite what I meant. Though, come to think of it, I wouldn't mind unwrapping that shiny silver disco dress you're wearing. It'd make a fitting coming-home present, don't you think?' It seemed she wasn't the only one whose inhibitions had been washed away by the alcohol. Rose's knees weakened for the second time that evening.

Mark reluctantly released her and steered her over to an empty seat under the tree. 'But before I do I'd better go and check on the grog. This lot could drink enough to sink the Titanic.'

Hearing Vance Joy's 'Georgia' blasting through the speakers, Rose stood up again. 'Don't be such a spoilsport, there's more than enough booze, and you have to dance to this with me. *She* ...' Rose began to sing, off-key. In her drunken state the lyrics seemed to make perfect sense. Hell, they made perfect sense drunk or not.

She didn't get any further: she suddenly noticed the expression on Mark's face. It was utterly bleak. 'Is my singing really that bad?' she asked.

Before he could answer, a tall woman in a skirt slit to mid-thigh, her sheer blouse undone several buttons lower than would normally be considered decent, and her dark hair in a cloud about her face, sashayed up and flung her arms around him. She had the kind of larger-than-life beauty that launched ships and inspired poetry.

'Hey, *we* were about to dance!' Rose nearly called out. She stopped herself just in time.

With a sickening realisation, she knew who it was. Her heart, which had been floating somewhere above the clouds only a moment before, now plummeted like a pheasant on the Glorious Twelfth.

Mark staggered slightly under the force of the woman's embrace. 'Isabella ... What? How? I thought you were in Barcelona?'

'I flew in this morning, and the news of your fantastical

win was all over the papers. I had to come and congratulate you. Mark, it is amazing. I am so proud of you. I knew you could do it. You are the hero.'

Standing only a few steps away, Rose couldn't help but hear everything. The smell of the heavy perfume that had followed Isabella's entrance made her feel queasy and her head spun.

So this is her. Isabella. Mark's wife. Fuck.

Suddenly sober, and feeling as deflated as a week-old party balloon, Rose knew that whatever flirtation she and Mark had going on paled into insignificance beside Isabella's claim. It also didn't help that the Spanish woman was terrifyingly elegant and composed, making Rose suddenly feel like a dishevelled, self-conscious teenager.

She turned away, blinking back tears, and found some glasses and plates to clear up. Operating on autopilot, she began to attack the debris of the party. A rumble of thunder sounded in the distance and Barnsie, who'd been tied up near the cellar door, began to howl at the sound. The air had become heavy, and clouds scudded over the formerly bright night sky.

Dan came up to her and gently took a glass from her hand. 'Oh, love, I can see you're upset. It's Isabella, isn't it?'

Rose nodded dumbly. 'Sorry, Dan, I can't...' She turned and fled to the barn, hardly registering the fat raindrops falling on her bare arms and splattering on the gravel. Barnsie, who'd been released from his tether, followed her in. She hadn't the heart to send him outside. She collapsed on the sofa, burying her face in the dog's damp fur.

CHAPTER 29

Peering out of the window the next morning, Rose could see that the sky was a blameless pale blue, as if the storm had washed it clean and hung it out to dry. There was a hollow feeling in her stomach as she remembered the party and Isabella's unexpected entrance. She'd thought Giles breaking up with her had hurt, but this was a kind of pain unlike any she'd ever experienced. Until last night she hadn't admitted to herself that she was in love with Mark, but now she could feel her heart – and her hopes and dreams – breaking into a million little pieces.

Her head pounded from the wine she'd drunk and her mouth and mood were as foul as a parrot's cage. There was only one thing for it. She tugged on her running shorts and a singlet, threaded her hair through a visor and laced up her shoes. The going would be muddy but she wasn't going to let that stop her.

Rounding the path that led to the cellar door she came upon the desecrated scene of the previous night's festivities: empty bottles scattered over the tables and littering the lawn, and a handful of cold sausages abandoned in the grease on the barbecue. She'd see to it all later; hopefully Astrid would help too. Now it was time to run – to run away from her disappointment, run until it couldn't keep up with her.

As she reached the top of the hill, she looked down on Trevelyn Cottage and wondered what would happen to it now. Vera and Violet were out of hospital and on the mend, but as the house was so badly damaged by the fire, they had gone to stay with some relatives instead. Rose ran down and picked her way along the weed-strewn paths through the vines and stopped in the veggie patch. It was overgrown, but she could see peapods of a decent size scrambling up a trellis and some baby tomatoes just starting to turn scarlet. She resolved to come back later on if she had time and give the patch a good weeding. She wanted to do something to help out her absent neighbours. She had to keep busy. Anything to take her mind off Mark and Isabella. She choked back a sob.

Turning back up the hill between the two properties, she hastened her stride. The late night meant that she had slept in, and no doubt the hungry hordes would be waiting for breakfast back at Kalkari. Regardless of how she might be feeling, she still had to feed everyone.

Sure enough, there was a clamour coming from the kitchen as she kicked off her mud-clagged trainers on the back verandah. She heard whistling, and walked in to find Jake frying up eggs and bacon while entertaining Leo and Luisa with silly faces and noises. He was pretty chipper this morning, she thought. There was no sign of Mark or Isabella.

'Doing me out of a job there, hey?' said Rose, trying to put a brave face on things. She was too proud to let anyone see her misery, particularly Jake.

'Well these two monkeys were starving, and so was I for that matter.' He smiled at her through his floppy dark hair, then expertly flipped the eggs over and slid them onto plates. 'Coming right up, guys.'

'What's coming right up?' asked Mark as he walked into the kitchen. His hair was newly washed, hanging in damp tendrils, and he looked fresh-faced and rested. He avoided Rose's eyes. 'What a party, hey?' he said to no-one in particular, grabbing a slice of toast and slathering it with butter and Vegemite. 'And how are you two rascals doing?' he asked, ruffling Leo's hair with one hand as he held the toast in the other, and then stealing a kiss from Luisa. 'I've got a surprise for you.'

'What? What?' cried Luisa.

'A surprise?' Leo was curious.

'Yep, come on. Help me put these things on a tray and we'll take them upstairs.'

'Upstairs?' asked Leo.

'Yes, mate. That's where the surprise is.'

Mark loaded up a tray with eggs, toast and juice and beckoned the kids to come with him.

Rose's heart sank. Any tiny hope she'd been clinging to that Isabella hadn't stayed, that there was still a chance for her and Mark, was cruelly dashed.

'You okay?' asked Jake, seeing her stricken expression. 'Uh-oh. The return of the estranged wife put a spanner in the works, huh?'

Rose didn't answer him. There was nothing to say. She could hear Luisa's excited laughter coming from upstairs.

Mark reappeared in the doorway. 'Rose, can I have a word?' he asked. 'I've got something over at the cellar door that I'd like to ask you about.'

'Sure thing,' she said, feeling like she was heading to the executioner. They headed out of the kitchen and onto the back verandah, away from the kitchen window. Once they were out of earshot of the house, Mark stopped, a look of contrition on his face.

'Rose, I'm really sorry about last night. Believe me: I had no idea that Isabella was going to turn up like that. But she is the kids' mother and until recently it was her home. I couldn't just kick her out. You and me, well, it's just really bad timing. Oh, Rose, I wish things were different, I really do, but right now I can't get involved. It's not fair to get you involved either. I've got so much stuff I need to sort out. I hope you understand.'

Rose nodded. She'd been expecting this. She really had no right to try and convince him otherwise.

'Look, Rose, the kids adore you. Everyone here likes you. Even Dan can't stop singing your praises. Between you and Astrid, you've really brightened things up around here. Kalkari is a much happier place to be. Please stay – oh look, I'm making a hash of this …'

She took a step back, putting as much distance between them as she could.

'I don't know, Mark. I need to think.'

'Okay,' he said, 'I'll respect your decision. I know I'm asking a lot of you.'

She turned away from him and walked towards the barn. The last thing she wanted was for him to see her cry.

Isabella wasn't the only new arrival at Kalkari that day. Before the Jimmy Watson win, Jake had managed to track down a source in the west of the state, and had been promised his special delivery would be on a truck within the week. 'The kids are going to be so excited,' he'd said as he'd explained to Rose what he was planning. 'I feel like a big kid myself.'

'Quick, Leo, Luisa, come and see what we've got,' he called into the house as a big livestock truck crunched its gears up the drive.

'What is it, Jake?' asked Leo as he followed him, racing around to the winery, Astrid, Rose and Luisa falling in behind.

'Whaddya think?' he asked, proudly indicating the creamy, pint-sized four-legged animals that were now skittering out of the truck, bleating and trotting around in the vineyard, checking out their new surroundings.

'What on earth are they?' asked Astrid.

'Woolly weeders!' he said, sounding very pleased with himself.

'What?'

'Babydoll sheep. They're going to graze in between the vines, keep the weeds down and add their own personal brand of fertiliser straight to the soil.'

'Crikey, mate!' exclaimed Dan as he came out of the shadows of the winery, scratching his head. 'Are *ewe* joking? Ewe – geddit?' He guffawed at his pun. 'The boss know about this?'

'Yup. Sure does. Got the go-ahead last week.'

'Aww, they're so cute,' said Astrid, gazing at them.

'Now, no grabbing one for a nice lamb roast, Rose,' he warned. 'These cost us a pretty penny.'

'I wouldn't dream of it. They look far too cuddly to cook,' said Rose.

'Can we pat them, Jakey?' asked Luisa.

'Well, I'm not sure how tame they are, but once they've settled in, you can have a go. Gonna need to train Barnsie up to keep 'em in line.'

Leo's eyes shone at the prospect. 'Can I help too?'

'Sure you can, mate. You're gonna be my right-hand man,' said Jake.

'Well I never,' said Dan, shaking his head. 'Never thought I'd see the day. So we're sheep farmers now too, hey?'

'You'd better believe it. These babies are gonna more than pay their way.'

CHAPTER 30

Rose was walking over to clear up some of previous night's mess when she saw a car heading up the drive. Not recognising it, she stopped to see who it might be. Perhaps it was the irrigation people arriving early. Jake had mentioned something about them at breakfast, but Rose hadn't really been paying attention. Her mind had been on other things.

The car came to an abrupt halt, wheels spitting gravel as it turned in a large arc. An elderly couple emerged. The woman had faded blonde hair streaked with grey and wore a tweedy green overcoat, teamed with a loudly patterned silk scarf knotted at her neck. The man was dressed almost identically, although he sported a checked deerstalker instead of the scarf. They looked like they'd stepped straight out of an alpine postcard.

'*Grüß Gott!* We are looking for Astrid.' the woman said.

'Have we come to the right place?' The woman's accent was unmistakeable.

'Hello there! Yes, you certainly have come to the right place,' Rose said. 'Welcome to Kalkari.'

'Oh good. We have travelled so far. I am exhausted,' the woman replied.

'Of course, you must be. Astrid's out at the moment with Luisa, but they should be back by lunchtime. Come this way and I'll get you something to drink while you wait,' replied Rose. 'Sorry about the mess here – we had a bit of a party last night. Kalkari won a big award.' She shepherded them to the bench under the she-oak, hastily removing several of the empty bottles that had fallen beneath it like so many dead soldiers. The woman raised her eyebrows before settling herself on the bench, but said nothing.

Rose's mind worked overtime. They were clearly Astrid's parents, but what on earth were they doing here? Astrid, she was certain, was not expecting them.

Rose hastily rinsed out a teapot and sliced up some leftover lemon tart from the party. Digging in the back of a cupboard, she located some pretty floral china cups and saucers. She guessed that Astrid's parents, her mother in particular, were the type who would appreciate them. As she came back out of the house carrying a tray laden with tea things, she saw the couple looking bemusedly around them, clearly unimpressed by the party detritus.

'I'm Rose, by the way. I work here with Astrid,' she said as she settled the tray on a nearby table.

'Ah, I see,' said the woman as she reached to pour the

teapot, lifting the lid to inspect it. 'I am Helga and this is Hans.' She pointed at her companion. 'We are the parents of Astrid.'

'I guessed you probably were. Astrid will be so thrilled to see you,' Rose said brightly. She was getting better at this lying thing.

She hurried back to the barn to retrieve her phone and warn Astrid of the new arrivals.

Astrid wasn't answering, so Rose sent her a quick text asking her to call urgently. Rather than sit around biting her nails, she went out again to start clearing up the remains of the party. Helga and Hans, it seemed, had finished their tea, and she could see them walking down the tree-lined drive, Hans hobbling along next to his wife, who was pointing at the vines and then throwing her arms up in the air. Rose could see her mouth opening and closing, but the breeze was blowing in the wrong direction for her to hear what she was saying. They appeared to be having an argument.

'Halloo, we're back! Anyone home?' Astrid called out as she huffed up to the back verandah with Luisa balanced on one hip. The house was silent. She carried the little girl through to the kitchen and set her in her highchair.

'Now, Miss Lulu, what is it to be? Cheese? Avocado?

A sandwich?'

'Soup, please!' demanded the little girl.

'Okay, then, I think there's some in here,' she said, opening the fridge and peering inside.

Rose had heard the car pull up, and jogged over from where she was still clearing up outside the cellar door. 'Hey, Astrid,' she puffed, out of breath. 'You'll never guess who's here.'

'I know. Thommo told me that Isabella is back. Oh God, that's all we need. That woman, she is batshit crazy. You'll see what I mean now for sure. '

'No,' said Rose. 'It's not Isabella.'

'Who then? Ryan Gosling?' Astrid giggled. 'He has decided to come to the Shingle Valley? Spill your beans, Rose. He's left Eva Mendes and decided to move to Australia. He heard you were here.'

'Umm, I'm surprised you didn't bump into them on our way up the drive actually,' said Rose.

'What, Ryan really is here? Tell me, yes? Come on, who is it really?' she asked, blowing on the bowl of soup she'd heated up for Luisa.

'We–ell,' said Rose. 'You might want to brace yourself for this.'

At that moment there was a knock on the door. 'Hallooo. Anybody there?'

The voice was muffled, but Astrid went white as a sheet and nearly dropped the bowl of soup she was holding. 'Oh, *mein Gott*. You are kidding me, yes?'

'No kidding around here, kiddo. The parentals have

come to visit,' said Rose.

'*Christus!* Oooh, sorry Luisa,' she said, covering the little girl's ears. Astrid's hands then went reflexively to her stomach, smoothing the bump. 'Oh, holy cows. This is the last thing I need. Can you pretend I'm not here?'

'I think it's a bit late for that.'

Astrid made a face and went to open the front door.

'Astrid, *liebling*.' Her mother inclined her cheek for a kiss. 'Where have you been? We have been waiting for you a long time.'

'*Mutti*, what a lovely surprise,' said Astrid, dutifully pecking her on both cheeks. 'If you had told me you were coming, of course I would have been here. I had no idea you were even thinking of travelling. It's such a long way to come. What are you doing here anyway?'

'You are our daughter, Astrid, in case you'd forgotten, and you have been away from home for a long time now. In any case, our old friends the Kaufmanns – you remember them? Well, they came to lunch a few weeks ago and were so enthusiastic about their visit to Australia, so we thought, well, why should we not come and surprise you, didn't we, Hans?'

'Hallo, *Prinzessin*,' Hans boomed as he held out his arms to her. 'How are you? It's so good to see you, *Liebling*. Let's have a look at you.'

'Astrid! What? Look at you. You have let yourself go? Tell me this is just fattening Australian food,' demanded Helga.

Astrid's loose top could fool most people, even her father, but not her gimlet-eyed mother.

'No, *Mutti*, it isn't.' She took a deep breath. 'This will be your first grandchild.'

'What on earth?' said Hans. 'But you're far too young to have a baby. Why, you're still just a girl yourself. What have you been up to?'

'Come on, father, do I have to explain that?'

Hans looked momentarily embarrassed. 'Who is responsible, hmm? I will have a few words to say to him. We didn't know you even had a boyfriend, did we, Helga?'

'Please don't be upset. It's all going to be fine. He's a good man, and he's going to take care of us,' Astrid replied, a determined set to her jaw. She didn't elaborate any further.

'Well, you will be coming back home, of course,' said her mother. 'Immediately. You're far too young and far too far away to cope with this on your own, whether the father is around or not. You're not even twenty yet! I don't suppose he plans to marry you, eh?'

'Young people today,' said Hans, blowing out his cheeks with exasperation. 'Perhaps I should have brought my shot-gun with me?'

'Father!' exclaimed Astrid, horrified.

'You think I make a joke? I do not joke about this.'

Astrid clutched her stomach. For a moment, Rose, who had been watching from the shadows of the kitchen door, in case things got really out of hand and Astrid needed her, wondered if she was ill. But then she heard her exclaim, 'Oh! I can feel kicking!'

Rose couldn't help herself and she rushed forward to

hug her friend. 'Oh, Astrid, really? Where? Show me! Can I feel it?'

The harsh expression on Astrid's mother's face didn't falter, but Astrid turned to face her bravely, her hand protectively on the curve of her belly. Rose stood by, her arm still around her friend's shoulders. '*Mutti*, I do appreciate you coming all this way to see me, but you can't take over my life. I'm happy here, really I am, and it's all going to be just fine. You'll see. Now, why don't you come in and we can get a room ready for you. You can take a shower and then come and have some lunch? I know Mark won't mind you staying for a few days.'

'Did I hear my name?' said Mark, who was just at that moment walking across the drive.

'So, you're the man responsible, I take it?' Hans Grosskopf glared frostily at him.

'I have no idea what you're talking about. And who, might I ask, are you?' replied Mark, looking both annoyed and perplexed.

'Hans Grosskopf. Astrid's father.'

'Oh, well, it's a pleasure to meet you, Hans. Astrid has been a wonderful addition to the team at Kalkari. I hope we've looked after her like a daughter.' Mark extended his hand.

Astrid's father ignored it, pointedly. 'A daughter? Is that how you see it?' Red veins stood out on his face.

Mark looked puzzled and ran his unshaken hand through his hair. 'Um, yes. Is that a problem?'

Hans looked ready to knock him to the ground.

'Oh, you're being ridiculous Papa,' said Astrid, exasperation in her voice. 'Of course it's not Mark who is the father.'

'Father?' echoed Mark. 'Whose father? Astrid, I thought this man was your father? Can someone tell me what's going on?'

'Oh *Christus*! I am sorry about this, Mark. I'd been waiting for the right time to tell you, but it seems Papa has let the dog out of the bag. I'm afraid I'm going to have a baby.'

'Bloody hell, really?' Mark looked astonished. 'I had no idea, Astrid. That'll teach me to open my eyes a bit more,' he said as he glanced more carefully at her midriff. You'd have to look hard to see signs of a bump under Astrid's smocked shirt. 'Are you okay? Is everything okay? Am I the only one who didn't know?'

'So he's not the one responsible? I seem to have the stick at the wrong end. Excuse me, I am tired and we have been travelling for so long,' said Hans.

Mark surveyed them both, speechless for a moment, then, seeing the funny side, began to laugh. 'Well, let's start again, shall we? Good to meet you, Hans, and ...?'

'This is my wife, Helga,' said Hans.

'What a nice surprise for Astrid that you've come to visit,' said Mark. 'Are you here for long? You're welcome to stay, of course. I insist. I'm sure the girls can sort out a spare room for you both.'

'Well, we can't be away for too long. You know how it is,' said Helga, 'But that is a very kind offer.'

'Why don't I show you to your room?' suggested Rose, hoisting Luisa into her arms and ushering them into the hallway.

Rose came down the stairs, having shown Astrid's parents to their room. She heard voices coming from the kitchen and paused, eavesdropping.

'So, Astrid. What's this all about, hey? Is there anything I can help with? Can you tell me who *is* the father?' she heard Mark ask.

'Oh, Mark, you must believe me, I did not plan this. I've been so scared, and I definitely wasn't expecting my father and mother to turn up on the doorstep. I'm going to keep the baby though. And Thommo's been great, really. I'd like to stay working here as long as I can, if you're okay with that.'

'Thommo Drummond, hey? Well, he's a steadier bet than Charlie, so you could have done worse, but things aren't going to be easy, no doubt about that.'

Astrid looked mournful. 'Oh, it's such a mess. Father is going to kill him, I know. I am still a little girl to him. And my mother is insisting I return to Austria.'

'Steady on now, it'll all work out, you'll see,' he reassured her. 'And in any case, I want you to stick around as long as you can, even afterwards if you can manage it. Unless you think you'd be better off going back home? The kids would want you to stay, I'm sure. They both adore you, Astrid. And they will love having a little baby around.'

'Oh Mark, that means so much to me.' Astrid gulped down rising tears. 'I don't want to go anywhere else, and I would hate to leave you all. But what about Isabella? Will you still need me to look after Leo and Luisa if she is back? Will you need Rose?'

'I have no idea how long Isabella plans to stay for, but I'm not holding my breath. The kids need some stability in their life, and they've had more of that in the past few months from you and Rose than Isabella's ever been able to give them,' he said firmly.

'Okay. I just have to convince my parents. I think they want to take me back to the Tyrol on the next plane.'

'Why don't you invite them to meet Thommo, for a meal or a drink perhaps? He's a good bloke, you know, and I've no doubt he'll be able to charm them, especially your mum.'

'I know he is. I'll do that as soon as I've had the chance to warn him, and Mark,' Astrid paused. 'Thanks again, so much. Your understanding means a lot to me.'

'Good. Now that's settled, is there anything for lunch? I could eat a buttered frog,' he said.

Rose smiled to herself. Thank goodness that had gone well. Astrid was two for two. Now all she had to do was win her parents around.

CHAPTER 31

A week later, as Rose was bringing in the dry laundry from the line, she rested the basket on one hip and paused, lost in thought. Seeing Astrid with her parents, difficult as that relationship obviously was, had made her homesick. She really missed Henry. Hell, it would even be nice to see her mum right now. The late afternoon sun cast long shadows, and Rose felt like the house was looming over here, with the hills beyond it: she suddenly felt very small and very far away from home. Mark was holed up in the winery and Isabella, it seemed, was here to stay, for the foreseeable future at least.

Isabella's main aim seemed to be to make Rose's and Astrid's lives as difficult as possible. Nothing was good enough. She complained about Rose's cooking ('too dry', 'too spicy', 'too cold') – though never in front of Mark, Rose noted – and found fault with Astrid's care of the children. 'I don't understand why they shovel their food in like that, honestly. Have you not taught them any manners?'

With Leo and Luisa, she blew hot and cold, one minute smothering them with affection, the next scolding them, irritated by their boisterousness. 'Sit up straight, Leo, you slump like a sack of oranges!' 'Be quiet, Luisa! I can't hear myself think!' She evidently liked the *idea* of being a mother, but perhaps the actual day-to-day demands were far too exhausting and beneath her, thought Rose sourly.

She was also all over Mark, trailing a hand along his as they sat at the dinner table, wrapping an arm around his waist, kissing him extravagantly whenever anyone else was around. 'Remember our honeymoon, darling?' she asked one night at dinner. 'That little restaurant just off the Champs Elysée? Rose, you really must try it when you're next in Paris. They way they cooked the lamb—' she poked at the chops that Rose had cooked as if making a point.

Patronising cow.

To be fair, Mark didn't seem to be responding, and in fact looked rather uncomfortable at Isabella's displays of affection, but it made Rose feel sick to watch the man she was crazy about being fawned over by another woman, even if that woman was his wife and the mother of his children. This thought, in turn, made her feel even worse. Isabella might be a complete bitch, but Mark was her husband, and Leo and Luisa her children. Rose was the odd one out, not Isabella.

It didn't help that Astrid's parents were also staying, so

Rose was busy cooking and clearing up huge meals for a houseful of people. She felt like she was running a fully booked B&B – one where none of the guests left tips or said so much as a word of thanks. Au pairs were usually expected to work around thirty hours a week. Seventy and counting was more like it at the moment. If she hadn't been so fond of the kids, and holding onto a shred of hope that Isabella might change her mind and leave, she would have been off like a shot, back to Bondi.

At least Henry had temporarily stopped hassling her for information. He was in Spain, embroiled in another winery takeover there. When she'd emailed him complaining about Isabella – 'Honestly, she's making life hell. I know she's doing it on purpose too. I don't know what Mark ever saw in her.' – he'd told her to stop whining and remember why she was there. He'd been uncharacteristically curt with her and Rose was hurt by his lack of sympathy.

She'd never felt so alone.

Removing the last of the wisps of fabric that passed for Isabella's lingerie from the line and resisting the urge to tear them to shreds and blame the washing machine – 'You must be careful. They are very expensive,' Isabella had warned – Rose trudged indoors, contemplating the prospect of another boring early night.

She'd just reached the barn when she bumped into Jake, who looked to be on his way out.

'Hey, Rosie, what's up? You look like you've got the weight of the world on your shoulders. Come on, it can't be that bad. Look, if it's any comfort, I don't reckon she'll be hanging around that long. I overheard her and Mark having a doozey of a blue on the phone when we were out in the vineyards this morning.'

Rose's spirits lifted fractionally. 'Really?'

He nodded. 'Anyway, fancy going to the pub? I'm meeting Angie and Deano and some of the others there.'

Rose had been tossing up between getting a head start on the morning's baking for the weekend or collapsing in the barn in front of the telly. *Exciting life I'm leading*, she'd thought.

'Sure, why not?'

As Rose entered the pub, she spotted Astrid and Thommo sitting with Astrid's parents on the far side of the room. Astrid flashed her an anxious look.

'I think they need back-up,' Rose muttered to Jake.

'Really? If I were you I'd be leaving that well alone.'

'I'm going over to give them moral support.' Astrid had had several conversations with Rose about her parents' insistence that she return to Austria with them and her own desire to stay at Kalkari, and how she might convince them of her wishes.

'Well, if you must, but don't say I didn't warn you ...'

Rose made her way over to the table. 'Mr and Mrs Grosskopf, how are you?'

The couple nodded, and Thommo pulled out a seat for her.

'I was just telling my mother about the hospital in New Bridgeton,' said Astrid.

'Oh, yes, I went there with Astrid for her scan. It's terrific. Very modern. There's a special birthing unit. Astrid's going to be in the best possible place, with the best of care.'

Astrid smiled gratefully at her friend for her support, but Helga frowned. 'It's not the hospital that I'm worried about. Astrid's place is at home, with her family.'

'But *Mutti*, I have family here now,' Astrid protested.

'Helga we have to let her make her own mind up,' Hans chipped in.

'Can I get you another drink?' asked Thommo.

'That would be nice, thank you, Thomas,' said Helga. 'This riesling is not so bad actually.'

'We like it,' said Thommo. 'It's a local drop.'

'So, can you be telling me, Thomas—' Astrid's father paused.

'Thommo, please. That's what everyone calls me.'

'Thommo,' he said. 'Tell me, just what are you intending with my daughter?'

'Father, this isn't the Dark Ages!' said Astrid, in an exasperated tone.

'No, it's okay, sweetheart, he's entitled to ask,' said Thommo. 'I have to admit this has taken all of us by surprise, but I intend to stand by Astrid, and do whatever she needs me to do. She can count on me one hundred per cent. And so can the baby.'

'Oh,' huffed Hans, the wind having been clearly taken out of his sails. 'Well, that's good, I suppose.'

'She is still of course going to come home to Austria to have the baby,' insisted Helga. 'There is no question of that.'

CHAPTER 32

'Santa come soon?' asked Luisa as she and Rose trooped over to the henhouse in search of fresh eggs the next morning.

The sun was already burning bright in the sky, with the promise of a scorcher to come, and Rose's head was pounding from one too many beers in the pub the night before. It had been a stupid idea to try to drown her sorrows. All she'd got for her trouble was a killer hangover.

Luisa's question reminded Rose that it was already mid-December: the holiday season was only a few weeks away. She hadn't given it much thought yet, but a hot Christmas was something she couldn't quite get her head around. If she'd been back in England, the air would be sharp with frost, darkness would be falling in the middle of the afternoon, and everyone would be bundled up in winter coats. It all seemed like another world.

'Yes, sweetie, not long now. What would you like Father Christmas to bring you?'

'An umbrella. A dolly. And Mummy stay.'

Rose gulped. She and Mark still hadn't talked about Isabella. In fact, they hadn't talked much at all since Isabella had come back. Only the fact that she couldn't bear to leave the kids kept her hanging on.

'Well, Lulu, let's hope Father Christmas brings you everything you want. Those sound like really good things to wish for,' she said as Luisa skipped off ahead of her. 'Now, how many eggs do you think the ladies will have left us this morning?'

Two days later Mark wandered into the kitchen while Rose was cleaning up the breakfast dishes. She was alone: Astrid was on her way to drop Leo at school.

'Uh, Rose, I'm not really sure what you had planned for the holidays, but Isabella's rented a house at the coast and apparently we're going up there for Christmas. Me and the kids, that is. We'll be back just before New Year's. So you can take some time off then if you want. I realised you haven't had a holiday since you started here in winter, so you're definitely overdue a break.' He looked uncomfortable.

Rose felt as if she'd had all the air knocked out of her lungs. She hadn't seen that coming.

'Oh, I see,' she said doing her best to hide the fact that she felt like she was dying inside. 'Well, that's good.' She tried to sound convincing. She was determined to put on a brave face and not let him see how upset the news had made her. He had his happy family back together, and she knew it was unfair to begrudge him that, but where did that leave her? She turned to face him. 'The kids will be thrilled. Luisa was just telling me how much she wanted her mummy to stay for Christmas.'

'Thanks for understanding. You're a gem.'

Rose didn't feel like a gem. She felt like raging about how unfair it was that her feelings didn't seem to be important to anyone. She felt sorry for herself, very foolish and more than a little pissed off. Had she imagined the words Mark had whispered in her ears only weeks earlier? Was he the same lying coward that Giles had been? Were all men so gutless, or was it just her own rotten luck?

'I do have some plans for the holidays myself actually, so some time off would be good. I had been meaning to ask you about it,' she lied. In fact, she didn't have the slightest clue how she'd spend the time. Perhaps holed up with a batch of triple-chocolate cookie dough and *The Notebook*?

'Oh good. Well, that's settled then.' Mark turned to leave, pausing to grab a slice of the fruitcake that was sitting on the table on his way out. 'Bloody good cake, Rose.'

In that moment, she almost hated him. How could he be so insensitive?

As soon as the kitchen was cleared up, Rose took off for Eumeralla. She needed to see a friendly face and catch up with the news from back home. After a quick chat with Bevan, she settled into her favourite corner at Sacred Grounds and switched on her laptop.

There was no news from Henry, which, depending on how you looked at it, was both good and bad.

She cast her mind back to family Christmases at home with her brother and mum and dad: going to church on Christmas morning, followed by a full English breakfast, then gift opening and a late turkey lunch, toasting the holiday with sherry and a decent claret, before Elaine inevitably fell asleep in front of the TV, leaving the rest of them to squabble over the purple-wrapped hazelnut caramel toffees in the vast tin of Quality Street that accompanied every Bennett Christmas.

She resisted the temptation to email him; she knew he was probably getting impatient at the lack of information she'd been able to give him. Despite Isabella's return and her frustration with Mark, she still felt her loyalties were divided. She had decided that the best course of action was no action for the time being. *Not much of a plan*, she thought despondently.

The only light in that dark day was a brief email from Philippe, who was back in Bondi. He mentioned that he was spending Christmas with Frostie and some other mates; they were planning a morning's surfing followed by a Christmas barbecue and plenty of booze. There was an open invitation for her to join them.

Well, she thought, *it's better than cookie dough and weepy movies*. And at least she didn't have to spend Christmas mooning around a deserted Kalkari feeling even sorrier for herself. The thought of some beach time, a sparkling ocean and the boys' company should have cheered her up, but she was in such a hole she couldn't see a way out of it. Nevertheless, she forced herself to email back to take him up on his offer.

'Guess what?' asked an excited Astrid as Rose returned to the barn one afternoon a few weeks later. Astrid's parents had left, and before their departure they had met Thommo's parents, an occasion that had gone very well, thanks to several bottles of vintage Windsong shiraz that had been liberated from the cellar. 'Thommo's invited me to spend Christmas with his family. They've been so great about the baby, and so nice to me.'

'That's wonderful news, Astrid,' said Rose, struggling to summon up the enthusiasm her friend felt.

'Hey, what's up? Where is the sunny Rose?'

'Nah, it's nothing, really.'

'I know you better than that. You're normally so happy, but not so much these last few weeks.' Astrid looked concerned. 'Oh, wait, is it about Christmas? Mark told me I could take some time off. He is taking the children to the coast to spend time with Isabella. Is that it? It's not a secret that before she came back you two had a bit of a thing going.'

Rose sighed. 'Yeah, but it was all pretty casual really, I doubt it meant anything to him. Now Isabella's back, I'm left feeling like a complete douche.'

'Don't be silly. Anyway, she's a total cow; he just hasn't seen it yet,' Astrid said firmly. 'And he will soon.'

'Yeah, well, I'm not convinced. They've got a lot of history together. Not to mention two kids!' Rose knew that Mark had been sleeping in the spare room at Kalkari, and she'd been clinging onto that bit of knowledge. But a week in an idyllic beach house? She'd lay bets that would seal the reunion, especially if Isabella had anything to do with it.

'Oh, Rose, I wish I knew how to cheer you up. Here I am, all loved up,' Astrid pointed to her belly, 'and you're so unhappy. What do you plan for Christmas? I'm sure I could ask Thommo if there is room for another.'

'Thanks, but I'm going to get away from here for a while. Philippe and Frostie are having Christmas in Bondi and they've asked me to hang out with them. It'll be nice to spend some time at the beach, too.'

'Oh, good for you. I am jealous. I could really do with some time on the beach, and cooling off in the ocean. Although I will not be fitting into my bikini anytime soon, hey?' Astrid said, trying to lighten Rose's mood. 'I guess no-one will be here at all at Christmas then. Jake is going back to Adelaide for a few days too.'

'Oh, is he?' asked Rose. 'Then it will be quiet here.' She was even more relieved that Philippe had saved her from a lonely few days. Time away might even help to give her some perspective.

Mark, Isabella and the two children left for the coast a few days after school finished up for Leo. Rose waved them off with a sinking heart mixed with a sense of relief. Isabella had driven her mad in the days leading up to their departure, insisting that Rose iron her entire wardrobe, as she couldn't make up her mind what to pack. Rose still had no idea what Mark might do about the situation with Isabella long-term, but one thing was certain: she was sick of being treated like a badly paid skivvy.

She stomped over to the barn to pack her things for her own road trip, vowing to try to keep her mind off Mark. She threw a couple of pairs of shorts and some tees into her backpack and added the dress she'd worn to dinner with Mark in Sydney. Astrid had kindly let her keep it. 'After all, what use is it going to be to me?' she'd insisted. As she folded it carefully, Rose remembered the thrill of that night. The night she'd first kissed Mark. Well, what a bloody mess that had gotten her into, she thought grimly as she tightened the drawstring on her backpack and clicked the clasps into place.

She ran into Astrid just as she was hauling the heavy pack to her car. The two girls embraced. They'd become firm friends in the months since Rose had arrived at Kalkari and she was going to miss her. 'Have a great time in the sun and the surf, and watch out for those Bondi beach boys.' Astrid winked at her.

'A bit of eye candy never hurts, hey?' said Rose, attempting to be cheerful as she heaved the backpack onto her shoulders and turned to leave.

She had seen Mark that morning, before he left. Before Isabella was up and about. 'So, you're off this arvo then?' he'd asked.

'Yup. I'm catching up with some friends in Sydney.'

'Travel safe, dear Rose.'

She'd looked up at him, surprised to see sadness in his eyes. Perhaps he wasn't as insensitive as he seemed? The tiny hope that they might find a way back to each other flickered and grew in her heart.

It grew stronger when, just as she was turning to leave, he'd pressed a small square package into her hands. 'Merry Christmas.'

'Oh,' she was embarrassed. 'But I didn't get you anything.'

He waved her away. 'Open it on Christmas Day.'

CHAPTER 33

Bondi was at its sparkling best, making it impossible for Rose to stay completely miserable for long. She sighed with pleasure when she spied the smooth crescent of golden sand, bronzed baking bodies and glittering blue ocean. It was so much busier than when she'd first been there, in the middle of winter. She parked her car in a back street and headed straight for Philippe's cafe.

'Rose! *Alors!*' he cried from behind the coffee machine. 'You made it!' He came around the counter and gave her a big hug. 'I'm finishing up here in five minutes. Why don't you sit down? Coffee?'

Rose looked gratefully at him. 'When it's made by you, how can I refuse?'

Later, as they strolled back to her car, companionably arm in arm, to collect her luggage, Rose found herself looking forward to the prospect of a few days chilling out at the beach. Even though it didn't feel the slightest bit like a traditional Christmas, perhaps it wouldn't be so bad after all.

The morning of Christmas Eve dawned warm and eyeball-searingly bright. She'd had a late night at the pub the night before with Philippe, Frostie and their mates, but nevertheless Rose woke early. Philippe's flatmate was away for the holidays, so she was camping out in his room, and the apartment was in a prime location, footsteps away from the beach.

She pulled on her running gear and headed out. It was still early, but the beach was filled with morning joggers, surfers and swimmers, all making the most of the holiday season. Frostie had warned her that on Christmas Day itself the beach was likely to be 'absolutely heaving, mate. You won't be able to move for pommie backpackers.' Frostie and Philippe had plans for a morning surf and then lunch with friends whose apartment overlooked the ocean. Passing the Icebergs club, Rose sprinted up to the path that wound its way along the cliff, headed for Bronte. It seemed like she wasn't the only one with that idea; the narrow path was congested with runners and walkers enjoying the spectacular views, and she had to duck and weave between them as she set off. Nevertheless, it was a great place for a run: the dramatic cliffs fell away to churning white water below and the coast stretched into the distance as far as the eye could see. It was a humbling feeling to stand on the edge of the land

and take in the vast blue of the ocean. It somehow made her problems seem very small and inconsequential.

On her way back from the beach, she ran into Frostie, who was wearing a rashie and carrying a board under one arm. 'Hey, pommie girl,' he called out, waving at her. 'Fancy a lesson? Surf's just about right. Later this arvo good for you?'

Rose nodded.

'Sweet.'

Rose spent the rest of the day shopping. She needed a swimsuit; there hadn't been much call for one in the Shingle Valley. Taking the advice of one of Philippe's friends from the night before, she headed to Bikini Island, apparently Bondi's finest swimwear emporium. Rose bypassed the bikinis; surely her boobs and bum would spill out of the skimpy triangles of fabric like ice-cream out of a cone.

'Just give us a shoutout if you need any help,' said the shop assistant. 'One-pieces are over there.' She bowed her head over her phone.

Rose was grateful for the girl's apparent lack of interest, and shimmied into the first suit she found that looked like it had enough fabric not to be indecent. Turning sideways she struck a pose. She was amazed by what she saw. It seemed that the months at Kalkari – the running and lack of chocolate – had had an astonishing upside. Every last bit of the flab that had previously hung in rolls around her middle had vanished; instead, reflected back at her in the mirror was a tall, toned, slim girl. Gone too were the cottage-cheese dimples that had once pockmarked her thighs. Her arse was no longer the size of a large county. 'Rutland, more like,' she muttered to herself, unable to wipe the smile from her face. She smiled at her reflection. Thank God for silver linings.

'That looks great! But are you sure you don't want to try a bikini?' The sales girl had roused herself from behind the counter and peered around the curtain. 'I don't mean to be rude, but you don't want to look like your nanna on the beach, do you?'

After some persuasion, Rose agreed to try on the skimpy item the girl held out.

Wonders would never cease. She couldn't believe her eyes. She actually looked okay. Better than okay, in fact.

Unable to choose between two of the rather miraculous bikinis the salesgirl had picked out – one in burnt orange and the other sapphire blue with a va-va-voom halter top that pushed her boobs up almost to her chin – Rose took both, enjoying the boost that a bit of much-needed retail therapy gave her, even if she nearly fainted when the girl told her the price. How could so little fabric cost so much?

Seeing the reflection of her now taut stomach and lean, muscled legs in the mirror had helped to chase away some of the pain of missing Mark, but she couldn't help remembering the look in his eyes when he'd first seen her at the dinner, going over in her mind their brief kiss, the feel of rightness when she was in his arms ... She was missing him, and Leo and Luisa, and Kalkari with an ache that was almost

274

physical. There was, however, a more immediate problem to deal with. The bikini had highlighted her country tan: brown arms, neck and legs and a pale torso.

Best go and do something about that.

She grabbed some sunscreen and headed to the beach to lose herself in a trashy novel. She had a few hours to kill before meeting Frostie for a surf lesson.

'Okay, darling, you're going to need a wettie. Just a shortie, I reckon. It's pretty warm in the water now – and a board.'

They were standing in a surf shop across the road from the beach. Rose could guess what a wettie was but had no idea what a shortie might be. She allowed Frostie to organise it all for her. She strolled over to a display of flashy white fibreglass boards that came up to her shoulder and idly ran a finger down the sharp, pointed tip of one of them.

'Think you'll be up for one of those, hey?' Frostie asked. Rose looked up at him enquiringly. 'Actually, we'll start you off easy on one of these big foamies,' he said, indicating a rack that had several towering foam boards lined up along it.

'But they look huge,' she said, protesting.

'You'll need an even longer one, as you're so tall, but don't worry, pommie girl, I'll see you right.'

He handed her a short-sleeved wetsuit and arranged to rent a large board. They headed across the road and down to the beach. Stopping on the sand, Rose wriggled her way into the wetsuit, grabbing the thick material and hauling it over her hips as Frostie ran through the features of the board. 'The sides of the board are called rails, right, and the front of the board is the nose.'

'Uh-huh,' Rose grunted as she struggled with the tight neoprene.

Showing her how to squeeze her shoulders together so he could zip up the back of her suit, Frostie explained that they'd be spending the first part of the lesson on the sand. Rose tried not to let her disappointment show. She was keen to get out into the water – the neoprene was making her sweat.

She copied Frostie's moves as he showed her how to lie on the board and then 'pop' up, pulling her knees underneath her and planting her feet sideways on the board.

'Ah, a goofy,' he said.

'Goofy yourself,' Rose replied defensively.

'No, that just means you're left-footed.'

'Oh, right then,' said Rose in a small voice, as she went back to practising.

After about half an hour, Frostie seemed satisfied with her progress and suggested it was time to head into the water. As they got to its frothing edge, Rose looked out at the ocean and suddenly felt a twinge of apprehension. The waves, which had looked so innocuous from a safe distance, were suddenly quite terrifying close-up. Determined not to let her concern show, she attached her leg rope to her ankle, hoisted the board under one arm and waded in.

Jesus, it's cold.

'I thought you said the water was warm?' she protested.

Frostie shrugged and she laughed. She continued forward, feeling a cool layer of water seep through her wetsuit and slowly warm up with the heat of her body. Once she was about waist-deep, Frostie told her to flop herself on the board as he steadied it. Feeling about as elegant as an elephant seal, she nevertheless did as he asked.

They headed out a bit deeper and he showed her how to dive under the oncoming waves, thrusting the nose of the board under the water.

Then it was time to try and actually ride one. Frostie helped to turn the board, with Rose clinging onto it, towards the shore, and she looked over her shoulder at a huge wall of green water that was heading inexorably towards her. At the last second, as the wave was almost upon her, he thrust the board forward and she was borne along on the crest of the wave. Rose completely forgot about trying to pop up and just held onto the board for dear life, thrilling to the ride as she sped into shore.

Spluttering, she stood up and shook the water out of her long hair. 'Ohhh wow! That was brilliant,' she called out as she saw Frostie heading towards her.

'Pretty cool, huh?' he said, 'Not bad for a first effort. Not bad at all.'

Rose was hooked, and they spent the next hour or so practising. Once, she even managed to get her legs underneath her and, kneeling, rode the wave into the shore until her fingertips touched the sand.

Realising that the light was fading and the sun beginning to set, they called it a day. Not minding the breeze that whipped her wet hair across her face, Rose laughed, exhilarated by the experience. 'That,' Rose said when they were back on the beach, 'was truly, really the best.'

'We aim to please,' Frostie said, laughing at her enthusiasm. He handed her a towel and she noticed as he turned away from her that he'd pulled down his own wettie and that etched across his shoulders was a tattoo of a pair of angel's wings. Rose smiled. Maybe it was a sign?

Seeking some comfort in the arms of the uncomplicated Frostie might be just the salve her heart needed. But as quickly as the thought occurred to her, she dismissed it. It wasn't the sign she was looking for.

CHAPTER 34

Waking on Christmas morning felt surreal. Rose gazed out of the window at the cloudless day. It was warm already, with just a gentle breeze blowing off the ocean, bringing with it a pungent, briny smell.

'Merry Christmas, *cherie*!' called Philippe as she walked into the living room. He was already dressed in boardies and was giving his surfboard a final rubdown of wax. 'I have an old softboard you can borrow downstairs if you like. Perfect morning, but we'd better get out there before the crowds. You ready?'

'You'd better believe it,' said Rose, knowing that spending the morning in the surf with her friends was just what she needed. She remembered her mum telling her that salt water was the best cure for anything, from a grazed knee to a sore throat – even a broken heart. She might have been right.

Before they left the beach later that morning, Rose messaged her brother a photo of Bondi, packed, as Philippe had predicted, with hundreds of swimmers and sunbathers, some of whom had even brought their Christmas trees down to the beach with them, and plenty of them on the way to their third or fourth beer of the morning, judging by the number of empties overflowing from the garbage cans. She gave her mum a call, but the line had an echo and they kept talking over each other.

'We're all very jealous of you being at the beach,' Elaine said. 'You must be having a brilliant time. Have a swim for me.'

Rose didn't have the energy to go into everything that had happened in the last couple of months, and in any case, her mum only ever wanted to hear good news. She gathered that Henry was on this way down later that day: Christmas Eve their time. She gulped as she hung up, suddenly feeling a long way from everything and everyone she'd grown up with.

But Philippe and Frostie didn't give her the chance to be sad for long. After a few hours down at the beach, they returned to the flat to shower off the salt and sand and then they got ready to head over to the North Bondi apartment of one of Philippe's mates. On her wanderings the day before, Rose had found a pale pink sheer cotton sundress, and now she slipped it on, slid her feet into a pair of sandals and twisted her still-wet hair into a knot at the nape of her neck, fastening it with the butterfly clip.

Her thoughts flew to Mark and what he might be doing this Christmas morning. Presumably playing happy families among a sea of presents. *Oh, presents!* She suddenly remembered the gift Mark had given her before he left. Burrowing into her pack, her fingers closed over the small square box and she pulled it out. Her hands shook slightly as she unwrapped it.

Inside was a tiny silver bunch of grapes on a fine chain. 'Oh,' Rose gasped as she held it up to the light.

It's perfect.

She turned to the mirror to put it on. When she saw the grapes shining against her brown skin, her heart contracted.

She felt like crying.

Frostie's mates, Kate and Em, had laid on a seafood feast, and Rose happily peeled herself a prawn, dipping it in a thick, garlicky mayonnaise before popping it whole into her mouth. The boys had brought a slab of beer with them and Rose's contribution was several bottles of Kalkari wine that Mark had also insisted she take with her on holiday. The girls poured themselves generous glasses and took them out onto the balcony, which overlooked the beach. *Wow*, thought Rose, *this is certainly a different way to celebrate.*

After gorging on the prawns, salad and wine, Rose didn't think she could eat any more, but Em marched onto the balcony carrying a flaming pudding. Rose had to laugh.

It was a boiling hot day but they were going to eat Christmas pudding?

'Oh, there's custard too, or brandy butter if you'd prefer,' said Em, catching the expression of mirth on Rose's face.

Rose leant back in her chair. 'Oh my God, I think my stomach's going to burst,' she said. 'That was amazing, thanks so much.'

'Philippe mentioned that you're a pretty talented baker,' said Kate. 'Did he tell you he's planning to open the cafe in the evenings, for dinner?'

Rose nodded. 'Yes he did. It's a wonderful idea. He'll make an amazing job of it, I know.'

'I'm going to be working with him,' said Kate. 'But there's always a place for a good pastry chef, if you're interested.'

'*Oui*, Rose, I was going to mention it, but I thought you were all set up out there in the valley,' Philippe added. 'We'd love to have you if I could persuade you to come back to Bondi.'

Rose was touched. And tempted. 'Gosh, thanks Philippe, but at the moment I've got two little kids depending on me, not to mention Ferment, our cellar door cafe.' *Not to mention a huge crush on my boss*, the voice in her head added. 'But it's nice to be asked, and, who knows what the future will bring. I might need to take you up on it one day; I'm not sure that my job at Kalkari will last forever.' *Particularly if Isabella continues to be such a complete witch*, she thought darkly.

'I don't think I'm going to need to eat for a week!' said Kate, stretching and patting her still-flat, tanned stomach.

'Time for a nap, I reckon,' said Em. '*Oui, ma cherie,*' agreed Philippe and they headed off to her bedroom.

Rose, Frostie and the others cleared away the remains of lunch and then took their glasses back out to the balcony, where the western sun was slowly setting. She looked out at the view, one hand on her silver necklace, tracing the shape of the grapes.

She looked across at Frostie, at his happy, open smile as he looked out at the ocean. Nope. It was hopeless. Her heart didn't beat faster when she looked at him. Her heart belonged irrevocably to Mark.

CHAPTER 35

Rose drove back to Kalkari a few days after New Year unsure of what might await her. She'd been away for just over a week, but, as much as she'd enjoyed the beach, she'd missed the Shingle Valley. She'd missed the early morning light as the sun rose over the hills, the huge skies and sudden crashing thunderstorms that sounded as though the whole world was caving in. She'd also missed the cheeky faces of Leo and Luisa. She wondered again what they'd got up to on Christmas Day, and whether they'd liked the presents she'd left for them. And she had missed Mark, far too much. She knew she had no right to miss him; Isabella was back and it was clear that the only role for her at Kalkari was as the au pair and manager of Ferment. She was just going to have to get over her feelings for her boss. Either that, or cut her losses and leave.

Her little car rumbled up the drive, scattering the baby-doll sheep into the vines on either side. As she came to a halt at the front door, she saw Mark, standing waiting for her, shading his eyes against the sun. She couldn't help it: her heart leapt at the sight of him.

She unfolded her long legs from the cramped car and stretched them out as she walked towards him. It was stinking hot, and her car's temperamental air-con had refused to work. Her shirt was almost soaked through with sweat.

'Hey there,' said Rose as she walked up to him. She was wary, feeling the distance that had sprung up between them.

'Hey yourself,' Mark replied.

'Where is everyone? I didn't think you'd all be back yet.'

'The kids are still up the coast with Isabella. Listen, Rose, come here. I need to talk to you; it's important.'

Rose went over to the verandah and he motioned for her to sit next to him.

This is it, she thought. *He's going to give me the sack, tell me it's best for them all if I leave.*

She steeled herself. She'd been expecting it. 'Actually, Mark, I think I know what you're going to say.'

He looked surprised. 'You do?'

'Listen, I know we started to have some feelings for each other, and you're a great bloke, but Isabella's back now and I know you need the space to mend your marriage. It's time for me to move on. I'm just getting in the way here.'

Mark grabbed her by the shoulders. 'No, no, my darling Rose, that's not what I've got to say at all.'

'It isn't?'

'No, nothing could be further from the truth. Things are over for Isabella and me. They have been for a long time – long before you arrived, even before she went back to Spain.' He sighed before continuing. 'She fell in love with me as a successful corporate guy: the guy with the big salary and the flash car and dinners in all the right restaurants. Not the penniless vigneron struggling to make ends meet. She got fed up with what she called my "complete obsession" with Kalkari, and the fact that we never went anywhere further than New Bridgeton, that I never did anything except work. She couldn't stand the fact that Kalkari took all our money and then some. The final straw came when we nearly went under last year. The bank put the squeeze on us and it looked like I was going to have to put the place on the market, to give up on my dream. It's only a loan from the Trevelyns that has kept us going this year. Now things are finally turning around, she's back, but it's too late for us, there's nothing there anymore. I think we've both realised that now.'

Rose already knew about the winery's precarious finances, but she was shocked to hear about Isabella's apparent change of heart. She'd thought the woman wanted nothing more than Mark back.

'But she's been all over you—'

'I think that was as much for your benefit as mine.'

Rose frowned. 'I don't understand.'

'She hates losing anything. Even if it's something she doesn't personally want anymore. But she's not really interested in me now, just the money.'

'And what about the children? *Her* children?'

'Well, she's missed them, of course, but I think it was easier for her to leave them behind than take them with her, believe it or not. While she's been back in Spain she's taken over the marketing of her father's winery, and that has meant spending a lot of time travelling – she didn't think it was fair to the kids to take them over there, take them away from their lives here and then hardly be around herself. She's not all bad, you know.'

Rose couldn't believe it. She could never imagine leaving your own children behind, no matter how difficult the situation was.

'She wants me to get rid of you, and Astrid. She thinks the kids have become too fond of both of you. But there's no way that's going to happen. You've been the only constant thing in their life recently and I can see how much you both adore them and they you, and quite frankly that's a good thing for them, not a bad one. I also couldn't manage without either of you – the wheels would well and truly fall off. We were only just holding it together before you arrived. But,' he looked at her with sadness, 'if you do want to leave, I completely understand. I know she's made your life hell. I've no idea how much longer she'll be around for. I can't kick her out just yet. We've still got a lot of logistics to sort out.'

Rose sighed. 'Okay, you've convinced me. I'm not going to go anywhere.' She paused. 'For now.'

Relief flooded over Mark's face. 'I'll sort it out, honestly I will. Just give me some time, Rose. Now,' he said, looking her straight in the eye, 'there's something else I really need to tell you. In fact, I've been wanting to tell you for months.'

'Oh?'

Mark looked anxiously at her. 'Rose, one of the reasons there is nothing between Isabella and me anymore is that I'm completely besotted with you. It's ridiculous and I know it's asking for trouble, but I just can't help it. I love coming home to the sound of your laughter as you play with Leo and Luisa, the smell of something delicious on the stove wafting through the house, the way you seem to make everything easier just by being there. You've made this old house a home in a way it never was before. *You* feel like home.'

Rose stubbornly stuck out her chin. 'You've had a funny way of showing it.'

'Oh, Rose,' he said. 'I'm so sorry. I've been trying my best to be fair to everyone. I think I've only ended up hurting you. It's such a bloody mess.'

He looked so distraught. Rose relented. 'Yep, it sure is,' she said softly.

Mark glanced up and saw the wistful expression on her face, and pulled her into his arms.

Sweaty or not, she never wanted him to never let her go. Ever.

He bent and put his lips to hers. She weakened in his embrace, desire flaring in her, all resolve of keeping her distance dissolving like ice on a hot pavement.

'Hot, isn't it?' he said with a wink.

Rose blushed. 'Sorry, the air-con in the car was on the blink.'

'That's not exactly what I meant,' he said, wrenching himself away, grabbing her hand and pulling her down the driveway. 'Come with me. I know somewhere we can cool off.'

'Now?' she spluttered, not particularly pleased that he'd released her just as things were getting interesting.

'You'll see,' he urged.

As they reached the bottom of the Kalkari drive, he veered left. He then took a sudden right, ducking into a copse of trees. Rose was glad he had hold of her hand or she would surely have stumbled on the rough ground. Emerging onto the other side of the trees, she saw the water. She knew the Shingle River, which wound a silvery path along the valley, ran close to Kalkari, but she hadn't realised there was a swimming hole so close by. Here, the banks had widened to form a deep pool, its smooth expanse ruffled only by a pair of ducks. It was several degrees cooler in the shade of the peppermint gums that grew along the banks. Mark shucked off his t-shirt and unbuckled his jeans, and finally Rose understood what he had in mind.

'Race ya!' he called, taking off towards the water.

She laughed nervously at the thought of diving in. She was so hot and sticky from her long drive but she had no idea what was in there. 'You're kidding, right?'

Mark's eyes held a challenge.

Oh my god, he's serious! She'd give anything to cool off, but she didn't like the look of the river's inky depths at all.

Completely unselfconscious despite now being naked, Mark had stepped onto the low bank and was preparing to jump in. 'C'mon, Rose, live a little!'

With a resounding splash he jumped feet first into the water. Watching him surface and shake the water out of his hair, Rose could see an echo of the exuberant boy he must have once been and her heart softened.

Yep, I've got it bad.

'I never even knew this was here,' she said.

'Yeah, well, I haven't even shown the kids yet. I want to wait till they're better swimmers, Luisa especially,' he called out.

'That makes sense.'

Mark looked at her. 'So are you coming in or do I have to drag you? I thought you were hot?'

His enthusiasm was infectious.

Well, if you can't beat 'em, join 'em

She pulled her sundress over her head. She did, however, keep her underwear firmly on. She wasn't as uninhibited as Mark obviously was. She waded in.

'Jesus, it's colder even than Bondi!' she said, gasping for breath, noticing the fine silt they had stirred up. She couldn't see her legs.

'You'd better believe it,' Mark said as he stroked over towards her, arms reaching to grasp her around the waist. He noticed the silver necklace glittering at her neck and held it between his fingers. 'Like it?'

Rose nodded. 'Love it,' she said, kissing him. 'Thank you, Mark, it's beautiful.' Then, with an impish grin, she wriggled out of his arms and stroked towards the far bank.

'Hey, where are you going?'

'Catch me if you can!' she sang.

'Oh, you're going to regret that,' he joked, swimming towards her.

Rose tried to stay out of his grasp, but he reached her in a few lazy strokes and dived down, not caring about the murky water, grasping her ankle. Rose felt herself being tugged downwards and she spluttered as her head dunked under the water.

'Hey!' she cried out as he released his grip on her leg and she bobbed to the surface.

Mark laughed and flipped water at her. 'Gotcha!'

The water was icy, and despite the heat of the day Rose's skin soon chilled, goosebumps rising on her arms. She shivered.

'Oh, you're getting cold.' Mark said, and they headed back to the bank. He scrambled out first and grabbed his shorts, then chivalrously extended an arm to help her up.

They gathered their clothes and Mark handed her his t-shirt to put on while he pulled on his shorts. 'C'mon, let's go back and dry off.' She had to stop herself staring at his broad, muscled chest and felt almost dizzy at the nearness of him. She longed to kiss him again.

When they reached the house, Mark suggested she wait outside on the verandah. 'Stand in the sun there and warm up. I'll be back in a flash.'

When he returned, she could see two towels under one arm, champagne flutes dangling from his fingers and an ice bucket and a bottle in the other hand. He set the bucket and glasses down on a side table and handed her a towel. Turning her back, Rose stripped off the now sodden t-shirt and bra and wound the towel around herself, squeezing her hair out and shaking it down her back. Setting the glasses down, Mark turned to twist the cage on the champagne. Deftly popping the cork, he poured two glasses, handing one to her.

'Happy New Year, darling Rose.' He raised his glass to her.

The champagne was icy and bubbles pricked her nose as it slipped easily down. 'Mmm,' she sighed appreciatively. 'Laurent Perrier Rosé. How did you know it's my favourite?'

'Would you believe a lucky guess? Oh, that and it was already in the fridge.'

'Well, I'm impressed,' Rose acknowledged. 'It's good to be back, Mark.' She wasn't ready to admit to him just how much she'd missed him.

'Yep, it was a bit quiet around here without you,' he replied, teasing her.

They sat and Mark reached for her feet, resting them on his knee and gently drying each one in turn, rubbing off the dust that had stuck to her soles.

'But weren't you up at the coast all this week?'

'I came back early.'

'Oh right. Was it that bad?'

He nodded.

They fell silent, and Rose imagined Mark was – like her – thinking about how they'd spent the previous week.

The sun coloured the sky rose and scarlet as it set.

Gazing out over the vineyards, Rose felt a sense of calm overtake her. All she could think of was being right here, right now. Nothing else seemed to matter. Sod the future. It could sort itself out.

The back of the house was out of sight of the driveway, so they were startled when they heard the stutter of an engine and then the slamming of car doors.

'Daaad!' Leo's voice called out. 'Where are you?'

'Oh, Christ,' said Mark in alarm. 'That'll be Isabella back with the kids. I wasn't expecting her until tomorrow.'

Rose had no time to collect her thoughts or do anything about the fact that she was dressed in nothing more than a towel, her hair in wet tendrils snaking over her shoulder.

'Halloo,' came Isabella's voice, as she rounded the side of the house. 'Oh, there you are, Mark.'

Isabella was the epitome of polished European resort glamour. Gold and black oversized sunglasses, blood-red lipstick, a matching tote, and a chic summer dress that looked straight out of *Roman Holiday*. Rose caught a whiff of her heavy, familiar perfume as she tried to shrink back in her chair – to become invisible. It was futile.

Great, glamorous estranged wife arrives, and here I am looking like something the cat dragged in. Again. Nice one, Rose.

Isabella's eyes flicked disdainfully over Rose's bare shoulders and legs. She arched one eyebrow at Mark, who had stood up, still wearing nothing but his shorts.

'Cooling off?' Her tone was icy. 'I do hope I haven't interrupted anything.'

Leo and Luisa came tearing through the house and out the back door, flinging themselves at Mark. 'Hey, guys, how are you? Look at you both! I swear you've grown in just a week.' He leant down and hugged them.

Rose clutched the towel tightly around herself. 'We had a swim. Such a hot day, you know,' she stammered to Isabella, feeling completely out of her depth. She flashed a look at Mark that said 'Help, get me out of here'. He gave her a grin that she supposed was meant to be reassuring but actually just made him look like a naughty schoolboy caught doing something he shouldn't have been.

Fat lot of help, you are, matey.

'So I see,' replied Isabella coolly, watching as Luisa toddled up to Rose and gave her a sticky hug. 'It looks as though it's not just the children who like Rose.' Sarcasm dripped from her voice. Rose wilted under her steely gaze.

'I'd better go and get changed. Excuse me,' said Rose, extricating herself from Luisa's grasp.

'That would be a good idea, I think, Rose.' Isabella's voice was mocking and made Rose feel even more ill-at-ease. *Oh God*, she thought as she hurried over to the barn to get dressed, *now Isabella really knows the score*.

Isabella stayed on at Kalkari.

Rose had to remind herself to be stoic. She was sorely

294

tempted to get the hell out of there as fast as the wheels on her little yellow car could carry her but, in a whispered conversation, Mark persuaded her not to leave.

'Please, Rose, it's just for a couple of days; I need some time to sort out all the details with her,' he pleaded. 'I meant everything I said to you. Please believe me. Just give me a few more days.'

As well as being incredibly beautiful, Isabella was also incredibly untidy. She insisted on carrying on loud telephone conversations in Spanish, leaving behind a trail of crimson lipstick–stained glasses and scrawled notes, and she expected Rose to cater to her every whim. She kept up her complaints about the meals Rose cooked, 'Per'aps, Rose, we could have something with a little less oil in it next time,' she said, after Rose had served up fettuccine carbonara one evening.

She also expected Rose to drop off her dry cleaning, run her errands and generally act as her maid. 'She asked me if I could find her some organic rosehip oil for Christ's sake,' Rose vented to Mrs B when she bumped into her in Eumeralla the next day. 'Do you think they stock that in the IGA?'

'Oh, love, you poor thing, I remember exactly what she's like,' Mrs B sympathised.

Rose gritted her teeth and acknowledged Isabella's requests with a thin veneer of good grace. She knew the woman was asserting her control, showing her who was boss, and, well, it had been – still was, really – her home. Rose was just an employee, something Isabella wasn't about to let her forget.

She drove Astrid mad too, but the Austrian girl took advantage of Isabella's presence and escaped with Thommo, who arrived promptly at six every night to pick her up and delivered her back at seven the following morning. Rose was surprised that Isabella insisted on getting the kids ready for bed – leaving a trail of wet towels and discarded clothes in her wake, she noted irritably – and so Rose was left to retreat to the barn, where she didn't even have the company of Jake to rankle her. When he wasn't out tramping the vineyards he was hanging out with the crowd from Lily-bells – he'd set his sights on Angie, and was doing his best to seduce her.

By the time the end of the week arrived, Rose was thoroughly pissed off. Even her usual morning run didn't improve her state of mind. She was fed up of waiting for the situation to change and was beginning to wonder if she wasn't being played for a fool by both Mark and Isabella.

Arriving in the kitchen to cook breakfast, she noticed several monogrammed Louis Vuitton cases were parked in the hall. Her spirits rose. It looked like, true to Mark's word, Isabella really was leaving. Wanting to keep well out of the way, she watched from the window as Isabella departed in a flurry of kisses for the children. Her heavy perfume hung in the air long after she'd left.

'She's really gone,' Mark reassured her later that day. 'We've talked and agreed it's all over.'

Rose was still not convinced. 'Are you sure? What does that mean for us, if anything?'

'It means I'm free of her,' he said simply. 'She's the kids' mother, I can never take that away from her, but that's it.'

'Are you sure?'

'Yes, I'm sure Rose. Trust me when I say that it's you that I want to be with. That is, if you'll have a jaded old bugger like me.' he grinned wryly.

He looked so sincere – and she really wanted to believe him. She cast her doubts aside and let herself be pulled into his arms, any lingering resistance weakening as his lips touched hers.

CHAPTER 36

When it finally happened, it was every bit as spectacular as she'd hoped it would be. The tension of the previous months had left Rose feeling like a dam waiting to burst. The evening after Isabella had gone, after dinner, and when the kids were safely in bed, Mark knocked softly on the door of the barn. Jake was away in Eumeralla with Angie, and they weren't likely to be disturbed.

No words were needed. Passion sparked in Rose from the moment Mark touched her, pulling her towards him and down onto the sofa. He tore at her clothes: buttons flew and her shirt fell in a heap on the floor. Reaching around to unhook her bra, Mark gasped as he took in the sight of her. Rose pulled his mouth back to hers, already missing the feel of his skin.

'Don't fight me,' he groaned. Wrenching himself away once more, he gently trailed a line of kisses along her breasts, then down towards her taut stomach and continuing on down. He pulled aside the lace of her knickers and explored the very centre of her with his mouth. A white heat engulfed her. She was beyond coherent thought as waves of pleasure pulsed through her, right to the very ends of her toes and the tips of her fingers.

Rose dragged his shirt off, exposing the wide brown expanse of his broad back, and the fine pelt of hair across his chest. She pulled him back towards her and kissed him hungrily. He raised himself above her, waiting.

'Are you sure?' Mark asked.

Are you freaking kidding me? What does this look like to you?

She didn't need to answer. She kissed him with all the pent-up longing of the past months, pressing every inch of herself into him. Reaching down, she grasped him, feeling him pulse beneath her hand and hearing his sharp intake of breath. She slowly moved her hand up and down, enjoying the solidness of him, the size of him, gently teasing him.

They rolled over so that she was above him and lowered herself onto him, riding him. They began to move rhythmically, slowly at first and then urgently, until the pleasure was almost too much to bear. Rose felt as if she were being drawn into a vortex, unable to escape the whorl of sensations that he was creating in her body, spinning almost out of control.

Rose was almost at the point of no return, when Mark stopped her and reached down for his jeans, fumbling for a pocket. He ripped open the square foil packet with his teeth and Rose helped him unroll it.

Slowly, gently, staring deeply into her eyes, Mark entered her again. Rose became oblivious to her surroundings as they rocked in an urgent rhythm, hip to hip, chest to chest. Waves of glorious pleasure began to wash over her and she was once again sucked into the vortex, spinning out of control. High on a precipice together, they came crashing down as the unrelenting force overtook them both. 'Ohhh, God,' she cried, as she came.

'Wow. That was pretty amazing,' said Mark as he got his breath back. 'Better than winning the Jimmy Watson.'

Rose gave him a disbelieving look.

'Well, it was up there with that, in any case,' he said with a bark of laughter.

'It was certainly worth waiting for, no doubt about that,' sighed Rose, utterly sated.

She fell asleep in his arms.

After that, they spent every evening together. Their nights were passionate, sweet and loving, but Rose began to suffer from lack of sleep, often yawning her way through her morning chores. She didn't know how Mark kept up the pace he did, heading off to the winery at sunrise every morning.

She felt drunk with love. Her eyes lit up whenever she saw him come through the door at the end of the day, and he always greeted her with a kiss, even in front of the kids. He hadn't said anything to them officially, but even Leo seemed to have taken the situation completely in his stride.

Rose had never been happier. She'd also never been busier. Ferment had taken off, as word spread through the valley and beyond. She'd even had a visit recently from Betty and Merle and the other CWA ladies, who'd all exclaimed over her muffins and wouldn't leave until she'd given them the recipe. Henry was still in Spain, and had stopped demanding updates.

Life, at last, was good.

vintage

noun

the act of gathering ripe grapes from a particular annual harvest; an exceptionally fine wine from the crop of a good year

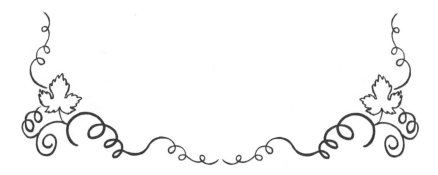

CHAPTER 37

The unrelenting summer heat continued, with the grapes growing round and fat, just as Astrid's belly did. The vines' shrouds of white netting were dropped on the ground like discarded undies.

'When do you think you'll be ripe, Astrid?' said Leo one day as they were guzzling lemonade in the shade of the verandah.

'Not for a while, I hope,' she replied, sitting down heavily and fanning herself. 'Though I can't imagine getting any bigger, or any hotter.'

The grapes, however, *were* very close to being ripe, and Mark announced over dinner with Rose that vintage would start in a few days' time. 'I don't think this weather will hold out much longer, and we can't risk any late-season heavy rains splitting the grapes,' he said. 'I'm afraid you won't be seeing much of me for the next six weeks or so. Dan, Jake and I will be working round the clock during vintage. There'll also be a gang of pickers coming in from Eumeralla every day. And Rose,' he paused, 'I'll need you to organise smoko and lunch for everyone. Mrs B can fill you in on what'll need to be done.'

Rose's heart sank at the thought of the extra work. She was already busy enough with Ferment. And she was in the strange position of being both Mark's lover and his employee. At times like this, it was awkward. 'I don't remember this being part of the deal. It's going to cost you, Mark,' she said, making light of her pique.

'Whatever you want, sweetheart, but we really need to keep these guys fed so we can get the grapes in on time, so your help will be much appreciated.'

'Whatever I want, hey?' a cheeky smile played about Rose's face. 'Let me have a think about that one … I might be able to think of a way for you to express that appreciation,' she teased.

'Alright, but whatever it is will have to be after vintage.' Mark's tone turned serious. She knew this was a crucial time for him and the vineyard, and that there would be plenty of hard work and long hours in the weeks to come.

Rose had been welcoming visitors to the cellar door cafe every weekend in ever-growing numbers. It was with a shock that she realised one evening, while checking her diary, that she'd been at Kalkari for more than six months. She was alarmed at how fast the time was passing. She wasn't ready to leave the valley. In fact, if she was totally honest with herself, she didn't think she'd ever be ready to leave.

The first day of vintage dawned clear, warm and bright, as each day had in the previous few weeks. The Aussie summer was set to be a record-breaker, according to Dan, who had consulted the almanac where previous years' statistics on weather, rainfall and vintage conditions were noted.

Rose was up early for her morning run, just as the sun was clearing the Shingle Hills, and as she paused at the top of a rise, she saw a minibus travelling up the road to the winery. Must be the pickers, she surmised, and yes, sure enough, as she reached home she could hear the chatter of the backpackers brought in to help handpick the grapes. They were starting barely after sunrise, with Mark preferring to have the grapes picked in the cool of early morning, keeping their temperature low as they went through the sorting line, the crusher and then into the big open fermenting tanks.

Heading over to the winery at lunchtime with platters of rolls and fruit, Rose set up on the table outside the cellar door, returning to the main house for jugs of iced water and a huge cherry and almond cake that she'd taken out of the oven that morning. It wasn't long before she saw the tractor rumbling up the drive, Jake behind the wheel, and its trailer piled high with picking bins full of golden, juicy grapes. Glancing over to the winery, she saw Mark and Dan waiting to receive them, eager to start the winemaking process. The excitement in the air was palpable as the first bins of fruit came in.

'Dig in,' she said to the pickers who had followed the tractor up the drive. Rose stood back and watched as the food disappeared faster than if a plague of locusts had landed.

'Okay, back to work now. No rest for the wicked.' Jake had finished unloading the grapes, and grabbed one of the few remaining sandwiches, stuffing half of it hungrily into his mouth. The pickers were lounging on the grass in front of the cellar door, some of them looking as though they were catching a sneaky forty winks. 'Hey, Rosie, how's it going?' asked Jake, noticing her standing there.

'Yeah, okay I think. They're a hungry lot,' she said, indicating the ravaged table.

'It's hard yakka, that's for sure. No wonder everyone's got an appetite,' he replied. 'Catch you later.' With that he rounded up the straggling pickers and motioned for them to climb on the back of the trailer. Rose shielded her eyes from the glare as it rumbled back down the drive, churning up dust in its wake.

So the days continued, with Rose putting out mountainous platters of food at smoko and lunch; the food disappearing almost as soon as she set it down. The heat was relentless; the skies cloudless and searingly blue.

'Bloody hell, look at me!' Astrid stuck out her legs in front of her. 'Fat as an old *hausfrau*,' she said, looking at her swollen ankles. The two girls were sitting on the back verandah, watching Leo and Luisa chase Barnsie around the backyard. The chickens were sensibly some distance away.

'*Christus*, it's so hot. Do you think it'll ever cool down?'

'Don't ask me. I'm as new to this as you are. Hey, do

you wanna come to the pub tonight? We can see if Mrs B will babysit. I feel like I've been stuck here all week buttering bread and baking.'

'Sure. I could do with a night out, even if I am only having lemonade.'

'Cool. I'll go and give her a call now.' Rose got to her feet and pulled open the screen door to the house, where, thanks to the thick stone walls it was at least a few degrees cooler. This was more than could be said of her accommodation at the barn, where the iron roof absorbed all of the daytime heat, turning into an oven.

They arrived at the pub just as the sun was setting and the cicadas tuning up. To Rose's surprise it was nearly empty. She spied the dreadlocked form of Bevan across the room and went over to see him.

'Hey there. How come it's so quiet in here, huh?'

'Vintage, babe. Everyone's too shagged to do anything but work or sleep.'

'Oh right, I should have guessed.'

Astrid set two glasses of beer and a pale orange-coloured drink down on the table. 'Two beers for you and a lemon, lime and bitters for me.'

'Thanks, darling, how're you doing? Growing a pretty decent bump there,' Bevan observed.

'Any bigger and I will pop, don't you think?' Astrid smiled and tossed back her long blonde hair. Even hot and tired from pregnancy, she still looked beautiful, thought Rose.

'Nah, you'll get bigger than that I reckon. My cousin was huge by the time she was due to push her little nipper out.'

'Thanks, that makes me feel so much better.' replied Astrid sarcastically. 'I just wish my mother was happier about me staying here to have the baby. I haven't heard from her since she went back to Austria. She won't even come on the line when I call up. My father keeps telling me to give her time and that she will come around, but she is a stubborn one.'

'Perhaps she'll mellow once she sees pictures of her new grandchild?' suggested Rose soothingly. 'Anyway, we're all here for you. Luisa can't wait to have a new playmate – she was telling me today how she was going to help you feed and bath the baby, bless her.'

Astrid looked around the deserted pub. 'Is it always like this at vintage?' she asked.

'Yep. Reckon so,' said Bevan. 'Pubs are quiet. Sacred Grounds is quiet. Everyone works their bums off and crosses their fingers that they'll get the grapes in on time, and hopes that Mother Nature doesn't decide to throw a wobbly at the last minute.'

They didn't linger. Astrid was exhausted, and apart from Bevan, there wasn't really anyone there to stay and chat to. Driving back along the dark roads, they wound the windows down to let in the breeze, the buzz of cicadas silenced as they gave up their evening chorus. 'So, Rose, do you think you'll stay? After vintage, I mean?'

'Well, I had planned to see more of the country before my visa runs out …'

'You don't sound very enthusiastic. It's Mark, isn't it?'

Rose nodded. 'Is it that obvious?'

Astrid laughed. 'Ya! Just about everyone knows what's

going on. At least it's stopped them gossiping about me.'

Rose reddened. 'Oh God, are they really?'

'It's all anyone can talk about.'

'Bloody small towns,' said Rose, but there was no malice in her voice.

'Well, I hope you stay. I didn't think I'd be staying here either, but it seems I am.' Astrid's hand traced the curve of her belly over the seatbelt. 'Getting myself knocked over to a one-night stand wasn't exactly smart, was it?'

'I think you mean knocked up,' Rose laughed. 'Yeah, not exactly a great plan, but at least it's worked out for you. Thommo adores you, you know.'

'Does he?' Astrid brightened. 'I hope so. And maybe it will work out for you too. Don't think; trust in here,' she said, placing her hand on her heart.

'Easier said than done. I've no idea what Mark's really thinking, but now is hardly the time to raise any of it with him. Mind you, I'm not sure when will be a good time.'

'I think he is scared,' said Astrid keeping her eyes on the road.

'Oh yeah?'

'Yes. After Isabella, he is scared to fall in love again, to trust someone else. But anyone with half an eye can see he's completely crazy about you. You two are good together. Stranger things have happened.'

Yep, stranger things have happened, thought Rose, remembering the real reason she'd arrived at Kalkari in the first place.

CHAPTER 38

The following week, all but the cabernet grapes were in, and most of the pickers had moved on to other vineyards in the valley. Rose popped over to the winery with some leftover cake from the cellar door, and watched in fascination as the last bins came in and were poured onto a long moving belt where several helpers sifted through the bunches. She breathed in the sweet, heady scent of crushed grapes that filled the air.

'Got to make sure there's no MOG in there,' said Mark, coming up behind her.

'MOG?' asked Rose.

'Material Other Than Grapes – leaves, shoots, rocks ... even the odd lizard. It happens. We don't want them stuffing up the wine,' he explained.

The sorted grapes sped along the belt and then disappeared into the crusher. An enormous black hose connected to the crusher fed the now porridge-like mixture of grapes into open square concrete tanks at the far end of the winery.

'That's when it becomes what we call the must,' said Mark. 'The grape skins and seeds form a cap which we have to punch down several times a day. If we don't do that, the whole thing will overheat. It's a workout. The thick concrete walls of the tank help the temperature stay constant.' he continued. 'And then, after the fermentation is complete, we press it and let it mature in these babies.' He pointed to the rows of barrels neatly stacked along one wall of the winery.

Mark, Dan and Jake had been working double shifts at the winery, and both Mark and Jake had several days' worth of stubble on their chins. All had dark shadows under their eyes. By rights they should have been cranky and short-tempered, but they looked exhilarated.

'Reckon this vintage is going to be a record-breaker,' said Dan when Rose returned to the winery later with some lunch. Mark and Jake had each left to catch a quick nap. He had to shout to make himself heard over the thrum of the crusher. 'We've done well to get all of Trevelyn's grapes in too,' he added. 'We should have no trouble filling the Channings order.'

'That'll be a relief,' said Rose.

'You're not wrong there, Rose, love. It'll take the pressure off big time. We might even be able to expand some more next year. I know Mark's got his eye on some more land further up the valley. And he's more chipper than I've seen him in ages. I even caught him whistling the other day. But that's got a lot to do with you too. I've seen how he is around you, how he looks at you when he thinks no-one's watching.'

Rose blushed. 'Yeah, well, it's no secret that we do kind of get on well,' she admitted. 'But just between you and me, I don't think it's more than a short-term thing.' Rose said, trying to play it down.

He looked surprised – and hurt. 'What makes you say that? I thought you liked it here? You've certainly made an impression on the place, what with the cellar door cafe and everything.'

A loud crack of thunder sounded overhead. Dan peered out the window. In the time they'd been chatting, dark storm clouds had swarmed over the previously blue sky.

'Bugger. That's the last thing we need. There's still a block of cabernet to get in. Better go rouse the boss.' Dan moved towards the door with unusual alacrity.

Rose followed Dan out of the winery door and back to the house.

She was in the kitchen when she heard the clomp of footsteps coming down the stairs. Mark poked his head around the door.

'Hey, Rose, are you up to much? Can you wield a pair of shears? We need all hands on deck. Wish I hadn't sent the pickers home early now. This storm wasn't supposed to get here until tomorrow.'

Rose finished drying her hands. She was dead on her feet, but didn't hesitate. 'Of course. Just show me what to do.'

They headed out to Mark's car and ran into Astrid and the kids, who were just coming back from Eumeralla.

'Hey, Leo,' called Mark. 'Wanna come pick some grapes with us?' The boy had been begging his dad for weeks to be allowed to help out in the vineyard, but Mark had thought he'd end up bored and only get in the way of the pickers, so had refused his pleas. Now, however, he needed all the help he could muster.

Leo's eyes lit up, 'You bet, Dad. This is awesome!'

'Well, I'm not sure awesome is the word I'd use about picking grapes during a thunderstorm, but I like your attitude, son,' Mark said, playfully cuffing him about the head.

The four of them jumped into the car, and Mark gunned the engine and sped off down the road.

Dan was on his mobile, speaking to Charlie at Windsong. 'Hey, mate, got any spare hands over there? This storm's threatening to break and we've still got the west vineyard to pick. Yeah? Great! We'll meet you there.'

Mark looked questioningly at Dan. 'What's the go?'

'Windsong got all their grapes in yesterday, so Charlie and Thommo and their crew are going to meet us over there. Reckon between us we can get the job done.'

'Hmm,' said Mark, looking anxiously at the sky. 'It's going to be touch and go.'

Within minutes they were at the first row of the west vineyard. When Rose got out of the car she noticed the temperature felt like it had dropped at least ten degrees. She shivered in the unexpectedly cool air. Tight bunches of fat purple grapes, their skins dusted with white bloom, hung below the leafy vines. Mark squashed a few between his fingers, examining the seeds.

'Well, they're brown, so that's good.' He crunched down on a grape, grinding the seeds between his teeth. 'Would have liked to have given them another day or so, but beggars can't be choosers. Let's get cracking.'

Jake, alerted by Dan, had driven the tractor down to meet them and began unloading the bins as each of them took a row and got to work. Louder cracks of thunder rumbled ominously overhead and the dark clouds made the afternoon light dim and eerie. Rose looked up as a flash of lightning illuminated the entire valley.

'Golly, this is gonna be some storm,' she murmured to herself, snipping bunches into her bin as fast as she could.

Thommo and Charlie arrived, and just as they got started another two cars pulled up. Rose spotted Deano and Mick from Lilybells.

'Heard you needed a hand,' said Deano, flashing a pair of shears at them.

'Mate, you're not wrong,' replied Mark, briefly looking up from his task.

They worked without stopping, till Rose's hands were blistered from the unfamiliar scissors and she thought her back would break from being bent over. The storm threatened, but apart from a few fat drops, the clouds didn't release their rain. She straightened up, her bin full again, wiping away dust from her face with the back of her arm.

'How's it going?' Mark came up beside her to collect the bin. 'You look all in.'

'Nah, don't worry about me. I'm okay. How's Leo doing?'

They looked back along the vines to where they'd

started. 'Still soldiering on. Reckon he's got a future in this if he's not careful.' Despite his concern about the weather Mark looked exultant.

'You love this, don't you?' asked Rose.

'Yep. Nothing like a bit of uncertainty to spice things up,' he said, grinning at her. 'Nothing's ever all plain sailing; that'd be boring. Glad we've got some help though. Otherwise we'd really be in the shit.'

Rose burst out laughing. Nothing like a bit of Aussie bluntness.

Dan called out from the next row, 'I don't know about you fellas, but I'll be glad of a cold one when this is all over.'

'I'll shout you all a beer or three if we get everything in before the storm breaks,' replied Mark. 'Now back to it, before we all cop a soaking.'

The final bins were being loaded just as the heavens opened. Rain fell in sheets. Rose still couldn't get over the way it rained in the Shingle Valley – as if God tipped an enormous bucket over the land. Jake headed back to the winery in the loaded-up tractor, seemingly unfazed by the wet, as everyone else took shelter in their cars.

'Well done, Leo. You were a champ,' said Mark.

'Thanks, Dad,' he replied, glowing with pride.

Rose sat up front with Mark and he placed a calloused hand over hers. 'You too, Rose.'

She winced as he squeezed her hand.

'We'd better get some salve on that when we get back,' Mark said, turning it over and seeing the raw, blistered skin where the shears had bitten into her soft palms.

317

'It is a tiny bit painful,' Rose replied through gritted teeth.

They returned to Kalkari, and they all dashed from the car to the winery, getting soaked to the skin on the way in. Dan went in search of the first aid kit to patch up Rose's hands, and Mark pulled a can of lemonade from the back of the bar fridge that lived in the corner of the winery office.

'Here you go, mate. Good effort today,' he said, cracking it open and handing it to Leo.

The boy slurped thirstily. Rose swallowed, suddenly noticing how parched she was.

'And this is for you,' Mark said, offering her a beer and taking one himself. 'Get that down you and then I reckon you should both go and get dry. Dan and I will see to the unloading.'

Oh, Dad, can I stay and watch?' pleaded Leo. 'I won't get in the way, I promise.'

'All right then, but keep close to me and don't touch anything,' Mark warned.

Rose ignored the sting on her palm as she grasped the icy bottle. It had been exhilarating – exhausting but exhilarating – to have brought the fruit in and beaten the elements. Cold beer had never tasted so good.

CHAPTER 39

The restaurant, Marilyn's (it was a Monroe-themed establishment, but happily the food was better than the décor), was lit by hundreds of candles that lent a magical glow to the faces of all those who'd been a part of the Kalkari vintage team.

'Wow, everyone's here, aren't they!' said Rose.

'Plus a few hangers-on,' muttered Dan, nodding in the direction of the blonde bob of Amanda Davis of Bellbirds, who was up from the city for the weekend and had somehow wangled an invitation.

Rose smoothed the front of her dress and fiddled with her hair, which hung down her back in a glossy wave. She felt suddenly self-conscious.

Looking up, she found Mark staring at her, an unreadable expression in his eyes. He leaned towards her. 'You look beautiful, Rose,' he said, speaking softly in her ear so that only she could hear.

Rose felt a thrill of pleasure at his words, and was reassured, but then noticed that Amanda was hovering behind them.

Amanda tapped Mark on the shoulder. 'Mark, darling, it's been too long. I heard the news about the Jimmy Watson. Congratulations, you must be positively ecstatic!' she trilled.

Mark turned towards her. 'Yep, it sure was a good day when we found out. The phone hasn't stopped ringing since and we've got orders for almost the entire stock. Couldn't have come at a better time.'

He turned back towards Rose, but Amanda wasn't letting him go that easily. 'So, tell me what you think of this vintage? Will we see another trophy-winning wine?' she winked at him conspiratorially.

Jake, who had been standing nearby and overheard their conversation, pulled Rose away. 'Come with me, Rosie. That trophy hunter gives me the irrits. But don't worry about her – she doesn't stand a chance. Anyone can see the boss has only got eyes for you. Anyway, let's go join the fun kids,' he said indicating the far side of the room, where Astrid, Thommo, Angie and Mick were sitting. They were already getting stuck into the reds by the look of things. The table was littered with decanters and bottles in various states of emptiness.

Rose looked back at Mark, but he was nose to nose with Amanda, seemingly deep in conversation. She let Jake lead her over to the table.

As she was about to sit down, she looked up to see a frail-looking Violet entering the restaurant, followed by her sister, Vera. Rose ran over to help them with the door, and embraced each of them in turn. 'Oh, I'm so glad you could make it. Look at you two! You're both looking so much better.' She beamed at them.

'Thanks, Rose, love. We wouldn't miss this for the world. Now, I understand there's a young man we need to meet. The one who's been looking after our vineyards. Can you point him out?' asked Violet.

'Oh, you mean Jake. Of course. He's just over there,' Rose gestured to the table where she'd been sitting. She waved to him to come over. 'Jake, this is Violet and this is Vera,' she said, indicating each of the sisters in turn. 'The famous Trevelyn sisters.'

'Ladies,' Jake said gravely, taking their hands and giving each of them a kiss on the cheek.

Oh, he's a charmer when he wants to be, thought Rose.

'It's a pleasure to meet you at last. I hope I've managed to treat your vineyards as you would have wished.'

'We'll see about that when we've had the chance to get back over there,' said Vera huffily.

'Now come on Vera,' Violet scolded her sister. 'Mark's done us a favour by taking them on and you know that. Besides, he assured me that he wouldn't do anything to them that we wouldn't do ourselves.'

'That's absolutely right,' Jake

Rose left them to catch up on the vintage, Jake enthusiastically quizzing them about the details of their biodynamic methods. On her way back to the table, she looked around the room. There was so much heightened emotion in the air: joy and relief at having made it through the frantic grape harvest, and anticipation about the wines that would be made from the juice now sitting in the barrels back at Kalkari. Mark – who had evidently shaken off Amanda – was sharing a joke with Dan; Astrid and Thommo were gazing lovingly at each other; and Vera and Violet were still chatting away to Jake. Rose felt her heart contract. In a few short months, these people had become her friends: her surrogate family. She couldn't begin to imagine having to leave them.

She really needed to come clean with her brother, tell Henry that she couldn't be his spy. Then she'd beg him to find another winery to buy. She resolved to email him in the morning and let him know that she couldn't go through with their arrangement. If that meant risking his anger, well, so be it. Rose knew now that she couldn't bear to betray Mark and her new friends, and she also couldn't stand the thought of Henry marching in and taking over Mark's business. She hoped that the success of the Jimmy Watson and the Channings order, which looked well on its way to being filled now the bumper harvest was in, would mean that Mark was in a much stronger position to fend off anyone interested in getting the winery for a bargain basement price.

She made her way back to the table and for the rest of the evening she set aside her concerns: she was with friends, and it was time to celebrate the successful vintage.

The next day, Rose was in Eumeralla, loading shopping bags into the trunk of her car, when she jumped at the honk of a horn beside her. She looked up, annoyed at whoever it was – and did a double-take. Was she seeing things?

'Hey, Rosie.'

What the bloody hell? She must be imagining it.

She was still trying to figure out if she was hallucinating when he called out again. 'It's been a long time between drinks.'

Oh my God, she thought, *it's really him.*

'Wh— what on Earth—?' She could barely speak for surprise.

'Well, I thought you might be a bit more pleased to see me than this,' Henry said, getting out of the car. 'Wow.' He blinked. 'You look amazing, Rosie,' he said, taking in her newly svelte figure. 'Incredible. Australia clearly agrees with you. I almost don't recognise this goddess in front of me.'

Rose got over her shock, squealed and leapt forward to hug him. 'Jesus! Honestly, Henry. Goddess, my arse! You nearly gave me heart failure. What are you doing here? Talk about a way to surprise me. I was just about to email you. You're supposed to be in France or Spain or somewhere, not the Shingle Valley, you ratbag!' Rose was thrilled to see her brother and squeezed him tightly, but her heart thudded inside her chest: she guessed why he was here. Things were about to get messy. Her two worlds would collide and the shit would hit the fan – unless she did something to prevent it. Just what that might be though, she had no idea.

'Thought I'd come and see how you were getting on. I had some appointments in Sydney and wanted to surprise you.'

'No kidding, you certainly did that. When did you get here? Where are you staying?' Questions tumbled from Rose's lips.

'I stopped at the pub and got a room there for a couple of nights. It'd be good to have a look around though. How about you show me the way to Kalkari and then you can walk me around the vineyards?'

Rose was flustered. 'Um, sure. No worries.' She needed some time to think, to prepare her argument and get Henry to back away from Kalkari.

'No worries? You're really down with the lingo, Rose,' he said with a smile as he turned back to his car. 'I'll follow you there.'

As she revved the engine and swung the car into the main road out of town her head spun. Hopefully Mark would be out in the vineyards and she could get Henry on his own. She needed to do some quick thinking and fast talking. She didn't want Henry spilling the beans to Mark about her real reasons for being there. With some effort, Rose kept her eyes on the road, but her mind was on the catastrophe that would surely result when Mark and Henry met. Henry wasn't known for his subtlety, and she knew that Mark would jump to conclusions – and in all honesty, the conclusions he'd likely jump to wouldn't be too far from the truth. In a blind panic, she crunched along the drive and pulled up outside the house.

'Niiice …' Henry let out a long, low whistle. 'That's quite a house you're living in. I can see why you like it here. A bit different to Clapham, hey?'

'Well, I don't actually live in the main house,' Rose indicated the rusted tin roof of the barn in the distance, 'that's me.'

'Oh,' said Henry. 'Got it.'

Rose tried to think of a delaying tactic. 'I need to start on lunch. Can I get you a drink?' she asked.

'Thanks. I'll take a seat out here for now, shall I?' he said, indicating the bench under the she-oak.

Rose didn't feel much like inviting her brother into the house until she'd had a chance to properly talk to him. She didn't want to be overheard, or worse bump into Mark. She was relieved that he was happy to sit and soak up the sun. 'Sure. I'll be back with some water in a sec.'

Still feeling flustered, she raced inside and bumped into Astrid and Luisa who were just on their way out.

'What's up, Rose? Did I hear voices? Ooh,' said Astrid, peering out of a side window that faced in the direction of the cellar door, 'Who's that?' She turned to look at Rose.

'Um, well, actually it's my brother. He had some business in Sydney and made a side trip to come and see me – check up on me more like.'

'He's a bit of a hunk.'

Rose shrugged. She wasn't surprised at Astrid's reaction. Henry had a seemingly endless parade of women that could be summoned at the click of his fingers, but despite the best efforts of plenty of them he'd managed to stubbornly remain a bachelor well into his thirties.

'You don't seem that excited. I thought you two were close?'

'Oh we are, and I am excited, really, just taken by surprise.' Rose hastily covered her tracks. She'd almost let her secret slip, and she could do without Astrid knowing just yet, though she felt sure it would all come out eventually and she'd end up looking like a traitorous cow. *Oh Christ*. She wished the ground would open up and swallow her, or at the very least that she could be teleported somewhere – anywhere – else, rather than have to face what was coming.

'Do you want lunch, little one?' She looked down at Luisa.

'We're going to Jethie's,' lisped Luisa.

'Play date,' said Astrid. 'We'll be back later this afternoon.'

'Have a good time sweetie,' said Rose, giving Luisa a quick hug.

As she watched them leave, Rose saw Astrid head off in the direction of the cellar door, not down the drive. What was she up to?

CHAPTER 40

'Here you go,' Rose handed her brother a glass of water and set a plate of sandwiches down on the bench, sitting down on the other side of him.

'I met your friend,' said Henry. 'Sweet girl,' he added thoughtfully.

Rose looked at him sternly. 'She's taken.'

'Steady on!' He put his hands in the air. 'I was talking about the little girl!' he protested.

Rose took a deep breath. 'So what really brought you here?'

'Like I said, sis, I had business in Sydney. I was in the neighbourhood.'

Rose gave him an old-fashioned look. She didn't believe that story for a second. She knew her brother only too well.

'Rose, may I see you for a minute?' Mark's voice boomed from the cellar door.

Oh shit. Mark. He didn't sound pleased. What was up?

She had no choice but to introduce her brother. He was sitting right there and it would have looked bloody odd not to. 'Sure, Mark. Um … Mark, this is my brother, Henry. Henry, this is Mark Cameron.'

The two men shook hands.

'G'day, mate,' said Mark. 'This is a surprise. Rose didn't mention you were coming.'

'Oh, it's just a flying visit, but I thought I'd come and check up on her. See how she's getting on.'

Rose dithered. She didn't know whether to stay and watch her world implode, or run away. 'Won't be a moment.' She fled to the barn.

She tried to convince herself that things really couldn't be that bad, that Henry wasn't about to betray her to her boss – the man she loved.

The man I love.

Yes, she did love Mark, she now knew, with every piece of her heart. Try as she had to deny it, there was no escaping the truth of her feelings. Gasping in horror as she realised that she'd stupidly left the two men alone together and that anything could happen, she quickly splashed water on her face in an attempt to calm herself down, patted it dry and then went back out in search of them.

Crossing the path back to the winery she noticed a lone magpie hopping in front of her and was reminded of the morning she'd first arrived at Kalkari. *That's right: one for sorrow*, she thought again. She could have done with a sign that all this confusion would be settled and everything would turn out okay, but it seemed the only signs were ominous ones.

Both men were so important to her: she wished they weren't on such a collision course.

She retraced her steps, but they weren't where she'd left them.

Oh crap!

She wondered what could have happened to them. Were they locked in mortal combat, or happily sharing a beer together? She couldn't stop her imagination running away with itself. She had no idea where they'd disappeared to. There was no sign of them at the cellar door or the winery. Short of running the length of the valley like a headless chook, she didn't know where to start looking, or what she'd face when she did locate them.

Other girls might pace the room or obsessively text their friends, but whenever Rose was worried – or bored, sad, or even happy, for that matter – she baked. A chocolate cake might help to take her mind off things. She headed for the kitchen.

'Mmm, that smells divine.'

Several hours had passed. But now Henry clattered into the kitchen and sat down in one of the wheel-backed chairs, making himself completely at home. How had he just wandered in like that? Most normal people would knock at the door. But not Rose's brother.

'Where *have* you been? I was worried about you.' she said nervously.

'Well, dear sis, I've been learning all about Kalkari. Mark gave me quite the tour, and then suggested I check out a few other places in the valley. There's nothing like a bit of wine tasting to loosen you up when you've barely slept a wink in the past twenty-four hours,' he said with a grin.

'I hope you were spitting, for your sake, mate,' Mark said, coming in.

'Oh Mark,' Rose was flustered. 'Hi.'

'Hi there, Rose. You've kept very quiet about your brother.'

Rose held her breath. Time seemed to stop.

'Mark's been showing me some of last year's reds, still in the barrel.' Henry filled the silence. 'Cracking wines.'

'Oh. That's good,' said Rose, trying not to sound too anxious.

'Listen, Rose, when are we going to have a chance to chat properly? I want to know everything that's been going on here. Your emails haven't given me a lot of detail,' said Henry.

'Um, how about we catch up tomorrow?' Rose was alarmed. What was Henry doing saying this right in front of Mark? But Mark, who was reaching across to put the kettle on, didn't seem bothered.

'Cuppa?' Mark asked Henry.

'Super,' he replied.

Neither Mark nor Henry seemed to notice that Rose was about to implode with nerves. They chatted away easily to each other about clones and trellising styles, pretty much ignoring her. If she didn't know better, they would have seemed like old friends catching up.

Astrid and Luisa returned, with Leo and Barnsie in tow. 'That cake smells delicious!' said Astrid, rubbing her stomach. 'This baby's gonna love chocolate, I just know it!'

Luisa climbed up into Mark's lap, and he fondly stroked her dark curls while continuing his conversation with Henry.

'Hi, I'm Henry, Rose's brother,' said Henry, introducing himself to Leo.

'Do you live near Tottenham too?' asked Leo.

'Well, not too far away. Have you ever been?'

'No, but I'm gonna. Rose's going to take me, aren't you, Rose?'

'Well, perhaps one day, Leo. We'll see.' Rose couldn't concentrate on anything but preventing Henry and Mark spending too much time together right now, but Leo seemed satisfied with that answer and followed Barnsie out the back door.

Rose hauled a large tin out of the oven.

'I see you haven't lost your touch, Rosie,' said Henry.

'She's got a talent, alright,' agreed Mark.

Rose wasn't feeling particularly talented. Instead, she was wondering how she could have gotten herself into such a ridiculous situation. Her boss, who she just happened to be head over heels in love with, and her brother were sitting in the kitchen chatting away like old friends, but her brother planned to steal Mark's beloved winery out from under him ...

Really, you couldn't make this shit up.

CHAPTER 41

'I've changed my mind,' Henry announced over a coffee with Rose at Sacred Grounds the next morning.

'What do you mean?' Rose asked. Henry had left Kalkari the previous afternoon and spent the night at the pub in Eumeralla. Sitting across from her now, he looked thoroughly rested and pleased as punch. She, however, had barely slept a wink thanks to worrying about what he was up to. The coffee she was drinking seemed only to add to her jitters.

'I'm not going to try to take over Kalkari. It has enormous potential, sure, but anyone can see the passion Mark has for it and where only he can take it. He's really managed to turn it around financially in the past year. Kalkari's not the prospect I'm looking for: I want something I can do more with. Something that's ripe for reinvention. A fixer-upper.' He paused. 'But I am interested in the valley. I think it's got a lot of possibilities.'

'Wait, what? You mean you sent me over here as your spy, asked me to dig around for any dirt you could use – made me feel like a *traitor*, I might add – and then just like that you tell me you've changed your mind?!' Rose was furious and relieved all at the same time.

Henry just grinned and sipped his coffee.

Something clicked in Rose's brain. 'Wait a minute. You never really needed me to spy on Kalkari, did you?' She pounded her palm against her forehead. 'You could have figured out all this by yourself. How could I have been so dumb as to not realise that?'

'Well, that's not *strictly* the case.' Henry looked shifty. 'Look, I was worried about you, moping around all day, wasting your life away. I wanted to give you a reason to pull yourself out of your misery, and I did want to find out more about Kalkari, though you're right, I could have found out what I needed without your help. But having you come over and nose around was a way of killing two birds with one stone.'

Rose whacked him around the head.

'Ouch! That hurt! Well, if that's all the thanks I get … Look, I'm sorry, Rose, but I knew you'd love it here, and it's clearly done you so much good. Just look at you: you're a different person to the sad sack who left London just a few months ago.'

Relief washed over her, but she was far from ready to forgive him. What were his plans now? 'So what does all this mean exactly?'

'We-ell,' her brother paused. 'Let's just say I've got wind of a steal of a deal.'

'You're kidding! Bloody hell, you don't half work fast. You've only been in the valley for twenty-four hours. How do you do it?' Rose was incredulous.

'Oh, you know, just keep my ear to the ground,' Henry winked. 'Let's just say that a conversation I had in the pub last night was very interesting. I also heard some stories about you.'

'What stories?' Rose was alarmed.

'You've been keeping quiet about some of the things you've been getting up to here, little sis.'

'What do you mean?' Rose's mind raced. Had he found out about her and Mark?

'A little bird told me that you've been running quite a cafe operation on the weekends.'

'Oh yeah, that.' Rose felt reprieved. He obviously hadn't heard any real gossip. She wanted to keep her relationship with Mark secret from her brother for the time being. For one, she didn't think he'd be too impressed that she'd fallen for her boss. 'So Mark doesn't know the real reason I came to Kalkari?' Rose asked hopefully.

'Don't worry, Rosie. Your secret's safe with me.'

Thank Christ for that.

A load lifted from Rose's shoulders and all of a sudden the day seemed very much brighter.

'So, spill – where is it?' she asked.

'You must know the little place just down from Kalkari? There was a fire there recently?'

'You mean Trevelyn's? Yes, of course I do. I've gotten to know Vera and Violet quite well actually. They're lovely old ladies. They're not selling, are they? They've been there for years.' Rose marvelled at Henry's ability to sniff out a deal but felt a pang for the sisters.

'Rumour has it they'd think about it.' Henry rubbed his hands together in anticipation. 'But if you know them, well, that's even better. Where do we find them?'

Rose hesitated. She wasn't sure how Vera and Vi would feel about giving up the land they'd farmed all their lives. On the other hand, she thought, they both seemed so much frailer all of a sudden. The fire had really shaken them up. 'I'm not sure we've got the heart to go back there,' Violet had confessed to her when they were in hospital.

'They were here two nights ago; they came to our vintage dinner. We helped manage their vineyards after the fire, and Mark buys almost all their grapes. I'll find out if they're still in the valley. I think they were staying with Mrs B.'

'Mrs B?'

'Brenda, the old housekeeper at Kalkari.'

'Lead on, little sis! Strike while the iron's hot, I always say. C'mon, I'm not getting any younger,' said Henry, draining his cup and getting ready to leave.

He'd always been in a hurry, even growing up, Rose reflected, as they bowled along the road to Eumeralla. Full of plans. It was certainly never dull to be around Henry. Exhausting and bewildering sometimes, but never dull.

As Rose had expected, they found Vera and Violet at Mrs B's, one of the pastel-coloured weatherboard cottages on the road leading into Eumeralla.

'It's lucky you caught us. We're off back up the coast tomorrow,' said Vera as she welcomed them in.

'Rose, how nice to see you again,' said Violet. 'And who's this handsome chap?' she batted her eyelashes.

'Vi, stop that! He's far too young for you, cradle-snatcher!' said Vera, going off into a cackle of laughter that ended in a hacking cough. 'Bloody lungs still not right, gawd save us.'

'I heard about the fire, Miss Trevelyn. I'm so sorry about that,' said Henry, turning on the charm.

'Well, thank goodness Rose here was nearby and saw the smoke. Otherwise we'd have been burned to a crisp.' Violet shuddered at the thought. 'Shall I put the kettle on?'

Henry brightened. 'I'd love a cup,' he replied. Henry liked tea almost as much as he liked wine.

As they settled themselves in the tiny kitchen, Henry began his sales pitch. 'Now, ladies, I won't take too much of your time, but I heard on the grapevine – whoops, bad pun – that you might be thinking of selling Trevelyn's. And if you are, I'd like to make you an offer.'

Violet looked surprised. 'News travels fast, doesn't it? Well, for the right price, and to the right person—' she glanced at her sister. 'We'd certainly consider it.'

'Steady on, Vi.' Said Vera. 'It's true, we have talked about it, but only in very general terms. I'm still not sure about selling up our family home, well what's left of it anyway.'

'I appreciate what a difficult decision it is,' said Henry. 'But my intentions are honourable, I can promise you that. I would aim to lease the vineyards to Mark Cameron at Kalkari. I understand Jake is doing a terrific job of managing them at the moment, and don't see any reason to change that.'

'Go on,' said Vera.

'I also plan to restore the house – it might make a good business, a B&B maybe. Perhaps even a restaurant?'

'Mate,' Violet laughed. 'You'll have a lot of work on your hands to knock it into shape. Have you seen it since the fire?'

'Perhaps. But I know what I'm letting myself in for. I spoke to a few people last night and I had a poke around there first thing this morning.'

'Well, it would be nice to see it restored,' said Vera. 'Even if we haven't the heart for it ourselves. I hate to think of it as a ruin.'

The two sisters looked at each other. Rose could see how torn they were, and hoped that Henry wouldn't push them too hard. They would need time to get used to the idea.

'I've got a figure in mind.' Henry retrieved a folded piece of paper from his top pocket and slid it over to them. 'I believe it's a fair one, but take your time. The last thing I'd want is for you to make a decision you might regret.'

Ooh, thought Rose. *Very smooth.*

Vera and Violet had promised to think about the offer, and Violet gave Rose an extra-long hug as they said goodbye.

'I can't believe you're really thinking of buying Trevelyn's,' said Rose as they hurtled along the Shingle Road.

'Well, actually, I can believe it, knowing you.'

'It's a good investment, dear sis. Land around here's dirt cheap compared to Europe. And the exchange rate's on my side too. Just need to get the paperwork in order and it'll all be sorted. You can help keep an eye on it for me. If, that is, you plan to stay on.'

Who had told Henry she might be thinking of staying?

Singing along at the top of her voice, Rose drove home along the winding road back to Kalkari, having dropped Henry at the pub in Eumeralla. She felt light as air. All her worries seemed to have disappeared like a puff of smoke.

She was eager to get back to the house and track Mark down. Now the vintage was over she needed to have a proper talk with him, find out where exactly they stood.

CHAPTER 42

As Rose pulled up at Kalkari, she noticed a navy blue BMW parked across the drive, with its driver-side door gaping open. Rose had to turn back to the cellar door carpark to leave her car. Tutting to herself about the careless parking, she walked back to the main house.

Rose heard voices. *Oh God. That accent.* She broke out in a cold sweat just hearing it. *Isa-bloody-bella.* Why was she back?

She warily rounded the corner and slowed down, eavesdropping.

'But of course, if you don't want to make this work ... Who knows how things will turn out?'

'Really, Isabella, don't you think you're being unreasonable? This is not just my future, but your children's too. Have you thought of that? I thought we had discussed everything, settled it.'

'The children will be well taken care of. I am not worried on that score.' Isabella's voice had a taunting tone.

What the hell is going on?

Realising that – whatever it was – interrupting was probably not the wisest course of action, Rose doubled back to the barn.

Later, as she was preparing Leo and Luisa's dinner, the heavy scent of Isabella's perfume wafted into the kitchen. Rose looked up to see her framed in the doorway, arms folded, the talons of her nails blood-red, crimson lipstick a warning slash against her olive skin.

'Ah, Rose, there you are.' Isabella's tone was condescending. She walked over to the dresser and leant casually against it.

'Isabella.' Rose was wary. 'Can I get you anything?'

'I think it is time we had a talk, no? It is an uncomfortable situation, I think?'

You're not wrong there.

Rose was silent, not wanting to give Isabella an inch. She continued chopping the onions in front of her, blinking her eyes against their pungency.

'Mark. My *husband*.' Isabella stressed the word. 'He is not serious about you, you know. He has – how do you say – an itch to scratch.' Isabella looked pleased with herself at the expression. In fact, Rose thought, she looked like the cat that had the cream, and not just a bowlful, but a cat that had licked the whole bucket clean. 'He is a simple man. He will take whatever is offered to him, what is put in front of him. On a plate. He is not too fussy, you know what I mean? But the fun is over. I think we know that it is time that you left us. Mark and I, we have a *partnership*.'

Rose was lost for words.

'This is not your home, but Mark, he is just too weak to say it. I heard that your brother is here. Perhaps it is time for both of you to leave, eh?'

Rose stopped chopping. She barely registered Isabella's words about leaving; she was more upset by her casual dismissal of Mark. The man Isabella was describing wasn't the man she knew, the man she loved. Mark was a thoughtful, considerate man, a man who loved his kids and his land and who always tried to do his best for those around him.

A red haze came over her and she gripped the handle of the knife tightly to steady herself. She could almost feel her blood boiling. 'I don't believe you. That's complete and utter crap and you know it. You just can't stand to see him happy. You can't stand the fact that he's found someone else, can you? Now that he's successful, now that someone else wants him, you want him back. Well you can't just click your fingers and expect him to come to heel. Life doesn't work like that, not anymore, not here. Things have changed.'

Isabella looked astonished at Rose's outburst. 'So the kitten has claws ... Meow.'

Rose turned back to the chopping board. In one hand she held the knife, in the other a glass of wine. She knew

which would do to the most damage. It would be so satisfying to plunge the knife in – not into Isabella's bitter heart,
she wasn't a complete psycho – but she could stab the soft
flesh of an arm, hold the point under her delicate chin …
She reined in her inner Dexter and did the next best thing.
With a graceful flick of her wrist, she turned and hurled the
contents of her glass at Isabella's immaculate snowy shirt.

Waste of a good red, but still, satisfying nonetheless. This
was one time Rose wasn't going to regret acting on impulse.

She fled the room, Isabella's outraged gasps of horror
ringing in her ears.

'Hey!' Jake protested as Rose burst onto the verandah and
slammed into him. She'd been running to the barn, knowing she had to get as far away from Isabella as possible.

'S—s—sorry,' she blurted, hot angry tears springing to
her eyes.

'Whoa there.' Jake grasped her with both arms and led
her towards the barn.

He closed the door behind them and gave her a hug. 'I
overheard it all. Jeez, she's a piece of work. God knows what
Mark ever saw in her. Good on you for standing up to her.
You know she was spouting absolute nonsense? Blind Freddy
could see how besotted Mark is with you. Nice work on the
red, too, by the way.'

Rose gulped. She was horrified at what she'd done. 'You
think?'

'Uh huh. Take it from me, she's just trying to get you out of the picture in any way she can. I reckon someone must have told her just how serious things were getting between you and Mark and she came back to remind him of his obligations.'

'Obligations?'

'She still owns half of Kalkari.'

Suddenly everything made sense. The hold Isabella had over Mark, why she so obviously had the upper hand, why she was so sure of herself. Rose groaned. What *had* she got herself into? It was hopeless. Mark would never be free of Isabella, no matter what he said to the contrary, and Rose would always be caught in no-man's land. While Isabella still had a share in the winery, she'd always be calling the shots, showing up without warning, poisoning everything. Was this really what Rose wanted for her life?

As it turned out, Isabella got exactly what she wanted.

After she'd calmed down, Rose began to think. The situation was always going to be complicated, she had accepted that, but this was too much. She didn't want to live her life in the shadow of a vengeful megalomaniac.

She briefly considered calling Mark to hear what he had to say about it all, but she felt in her heart there was no point. There was nothing he could say to make the situation any better. There was nothing that would change it. She knew what she had to do: it was time to cut her losses and get out of the valley. She rang Henry instead.

Reaching the barn, she began throwing things into her backpack. She could barely squeeze all her stuff in – it seemed to have multiplied in the time she'd been at Kalkari – and regretfully had to leave the glamorous dress that Astrid had given her hanging in the wardrobe. No matter, it would only have reminded her of happier times.

Barely fifteen minutes later, she was all packed up. Just as she was fastening the last strap, Jake walked in to the empty bedroom. 'What the bloody hell! Rose? What's going on?'

'I just can't do it anymore, Jake. I'm sorry. I'm in the way here. It'll be so much easier for Mark if I'm not around to complicate things. He's got enough on his plate. It's for the best, really.' Jake went to interrupt her, but she held up a hand to stop him. 'There's nothing you can do to change my mind. I'm leaving with Henry and going back home to England.'

Jake looked at her in surprise. 'I thought you were tougher than that,' he said quietly.

'Yes, but I'm not an idiot. Now, please just let me go.'

He sighed, resigned. 'I'll not get in the way of a woman whose mind is clearly made up. But I think you're making a big mistake.'

'No, the only mistake I've made is hanging around here far longer than I should have done. I've been a fool.'

Jake shrugged. 'No, Rose,' he said gently. 'You're far from a fool.'

'Whatever. Would you be able to do me a favour? Do you think you could let Mark know? He's over at the far end of the valley and there's no coverage. I've tried, but I can't reach him.' She was lying. She hadn't tried to call, but Jake didn't need to know that.

'Of course.' He looked at her sadly. 'But I'm sure he'd rather hear this from you. Can't you wait a few more hours?'

'No, I'm afraid not. I've a flight to catch later today.' Rose was lying again, but now the decision was made, she wanted to get out of Kalkari as soon as she possibly could.

Rose heard the beep of a horn. She took a last look at the place that had been her home for the past few months. She refused to cry, but inside she felt like the door was shutting irrevocably on something that had been so good – the truest thing she'd ever known. Feeling a knot tighten in her stomach, she did her best to breathe through the pain.

Henry loaded her backpack into the boot of her car and they drove in convoy to New Bridgeton, where he offloaded his hire car.

'You're sure about this, sis? You're not being too impulsive?' he asked as he settled himself in the passenger seat next to her.

She bit her lip and nodded. 'Absolutely.'

CHAPTER 43

'Cherie! C'est magnifique to see you.' Philippe's welcome was enthusiastic.

She had shown up at Rustica, Philippe's new restaurant, straight from dropping Henry at the airport. She'd lied when she told Jake that she was going back to the UK. She wasn't quite ready to leave Australia, and was hoping to hang out in Bondi with her friends for a while before setting off to see more of the country.

She tried in vain to stop the tears from pricking her eyes as Philippe hugged her. 'Hey, Rosie, what is it? Why do you look like you are about to cry?'

'Nothing, really,' she said, brushing her hand over her swollen eyes. 'Just pleased to see a familiar face. Can I come and crash with you for a few days?'

'Of course! But why are you here? What about your job?'

Rose poured out the whole story.

'Well, I am so very sorry to hear this, poor Rose, but his loss is my gain. If you're not busy tomorrow, do you think you could help us out? My pastry chef just quit and I am – how do you say – up the creek,' he looked hopefully at her. 'In fact, I need someone permanently if you think you might be interested.'

'Really?' Rose couldn't believe her luck. 'Are you sure?'

This was just what she needed: working in a busy kitchen might be the best way to take her mind off things. It was a much better plan than going sightseeing, which would leave her way too much time to dwell on the mess she'd got herself in. In the state she was in, the scenery would doubtless be blurred by tears in any case. A small part of her worried that she would be completely out of her depth in Philippe's kitchen, but she quickly dismissed the fear. *To hell with playing small*, she thought defiantly. *Time to jump in, boots and all.*

'*Je ne vinaigrette rien*,' she said with a weak smile.

'*Pardon?*' asked Philippe, puzzled.

'Never mind,' she grinned. 'Okay, I'm in. If you think I'm up to it.'

'Never a doubt.'

'So, what's on the menu?'

'I'll fill you in tomorrow,' Philippe tossed a set of keys at her. 'You can crash at my place for now. Frostie's moved out and there's a spare room – if you don't mind sharing it with a few surfboards, that is.'

The next day, he took her through the – mercifully brief – dessert menu, and explained that they'd already got most of the preparation needed for service that night underway. 'Why don't you change into these,' he said, handing her some starched chef's whites, 'and then get your skinny *derrière* back in here as soon as you can.'

Rose's mouth twisted into a wry smile. She had never thought anyone would ever call her arse skinny. When she returned, she was thrust into the tiny, cramped kitchen with Philippe and two other chefs. She didn't have time to be nervous.

By six o'clock there was a line forming out the door, and she could see it snaking along the path as she peered outside. 'Bloody hell, Philippe. You didn't tell me you were doing this well.'

He laughed, '*Oui*, what can I say? Seems we're flavour of the month. I reckon it's the cocktails that Benji mixes.'

'You're far too modest, mate. Didn't we have a coupla food reviewers in just last week? Word's out,' called Benji from the bar.

'I think that's who they were. They ordered almost everything on the menu, shared all the dishes, and sat there taking notes on their iPads. Benji tried to eavesdrop but didn't give us much. Whole lot of use *he* is,' Philippe replied, chucking a dishcloth at Benji.

As Rose meticulously sliced fruit and caramelised sugar she realised that she found comfort in the familiar procedures. Philippe had created a little bit of rural France in Bondi, fashioning the cafe into a kind of weathered

Provençale fisherman's shack, with bleached boards on the floors and walls. It was incongruous, but somehow it worked. Attracting nostalgic Euro expats and hungry locals alike, Rustica was also proving to be a hit with the hip but notoriously fickle Sydney dining crowd, and the adrenaline running through the kitchen was infectious. Rose was impressed as she saw the simple, flavoursome dishes placed on the pass. Philippe was running a clever operation. She didn't want to let the side down with the desserts, and was relieved when he gave her a slap on the back of approval as she put the finishing touches to the first few orders. She hoped his confidence was not misplaced.

As the days passed, Rose settled into a groove and she was thankful not to have too much time to dwell on Mark and everything she'd left behind at Kalkari. Philippe had reiterated that the job at Rustica was hers if she wanted it. She decided to put off her plans to travel and became completely absorbed in her work. It was only when she finished late at night that she felt the now familiar ache in her heart. She missed Luisa's cheeky face, Leo's serious one, and wondered what Astrid was up to, but more than anything, when, wired from a long shift, she lay awake in bed, she missed Mark. The special smile he saved only for her, the satiny feel of his skin against hers, how her heart beat faster when he held her. Her heart twisted again and she rolled over and over, willing sleep to come and give her the oblivion she craved. With a strength she hadn't realised she possessed, she had deleted his number from her phone. It was all too complicated; if she never ran into Isabella again it would be too soon.

The broken nights meant that Rose was groggy and tired in the mornings, with eyes as gritty as sandpaper, but she forced herself out into the sunlight, running or swimming laps in the ocean pool until her lungs felt like they would burst. It seemed impossible that everyone she saw around her could be so happy and carefree when she felt completely numb.

But Rose loved the work she was doing, and, with the approval of Philippe, had made some changes, incorporating new flavours and putting a twist on some of the original dishes. 'Chocolate parfait with candied beetroot, Rose? Are you sure?' Philippe had asked. It turned out to be one of the most popular dishes on the menu. At last she was getting to stretch her culinary wings and put her training into practice, and she felt a growing self-confidence. Perhaps this was one thing she might not screw up.

One afternoon, as she arrived at work, she noticed that Philippe seemed less like his usually laid-back self. '*Alors!* Take a look at the bookings – we've got one of the city's top reviewers in tonight. Benji reckons this is him,' he said showing her the list, 'isn't that right Benji?'

Benji nodded from behind the bar.

'Everything must be perfect,' he said, worriedly running through the menu again, checking the *mis en place* was completed to his satisfaction.

'I don't know what you're so bothered about. This place is jam-packed every night; we couldn't be busier if we tried. Who needs reviewers, anyway?' she said.

'We do, Rose. I've got a massive bank loan to pay off, and we need the locals to keep coming through winter,' he replied.

'Right,' she said, at last understanding where he was coming from. 'Well, let's get to it then.'

A little after eight o'clock a middle-aged couple came in and sat at the table nearest the window. 'That's them,' hissed Benji, coming into the kitchen backwards. 'I'm sure he's wearing a wig.'

The atmosphere in the kitchen cranked up a notch. Philippe, who normally never shouted, started yelling orders.

Rose wanted to tell him to chill out, but decided to stay out of it and bent her head over her station.

'I think they liked it,' reported Benji after they'd gone. He'd been not-so-surreptitiously eavesdropping from the bar. 'I heard definite murmurings of appreciation.'

'And they ate everything on their plates,' added Kate. 'Restaurant reviewers almost never do that.'

'Really?' Philippe looked hopeful. 'Well, we did our best. Well done, everyone, you all made us look good tonight,' he said speaking to the assembled team. 'Now who wants a drink? I know I do. Benji, let's have a large jug of Blonde Française, *tout de suite.*'

CHAPTER 44

R ose had forgotten about the reviewer's visit as she went for a late-morning jog along the beachfront several weeks later. The days had become a blur of run, work and sleep, and seemed to merge into one another until she could barely remember which day of the week it was, let alone what month. She did notice that the air was cooling and the beach was less crowded, but things at Rustica had, if anything, gotten busier, and the menu had changed to focus on hearty soups, rich, garlicky fish dishes and pot au feu. Rose was experimenting with Calvados-soaked brioche, crème anglaise, and pear and anise compôtes. The luscious ingredients didn't tempt her though. The jeans she'd bought in the valley were now loose and she'd had to make yet another hole in her belt to keep them up. Philippe chided her for becoming too thin, but she paid no attention to his words. Somehow there was never time for more than a hurried staff meal once a day, the fridge in the flat she was sharing with Philippe never contained anything more than a few dried-out lemons and a bottle of vodka and her appetite wasn't up to much in any case.

Freshly showered, she shrugged into her chef's whites and walked the few hundred metres to the restaurant. A busy lunchtime crowd hung around the outside tables, soaking up the sunlight. She was almost knocked off her feet as she pushed through the front door.

'Rose!' Benji lifted her up, spun her around and kissed her on both cheeks before setting her down again.

'What was that for?'

'Read it, go on!' he urged, flourishing a newspaper at her, beaming from ear to ear.

'This summer's sensation, Rustica, lives up to its reputation as the hottest ticket in town. But don't just come to ogle the beautiful people ...' she read. 'And don't let the laid-back vibe and sun-bleached surrounds fool you. There's some seriously good food coming out of this kitchen ... Rustica, *nous sommes enchanté!*'

'Fantastic! That's just brilliant!' Rose was thrilled for Philippe and the team.

Don't stop reading, Rosie, go on,' urged Philippe, coming out of the kitchen.

'UK ring-in Rose Bennett has upped the stakes on the dessert front, with a died-and-gone-to-heaven selection of sweet courses that put a contemporary spin on some classic Provençale favourites. Our pick? The luscious bruleed tarte

353

au citron scented with rosemary. It's as sweetly delightful and surprising as the place itself.'

Rose choked up. 'Aww, that's wonderful.'

'Wonderful?' asked Philippe incredulously. 'That's bloody brilliant. This guy is so hard to please, especially when it comes to desserts. You should be thrilled.'

'And look,' chimed in Benji, 'they've given us fifteen out of twenty. That's a bloody hat!'

'Hat?' asked Rose, not understanding.

'Chef's hat. It's like a star system. It goes from one to three hats. One hat is bloody great for what we're doing, especially as we're operating basically out of a cafe.' Philippe explained.

'The phone's been going crazy since the review came out this morning,' Kate added. 'We're booked through till next month.'

Rose saw how ecstatic Philippe looked. The pressure to succeed had been weighing on him heavily and there were lines of stress etched on his face that hadn't been there when she'd first arrived in Sydney and caught up with the carefree barista with little more to worry about than the next day's surf report. How times changed a person, she thought with some irony, catching sight of herself in the mirror, seeing the pants that now sagged in the bum and hollow eyes that spoke of too many sleepless nights. She resolved there and then to stop wallowing and start living. Too bad that she'd broken her heart over a man she couldn't have. There was more to life than beating yourself up over things you couldn't change.

'So how are we going to celebrate?' she said with a grin.

'With more hard work!' said Philippe, sighing dramatically. 'But it'll be fun.'

'Always,' agreed Benji.

Still on a high from the review, Rose hurried to work the next afternoon. Philippe had given her a shift off and after a much-needed sleep-in she'd had time to get her hair cut; instead of the heavy rope that hung down her back, it now swung glossily about her shoulders. She felt lighter in spirit too. The extra sleep had helped diminish the dark circles under her eyes, and she'd even managed a bowl of fruit, an almond croissant the size of her head and an enormous latte for breakfast. There had also been a double rainbow arching over the ocean as she sat on the apartment balcony. A good sign, even though she was trying not to put so much faith in superstitious nonsense anymore.

'Hey Rose,' Benji greeted her with a low whistle as she arrived at the restaurant. 'You look great. Like the hair, babe.'

'Thanks mate, about time I did something about it huh?'

'Well you picked a good day. There's someone to see you over in the corner. He's been here for a while. Wanted to wait.'

Rose peered to the back of the room. Her heart almost stopped beating. Her breath caught in her throat. The clamour of the noisy restaurant faded into the background as she saw the face that she'd wanted to see for so long. One that had haunted her dreams.

Was it really him? Damn, but he looked good.

She took in the dark hair with its sprinkling of grey, the deep green eyes and sensuous mouth, feasting on the sight of him. She had no idea why Mark was here. How did he even know where she was working? What was he doing in Sydney? Maybe he was in town and had just come to look her up as an old friend, she reasoned, trying to quell the butterflies jostling in her stomach.

Nervously wiping her hands on her pants, she walked over to his table.

'Hi Rose,' Mark said, looking up at her.

She was unable to look away. Staring at him was like warming yourself at a blazing fire when you were freezing cold. She was helpless. She'd been telling herself that she was moving on, finding other things to make herself happy, but one glance at his face, so beautiful and so familiar to her, and she was lost again.

'Hi yourself,' she said carefully.

'Can you sit down? I'd really like to talk.'

'Umm, I was about to start work actually.'

'Please?' He pleaded with her. 'I really need to speak to you.'

'Is there anything left to say?'

'Please, just hear me out,' he begged.

'I'm trying to forget you Mark. To forget everything about the Shingle Valley,' she whispered. 'This doesn't help.'

Mark looked wounded.

Rose softened. 'Let me see if I can take a break for half an hour or so.'

She went into the kitchen, her hands shaking as she

pushed on the swing door. Philippe looked up. She didn't have to say anything. 'Go, take all the time you need,' he urged.

'Thanks,' she mouthed, and swung back into the restaurant.

'Let's walk,' Rose suggested. She couldn't sit still: there was far too much nervous energy rushing through her veins. She also didn't want Benji and half the restaurant eavesdropping on her conversation.

They made their way down to the beach. Mark jumped from the stone wall onto the sand and held out his hands to her. She ignored them: she didn't trust herself to touch him and be able to let go again. She jumped down beside him and they walked along the water's edge as the frothing waves sucked at the dark gold sand. She took a sideways glance at Mark, going weak at the memory of his mouth on hers, the feel of him, the sound of his voice, the curl of his hair, the spicy, soapy scent of him. They were all so familiar to her. She forced herself to look away. She didn't want him to notice her staring.

'So, how've you been?' Mark asked.

'Fine, thanks,' she replied. Then, after a beat, 'Mark, let's not make small talk. Why are you here?'

'Jake showed me this,' putting his hand in his pocket, he pulled out a crumpled newspaper cutting and thrust it at her. The review. 'I had no idea you were still in the country. Jake told me you went back to the UK. But as soon as I saw this I had to come and see you. What happened?'

It was Rose's turn to look uncomfortable. 'I decided to stay in Bondi. Philippe had a job going ... I wasn't ready to go back to England, but I wanted you to think I'd left the country. I didn't want you to try and contact me. It was all too much, with Isabella—'

He nodded. 'You've done so well, Rose. You really deserve this.'

Rose gave him a small half-smile. 'Yeah, well, it's been quite a ride.'

'There's something I need to tell you. Why I had to come and see you as soon as I found out you were here,' Mark ran his hands through his hair. 'Rose, I'm not one for fancy words.' He took a deep breath. 'All I can say is that I'm here because I love you. I miss you. I miss your sunny smile, your laughter, every part of you. I'm half a man without you. Home is not the same without you there. You're the first thing I think about in the morning, and the last thing at night. I can't live without you, Rose.'

Rose couldn't believe her ears. This was everything she'd wanted to hear, for such a long time. But there was still an obstacle. A pretty immovable one at that. 'But what about Isabella?'

Mark took her hand in his and she trembled as she felt his warm, strong touch. 'It was all about the money. It was only ever all about the money. When I won the Jimmy Watson she was back in a flash. But I'm finally free of her.'

Rose still didn't believe him. 'Really? But that's what you said last time.'

'This time it's really true,' he insisted.

'Oh, Mark, a lot's happened. I couldn't come back, not anymore, not now …' Rose's voice trailed off.

'Right, yes, I understand. Of course.' Mark looked devastated. 'Pretty foolish of me to come and think I could persuade you back, hey? You've achieved so much here. Look, perhaps I can see you when I'm in Sydney? I can get here every week or so. I really want to work something out Rose. I don't want to lose you again. I've never been more certain of that.'

Rose was torn, but resolute. 'I'm sorry, Mark, I just can't. I can't share you.'

'Share me? What are you talking about?'

Rose was exasperated. 'Do I have to spell it out?'

'But I thought I explained. Isabella has gone. Back to Spain. She left a few days after you did. In any case, when she does see the kids I'll be there to stand up for you. In fact, she's promised that when she does come to see them she will stay in Eumeralla, not at the house. You won't have to take any nonsense from her ever again. I've told her how I feel about you. She's agreed to a divorce.'

'Oh.' Rose was floored.

'And the kids miss you so much.'

'I miss them too,' cried Rose, thinking of Luisa's merry dark eyes and Leo's shy smile. She paused, letting the full meaning of Mark's words sink in.

He looked so forlorn. Her heart broke for him.

'Oh, Rose, won't you believe me when I tell you just how much I've missed you, longed for you? I never want to let you go again,' he said fiercely. 'But I understand if you don't want to leave Sydney. I can see how well you're doing here. You're doing what you're really good at, what you were meant to do.'

'No. That won't work.' Rose was definite.

She saw his devastated expression and took pity on him. 'I'd want to see more of you than just every few weeks. Just quietly, life without you isn't all it's cracked up to be either. All the newspaper reviews in the world don't make up for being with the one you love and knowing you're loved to bits in return.'

Realisation dawned on Mark's face. 'Really?'

'But Mark ...' she paused, moving away from him and biting her bottom lip. 'There's still something I need to tell you.' She had to come clean with him. It was now or never.

CHAPTER 45

Rose swallowed. 'I, um, well, I didn't really come to Kalkari just to be your au pair.'

'I know.'

Rose was gobsmacked. 'What?'

'Henry confessed. He also told me you make a bloody awful spy. He said he got absolutely no useful information from you at all.'

Rose looked up, mortified, but was astonished to see the glint of amusement in his eyes.

'Oh, Mark, don't tease me. I'm not sure I can take it,' she wailed. 'I've been feeling awful about that for months.'

'Forget about it,' Mark took her hand. 'Anyway, there's something you didn't know, too.'

'What?'

'I didn't meet Henry when he showed up in the Shingle Valley. We met each other when I was in London. It was then that he asked me to look after you, and said that he'd told you to spy on Kalkari for him – not that he had planned to do much with what you might have been able to tell him, in any case. He said it was more of an excuse to get you out of the country and give you something to do with yourself. He knew you'd never leave London unless he gave you a really good reason to. He knows you well, sweetheart – you're always so quick to help others out. It's one of the things I love most about you.'

'What the hell? I spent all that time feeling guilty about having to betray you and the whole time you knew what was going on?' Rose was suddenly livid. 'God, I'll kill that brother of mine when I see him. He completely played me.'

'Don't be so hard on him. He only wanted to do what was best for you.'

'Humph. Well, he'd better stop interfering in my life from now on.'

'Forget Henry, Rose. Will you really come back? Back to the Shingle Valley? Be mine?'

'If you're asking,' she said, suddenly shy.

'Oh, you'd better believe it, Rosie: I'm asking.'

'Okay, but if you don't kiss me soon I'll not be answerable for the consequences.' Rose revelled in her boldness.

Mark looked at her and a huge smile spread across his face. He didn't need any further invitation. He held out his arms.

Rose looked into his eyes and she couldn't hold back any longer. She fell into his arms and breathed in the dear, familiar smell of him. She raised her face and pressed her lips to his, drowning in the sensation.

After a few moments, Mark reluctantly drew away from her. 'Wait a sec.'

'What?'

'There are a few other people who'd like to see you. I figured if I couldn't persuade you, they might be able to.'

Rose was puzzled.

'Come with me.'

He took her hand and they walked to the far end of the beach, where she could see two small figures and a taller one pushing a stroller that looked like it had been engineered by NASA. The children!

She broke into a run. 'Leo! Luisa!' she called out, her voice carrying on the wind towards them.

They looked up and, seeing her, raced to meet her.

'Hey, guys. How are you?' Rose laughed, the sound coming deep from her belly. The sound of joy. She hugged them each tightly, showering them with kisses.

'Wosie!' cried Luisa. 'Wosie! We've missed you.'

'So have I, babycakes, so have I.'

'Astrid had her baby,' added Leo, pointing proudly at the stroller.

'Hey there, Rose,' said Astrid, catching up to them and enveloping Rose in a huge hug. 'Come and meet Max.'

'Oh Astrid, he's even cuter than the pictures you emailed me. I'm so sorry I couldn't be there for the birth.'

'Don't even worry about it. I had Thommo, who was just wonderful. He's such a proud papa.'

After Rose had cooed over the gorgeous, fat, fast asleep bundle in the stroller, Mark pulled her away again. 'Rose, there's something else.'

'Something else?' What more was in store? Rose didn't think she could stand any more surprises.

'Yes. Hopefully this will convince you beyond any doubts. I assume you don't know this, but Isabella actually owned half of Kalkari.'

Rose nodded. 'I heard.'

'When first I set up the business she invested her money – from her family's business – in it too. When she went back to Spain last year she used it as a weapon against me, threatening to sell her share to a rival winemaker in the valley. She told me she desperately needed the cash – she had taken over her family's winery in Spain and wanted to expand. I spent all of last winter trying to raise enough to buy her out, and playing for time. I didn't tell you about it, and now I realise I probably should have. I guess I didn't want to scare you off. Now I'm finally free of her, even if it did cost me over the odds.'

'But how could you afford to buy her out?'

'Actually, I've gone into partnership.'

'What? Who with?'

A lightbulb exploded in Rose's brain as she put two and two together. 'You're kidding me. Henry? Really? No way!'

'Got it in one,' Mark gave her a grin.

'Hang on, let me get this straight. Henry now owns Trevelyn's and half of Kalkari? What's he trying to do, buy up half the Monopoly board?'

Mark laughed. 'And I couldn't be happier. He's got no plans to interfere in the way I make wine, and he's even got plans for a further injection of capital.'

'Oh God. You're going to be stuck with both of us!'

'And I couldn't be a happier man, Rose Bennett.'

CHAPTER 46

As she walked up to the top of the hill above Kalkari, Rose could see her breath: the vapour hovered in the freezing air. Reaching the top, she stopped to take in the scene that lay below her. A bleak landscape of dormant vines, stripped bare, emerged from the mist. The sun was rising over the Shingle Hills and a shaft of light broke through the clouds, illuminating the valley below. A blessed land. Her land now. She belonged to it as much as she and Mark belonged together, though she was still incredulous that a small part of it was all hers.

She pulled the zip on her jacket up to her chin and was glad of the beanie that covered her hair. 'Christ, it doesn't get any warmer out here,' she muttered to herself. The summer had been so long and scorching, she'd almost forgotten just how cold it could get in winter in the valley.

To her left, the red-tiled roof and white walls of Trevelyn's could be seen starkly against the hillside. She couldn't resist going over for another look. Shucking off her muddy boots on the front verandah, she reached for the front door. It was new, but old, like much of the renovations that had been done over the past few months to resuscitate the fire-damaged building. They'd been able to make good use of a load of timber and bricks reclaimed from a decommissioned church further down the valley. 'You've transformed it into something really quite miraculous,' Mark had said just the day before as she had proudly showed him around the finished project.

She pulled a key from her pocket and inserted it in the shiny brass lock. The clean, sharp smell of fresh paint assaulted her.

Rose padded down the hall and into the sparkling new kitchen. While the rest of the place had a rustic aesthetic, the kitchen was state-of-the-art, with enormous industrial ovens, gas ranges and a huge walk-in coolroom already stocked with meat, fish, fruit, vegetables and vats of milk and cream. She'd hired two young chefs to help her and together they had already completed most of the *mise en place* for the pre-opening dinner that was planned for that night, including the dessert: three perfect six-layer chocolate glacé tarts that sat glossily on the coolroom shelves.

Putting a heavy kettle on the range to boil, she rummaged around in the storeroom for tea. Spooning some leaves into one of the restaurant's new denim-blue Japanese teapots, she glanced through the open kitchen into the space before her. The old house had been completely redesigned, with the ground floor now a single open space. Tables for two, four and eight surrounded an enormous timber central table that was laden with heavy vases of greenery and fragrant winter blooms.

Tea brewed, she stepped outside. Dew trembled on the canes and the mist had begun to clear. It was going to be a beautiful day. Beautiful but cold. Not that it would be a problem at the restaurant – she'd insisted on the best under-floor heating on offer, as well as a cosy open fire at one end of the large dining room. After her experience at the barn, she'd refused to skimp on the heating.

As she clasped her hands around the mug, she thought about all the work that had gone into realising her dream of a small country restaurant and provedore. She'd travelled the length and breadth of the valley, cajoling the best ingredients from local producers: bespoke cheeses from the Shingle Dairy, olive oil from a farm on the other side of Eumeralla, lamb and beef from nearby farms, and eggs from her own brood of chickens, each one named after her favourite cooks and chefs – Alice, Julia, Ina, Elizabeth and Kylie. She'd overseen the renovations, enlisting Astrid's help to create a warm, welcoming feel. Astrid had also designed the signage: one hung proudly from the eaves and another stood at the turn-off from the Shingle Road. Trevelyn's Pantry. There had been no question about the name.

The opening was tonight – Vera and Violet were the guests of honour (they were now settled happily in a small stone cottage just off the main street of Eumeralla), and family and friends, including Dan, Bob, Charlie and Thommo, Astrid and Bevan and Angie, Mrs B, Deano, Ben and Jake would be coming – as well as half the valley, it seemed. And, of course, Mark. Mark who made every day a joy and a delight. Mark, her champion and her comfort, her lover and her friend.

Draining the dregs of her tea, Rose returned to the restaurant.

She had work to do.

ACKNOWLEDGEMENTS

I owe an enormous debt of thanks to a number of people, without whom *Rose's Vintage* would never have seen the light of day.

First and absolutely foremost is my agent, Margaret Connolly, who saw a diamond in the rough and who, thanks to her sage counsel, continual encouragement and belief in me as a writer, has made everything possible.

To my sister Becky, who was the first to read the initial pages (which ended up on the cutting-room floor, gulp): your encouragement, endless plot powwows and no-bullshit advice kept it real and kept me going.

To four of my early readers, Mercedes, Di, Jane C. and Jane R. – you were more enthusiastic about Rose and the Shingle Valley than I dared hope. To Sanchia and her eagle eyes, for reading it at its final stage. And yes, there will be more Shingle Valley shenanigans, I promise!

To the original Pirates – you know who you are – for your enthusiasm, irreverence, inspiration and belly laughs.

To Max Allen, for his fascinating and inspiring survey of Australian biodynamic and organic wineries, *The Future Makers: Australian Wines for the 21st Century* and to the good people at Short Sheep winery, for educating me in the finer points of keeping Babydoll sheep among other useful things. Any mistakes in relation to winemaking practices are entirely my own.

To Ali Watts, for her encouraging words and stellar advice. To my publisher, Jeanne Ryckmans (who tells the best *true* stories!), for completely understanding my vision for the book, and my calm and kind editor, Kirstie Innes-Will – the book is so much better for your hard work and spot-on suggestions.

Kayte Nunn is a freelance book, magazine and web editor and the former editor of *Gourmet Traveller WINE* magazine. She writes on travel, health, wellbeing, parenting and lifestyle topics, and has been short-listed for local and international short-story awards. She is a mother to two girls. This is her first novel.